Brockenhur
and the
Two World Wars

Compiled by
John Cockram

Photographic work by
Tony Jackson and
Richard Williams

Cover drawn by
Gervase A. Gregory

Published by the Author in aid of The Royal British Legion Poppy Appeal

The King commands me to assure you of the true sympathy of His Majesty and The Queen in your sorrow.

He whose loss you mourn died in the noblest of causes. His Country will be ever grateful to him for the sacrifice he has made for Freedom and Justice.

Milner

Secretary of State for War.

SENT TO EACH BEREAVED FAMILY

PREFACE

By

Major General J C Woollett CBE MC

The Millennium is a time when we need to understand the past as well as look to the future. The village War Memorial commemorates the 86 men from Brockenhurst who died for their country in the two World Wars. As years go by, and before memories fade, more information needs to be recorded about them than just a list of names.

The Brockenhurst Branch of the Royal British Legion therefore agreed that research should be carried out and the resultant information be put together into a book. Many village families have contributed information, which has been integrated with background research and written in its present format by John Cockram.

Robert Banister - whose two eldest brothers were killed in the Second World War - sums it up clearly by saying

> *"I am very pleased to assist in any way I can as this seems a very appropriate and timely venture, to honour those who gave their lives so that the world could enjoy a half century of relative peace."*

The book sets out to explain how the individuals concerned belonged to the village and the events that led to their deaths. In this way their lives and their sacrifice can be recorded for future generations, most particularly for their relatives.

We are very grateful to the people of the village, who have contributed so helpfully to enable this Memorial record to be completed. I will conclude by quoting again from Robert Banister:

> *"When you have read Jimmy's final poem on page 249 and appreciated the question it poses, you will understand why I am so pleased the Legion is compiling this Millennium Record."*

JOHN WOOLLETT
President
Brockenhurst Branch, The Royal British Legion

INTRODUCTION

I never read the Introduction to a book, as I always want to get straight into the book itself.

Some explanation of the scope of this book must, however, be offered, as it is not simply a chronicle of the War Memorial. The aim has been to attempt to describe the effect that the two World Wars have had on this small village in the New Forest. Thus whilst the recording of the names and histories is a large part of the book, information on the framework of the village before 1914 is given to provide a reference to enable you to judge how the village was affected by the war years. This aspect is, perforce, selective and very dependent on the personal recollections of villagers. Despite the passage of time such memories reflect the priorities of youth and provide a glimpse into the immediacy and values of the wartime years. We live now in a vastly different age. The book therefore includes information which I hope will make the experience of the village intelligible to those who, happily, have never experienced war, rationing - or even a village without main drainage!

Relatives may wish to visit graves or memorials and to this end the reference of the grave and its cemetery or the panel number of the Memorial is given at the end of each personal memorial. The names of villagers who died are shown in **_bold Italics_** to distinguish them from those who returned.

This book sets out, therefore, to recall and record the impact on the families in the village over both wars and the intervening years. To this end I have recorded those who died in chronological sequence so that the impact on the village, month by month and year by year, can be understood. The shock of the news of **_Harry Waterman's_** death in the fourteenth week of the war can be appreciated. The loss of eight villagers in 1915 defending the Ypres Salient, of four fighting on the Somme in 1916 and three at Passchendaele in 1917 gives reason for why these places still strike a chord within us today. The death of **_Ron Chalk_** six weeks after the Second War broke out had the same shock effect. The news, on Naval families, of the five men lost at sea in 1941 would have been matched later on in 1943 in other families as bomber crew losses mounted and soldiers were killed in the battles of North Africa and Italy. I have included a simplified history of the military background to the events leading to the deaths of villagers in order to give the scenario for their sacrifice.

The First World War names have been mainly researched from written sources as the records that survive - many were destroyed in the Second World War by enemy action or Fire Service preventative action - in the Public Record Office are only now becoming available for consultation. The oral tradition still survives but in small measure only. It is, anyway, at this distance fallible. Brockenhurst Church was "of unknown dedication" until 1912 when the discovery of a will dated 28 August 1539 revealed its dedication to St Nicholas. How can the name of the village church be forgotten in the oral tradition?!

As the village policy appears to have been that everybody was equal in death, so names and initials only were inscribed on the War Memorial. This has dictated the necessity to cross-reference all names to get at least two different sources of information to confirm the extant military details as well as linkage with Brockenhurst. This has been achieved by consulting the resources of the Regimental Histories, museums, Public Record Offices, local libraries and Parish Records as well as talking to people. This discipline gives provenance to those identified but has failed in the case of *Sydney Richard Payne.*

One disappointment has been the inability to track down the Minutes of the Sub Committee that must have been established for the War Memorial Project and, indeed, to determine the names thereon. Why do the names on the boards of the shrine – now in St Nicholas's Church porch – not tally with those on the War Memorial? In some villages it has been a requirement to be born or to reside in the parish before a name can be entered on the Memorial. Yet in the case of Brockenhurst twenty-five men who died in the war were born or resided in the village, but their names have not been recorded on the Memorial. These men have not yet been researched and do not, therefore, have personal memorials in this book. According to the War Memorial five villagers died in the 1916 battles on the Somme. In fact village families suffered the loss of eleven of their men folk. This multiplier effect is also visible for the battles in Gallipoli, Mesopotamia, Passchendaele and the final advance to victory in 1918.

The Second World War has required a different approach as the records have not yet been released for public inspection and personal memory is so much fresher. It is arguably also more interesting as the pen portraits are more personal and more immediate. In the Second World War, also, Brockenhurst was directly involved in the war in a way never before experienced and suffered its own losses.

Caveat. As Don Cording has said - in a sense this book can never be finished, as there will always be new material that will surface after its publication.

Feedback. Despite trying to back all statements with evidence, all mistakes are my very own. Reader's comments and information will both, therefore, be very welcome.

July 2001   JOHN COCKRAM

Published by John Michael Cockram of Brockenhurst, Hampshire SO42 7RX.
Copyright John Michael Cockram 2001

ISBN No.: 0-9540972-0-3

Contents

ACKNOWLEDGEMENTS

What has been a great joy during this research has been the willing and prompt help received from the village, from museums, libraries, newspapers and other organisations.

Help from the families of those who died has come from Eileen Abbott, Robert Banister, David Bartlett, Jane Chalk, Owen Clark, Archie Cleveland, Angela Coles, Elsie Cooper, Donald Cremer, Ursula Davies, Bill Dunkinson, Ray Dunkinson, Kay Elphick, Ian Hayter, Michael Hodder, Peggy James, Minerva Kitcher, Sue Lynes, Peter Perfect, Bliss Phillips, Rosemary Seccombe, Bruce Smith, David Jackson-Smith, John Street, Ruth Walker in New Zealand, Caroline Waterman and Ursula Weeks. From talking to surviving relatives of those who died it is very clear that the losses of 55-60 years ago are still keenly felt.

Local material has been willingly provided by Nina Ball, Primrose Blaikie, Len Burton, Russ Ferrett of the Fire Service, John and Kay Jolly, Molly Mueller, James Paterson, John Purkess, M E Reed, Mary Roberts, Ruth Rollin, Peter Sweet, Olive Wallis and Caroline Waterman.

Graves have been keenly hunted in St. Nicholas Churchyard by Sophie and Kate Denton and Julie Hodkin. Gordon Glenton has kindly cleaned graves for photographic purposes. Mary Pattison has checked the Register of Graves.

Researchers include Muriel Bishop, who solved the Ash and Donaldson cases, Don Cording - whose knowledge of the P.R.O. and the British Census has been invaluable, Derek and Gwen Howe for their interview skills, and Carole Standeven, Peggy and Jude James for their local knowledge. Stan Stancliffe (Jnr.) has been the Canadian link, as has Clare Church for New Zealand.

World War II material - "The War at Sea" was written by Loftus Peyton-Jones whilst "The Air War" has been provided by Jack Brindley and "The Home Front" contributed by John Purkess. John Alexander, Ted Brown, Robin Budgett, Dot Jenkinson, Peggy and James Jude, Peter Kendell and John Woollett have formed the team of proof-readers.

Susan Hill of the Southampton Archives Service, Gavin Edgerley-Harris of The Gurkha Museum at Winchester, Mr Mick Bardwell, BEM, of The Royal Hampshire Museum, Giles Smith of the Tank Museum at Bovington, Peter Kent of the Imperial War Museum, The Royal Navy, the Submarine and The Royal Marine museums at Portsmouth have all provided prompt and willing assistance; as has also been given by the DAILY ECHO and the LYMINGTON TIMES.

Photographs have been provided by many of the above organisations and individuals. In addition, specific photographs have been taken by Nina Ball, Brockenhurst College, John Elliott and Richard Williams. The War Memorial on the cover has been superbly drawn by Gervase A. Gregory.

Five people, however, have been so essential to the project that it could not have been completed without their assistance. Tony Johnson has provided many of the village pictures that make the text come alive. Clare Richardson has been so patient and professional in word processing my scribble. Thelma Stollar has researched the London museums and generously contributed towards the costs of the venture. Richard Williams has been an absolute wizard on scanning and enhancing the illustrations as well as writing some of the text. Finally, my wife, Gill, whose strong support and patience has included the sacrifice of her dining room table over the past two years.

I also greatly appreciate and acknowledge the help and support provided by the Brockenhurst Branch of The Royal British Legion, for this, their Millennium project, by the Parish Council who have also adopted it as an official village project, and The Friends of Brockenhurst - without who's generous financial assistance this book could not have been published.

Finally I must thank Terry Ozanne and his splendid team at Hobbs the Printers, for their unstinted help in getting this book printed.

To these, and to all that have so enthusiastically helped and encouraged me - not forgetting that splendid man George Murdoch - I am very grateful.

SOURCES

The three main sources have been the **War Graves Commission** (now on the Internet), **Soldiers Died** in the Great War and the **Public Record Office**.

The New Forest Magazine, the **Parish Magazine** and **The Brockenhurst Bulletin** have all been trawled, where available. They are unique primary sources of local information.

Books consulted are given in the Bibliography at page 283.

Grateful thanks to the following for permission to use their
    Original artwork:
        AIR International for pages 181, 199, 254.
        David Howley for pages 217, 223, 229.
        Wharncliffe Publishing for pages 21, 44.
        Aeroplane Monthly for page 240.
        Arthur Banks for maps on pages 85, 95, 174, 180, 197.
    Photographs. Imperial War Museum for photographs on pages 17, 28, 61,
        98, 134, 135, 183, 185, 188, 192, 193, 195, 205, 212.
    Articles. **THE ECHO** for articles on pages 207, 252.

Copyright. Every effort has been made to secure copyright approval were sources have been reproduced.

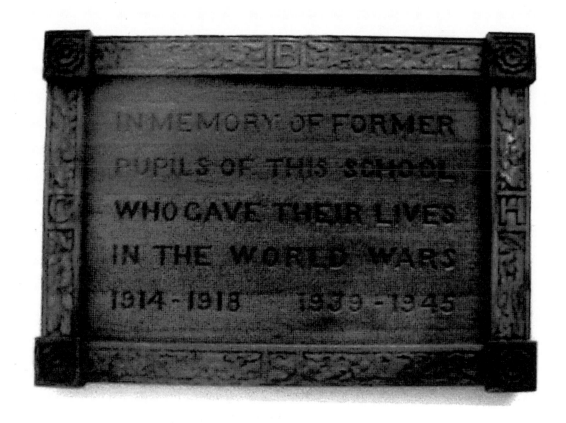

THE MEMORIAL AT BROCKENHURST COLLEGE

The First
World War
1914 – 1918

THE VILLAGE AND 1914

Mrs Eileen Abbott (Nee Pope) of Lyndhurst recalls Mrs Povey's father's description of Brockenhurst before the Great War:

> *"There were few industries, the boys worked on gardens, on the railways, or at Popes - where toy wooden horses, brush heads, table legs, banister rails etc. were made and sent all over the country. The Turnery Works were destroyed by fire in 1909, but reopened at Balmer Lawn. Lunn Brothers also had a sawmill there but afterwards moved to Sway.*
>
> *The girls either went into service (a very few worked in shops then) or did dress making. There were three dressmakers in the village to whom girls could be apprenticed for two years, for little or no wages. Married women did not go out to work, but many cottagers took in washing - there then being no public laundries. The bigger houses - the Park, Hincheslsea and Careys all had their own private laundries.*
>
> *Practically all cottagers kept pigs and fowls, and some kept ducks and geese. Many villagers also kept cows which roamed the forest in the daytime and returned home at night to be milked and bedded down. "Soldier" Smith, who lived at Wide Lane Cottage, kept a number of cows. He also had some knowledge of cattle ailments and was considered a vet. He could also charm away warts. On the opposite side of the road the tenants of Bartlett's cottage (now demolished) also kept cows as did dozens of others, especially those whose houses adjoined the open forest.*
>
> *Where the War Memorial now stands, there was once a pond where the cattle drank and where children loved to slide when it was frozen over in winter."*

Against this background it is easy to understand why the brothers *George* and *William White*, with other village lads, emigrated to Canada. One can also have sympathy for those boys - *Thomas Moore, Charles Tucker* and *Harry Waterman* - who decided, before 1914, to "go for a soldier": or to join the Navy - as *Selim Chandler* and *"Nip" Pope* did. The discipline and living conditions of the Services then may appear harsh in today's terms, but at least it represented three square meals a day and all found at a time when such basic requirements were not always guaranteed.

The need to find work away from the local area is also reflected in the distant locations where villagers enlisted e.g. Swansea, for *Thomas Dove*, Birmingham for *Alfred Beard* and Loughborough for *Alex Macintosh*.

The Parish Registers of Marriage. Many of the villagers who went to war were married men. In 1902 William Povey (see page 86) married Harriet Eliza Burton. This photograph was taken outside Norton Cottage, Park Close, Brockenhurst.

WILLIAM and ELIZA POVEY

JOHN BURTON   FREDERICK BURTON

HARRIET BURTON

The Smithy. It paid to advertise!

THE VILLAGE SMITHY - THE FORESTERS PUBLIC HOUSE IS IN THE BACKGROUND

The School photograph of the class of 1899, with its headmaster, is emotive.

Twenty-one boys were in the class. Eight of the boys in the picture were serving at the outbreak of war in which four of them were to be killed. Of those who enlisted after war was declared, four more were to die.

CLASS 1 IN 1899

Mr J. D. Tombs, the headmaster, is second row from the back on the left.

Back Row	George Woolacott	(3rd from left)	Served in Royal Marines.
	John Hibbs	(4th from left)	Killed 1918.
	Harry Waterman	(2nd from right)	Killed 1914.
Second Row	*Will Stride*	(3rd from right)	Killed 1918.
	Percy Wingate	(Left)	Served in Army.
Front Row	Bert White	(2nd from left)	Served in Army.
	Charlie Tucker	(4th from left)	Killed 1915.
	George Smith	(Right)	Served in Royal Marines.

Village Football was an important activity for youngsters.

Brockenhurst National School Football Club
1905 - 6.

| MR G H GENDALL (HEAD MASTER) | H EMMS | F JENVEY | T GREEN | C BURTON (HON.SEC) | W BUTT | W NINDEBANK | C PERKINS | A.S. IMBER (HON.TREAS) |

| W BURTON | F WATERMAN | B GULLIVER (CAPTAIN) | A MOODY | B BURTON |

These young men were mostly 13-14 year olds who, in the war years, would have been very recruitable 19-23 year olds. Whilst it is not known how many of the team joined the Royal Navy or Royal Marines, those who served in the army all survived the war.

The Burton and Waterman families, however, were destined to lose, not only their own children, but other relatives in the conflict.

Quoits. Quoits was a very popular game for villagers before the First World War. It was played at the bottom of Church Lane where the Commemoration oak trees now grow.

Bill Harrison is identified on the original photograph as the man on the right. As it was taken about 1910/12 others in the group would have also fought in the war.

The Fire Brigade was established after the great fire in Pope's toy factory. Arthur Stevens, who was a fireman for 24 years, served in it when it was located in Fibbards Road. Whilst this photograph was taken in 1920 the brigade was still equipped and uniformed as it had been before 1914.

J. MARTIN   F. HAYWARD J. STEVENS F FIELD P. MAHER J. JENVEY G. CHALK   W. HIETT   F. SLADE
Hon Sec   *Chief*   *Foreman*
                                                                       Officer
           W. SLADE   R. MAHER   A. BOWDEN
              Call boy

The Post Office was an important part of the village and Eileen Abbott remembers it as being close to the level crossing. Arthur Stevens, now 91 years old, remembers that it moved temporarily to the corner site next to where "*Pot Pourri*" is now, before it transferred over the road in 1909 to its present location.

JESSE SQUE   **JACK WATERMAN**

"NIP" POPE

The village band was an essential element of the social life of pre-war Brockenhurst in the days before radio, television or a local cinema.

This photograph was taken outside the Hinves' house in Tattenham Road and shows four family members of the band.

Charles Hinves is in the foreground, with his sons Leonard, (left), *Alan* and *Harold*, (right).

All three sons joined the Army during the war.

Len was captured by the Germans in their offensive of 1918.

Alan was killed at Gallipoli in 1915.
Harold was killed on the Somme in 1916.

In the 1911 Census the village (of 5,994 acres) had a population of 2,048 comprising 972 males and 1076 females. This represented 483 family units.

Roll of Honour, 1914. Stevens, the local printers whose printing house was behind what is now Londi's shop in Brookley Road, published a "Roll of Honour" early in the war showing

"Brockenhurst Men who are serving their King and Country,
in the Army, Navy and Marines, at the time of
the Great European War, 1914."

This list is not definitive as it was compiled in response to a request from the Vicar, Reverend Arthur Chambers, for information on those serving. There are also inaccuracies - for instance ranks are not given for either Sir Berkeley Pigott or I. R. Walker-Monro, and the regular officers of the Large family are not shown. Nevertheless it is an impressive statistic that this small village could take pride that it had at least 105 men in uniform at the beginning of the war.

Men serving in the Navy. Twenty-one villagers are shown as serving in the Navy in 1914. Two of these were officers - Lieutenant commander *Victor Bowden-Smith* and Lieutenant-Commander J. Patterson, who was a Naval Padre. F. Smith and F,. Young were both Petty Officers and the remaining seventeen Ratings. Of these *Selim Chandler*, *John Hibbs* and *Percy Pope* were not to survive wartime service.

Men serving in the Army. Of the eighty men in the Army Lieutenant Colonel C. Logan is the senior officer, the two Willis brothers are shown as Captains, the three Dent brothers as Lieutenants - as is G White and both *Robert Groome* and *Richard Tillyer* are 2nd Lieutenants. The three Sergeants listed are P. Sherrard, P. Smith and *Harry Waterman*. Corporals R. Fairweather and A. Wingate are also noted. Of the remaining sixty-six men *Charles Christopher, George Clarke, John Gates, William Harrison, William. Cleveland,. John Lancaster, Thomas Moore, Christian Patterson, Fred Sibley, Len Smith* and *William White*, were all to die from war service.

Men serving in the Royal Marines. Sergeant G. Smith and three men were in the Royals at this time. *William Stride* was destined to be killed two days before the end of the war.

Liar's Den Gazette Whilst life was hard and times difficult the village clearly had a corporate sense of humour. Stevens, the local printers, issued a local newsletter apparently called the "Liar's Den Gazette".

In 1974 a local paper reminded readers of the problem of noise pollution in the village before 1914. This led Mrs Crouch, of Sway, to send the following letter to the paper on 14 September 1974 enclosing a postcard giving the humorous view of the villagers at the time on the subject.

Sir,

I have read with great interest about the "cows" taking their strolls in the village of Brockenhurst. It seems to me somehow these poor creatures have placed a hoo-doo on the inhabitants – hence I enclose a postcard printed before the first war, when my father, **Fred Johnson**, was a young man, later to be killed at Ypres in 1918, whom I have always given to understand from my mother gave a helping hand to disrobe "Dan Minty's" cows of their bells – a perfect nuisance so they say!

Lucy E Crouch,

THE BELLS OF BROCKENHURST

About eight days ago, Sir,
(As I have seen to-night),
Two cows strode through the Village Street,
(To this they had a right);
They walked & walked & talked & talked,
And bore themselves with pride,
As if to say "We know we are,"
"the hope of Riverside's."
But sad to say when night arrived,
The bells that each did bear,
With strap and buckle all complete,
Did vanish in the air,
Some wicked person must them "pinch"
And thereby break the law.
But the 'music' had a nuisance been,
And made the public raw.
Now on the walls and hoardings plain,
A notice you may scan,
With riches promised to the one,
Who will denounce the man;
But perhaps the best that we can do,
Is pack up our valise,
'Ere the Shoppe again on the mark,
And telephone the police.
Maybe these cows, on "rations" thin,
Unfit to bear the strain,
By some mishap slipped through the strap
Which makes the thing quite plain,
If so when next those beeves we see,
Unless this ad-vice fails,
They'll walk the street with bells all tied,
Upon their lovely tails.

Printed and published by the "Liar's Den Gazette"

THE HAMPSHIRE REGIMENT

As 15 out of 50 army names on the war memorial served with the Hampshire Regiment it might be helpful if the organisation of this regiment was explained. Whilst to any member of the regiment it is, as an entity, unique – its structure is largely common to other infantry regiments of the time.

In 1914 The Hampshire Regiment consisted of: -

Regular Battalions	**Where stationed in 1914**
1 Hamps.	In Colchester
2 Hamps.	In Bengal, India
3 Hamps. (Special Reserve)	Mobilised 7 August 1914 in Isle of Wight. A training unit whose task was to "feed" the battalions on active service.

Territorial Battalions

1/4 Hamps.	}	At annual camp in Bulford
1/5 Hamps.	}	Volunteered for overseas
1/6 Hamps.	}	9 August 1914
1/7 Hamps.	}	

2/4 Hamps.	}	Formed as second line units
2/5 Hamps.	}	for home defence.
2/6 Hamps.	}	Volunteered for overseas
2/7 Hamps.	}	December 1914

1/8 Hamps.	(Isle of Wight Rifles)	Formed 2/8 Hamps. in December 1914
1/9 Hamps	(Cyclist Battalion)	Formed 2/9 Hamps in September 1914

Service (Kitchener) Battalions

One (K) battalion to be raised for each new Kitchener Army.

10 Hamps.	Embodied at Winchester	K1 attached 10 (Irish) Division
11 Hamps.		K2 attached 16 (Irish) Division
12 Hamps.		K3 attached 26 Division
13 Hamps.	Became 34 Training Reserves	K4 attached 32 Division
14 Hamps	(1st Portsmouth)	K4/K5 (April 1915) attached 39 Division
15 Hamps	(2nd Portsmouth)	K5 (September 1915) attached 41 Division
17 Hamps	(orig. Hampshire Brigade)	Formed 1915, for Home defence

Other Battalions

16 Hamps. (Local reserves)	Formed September 1915. Retitled as 97 Training Reserve
18 Hamps. (Home Service)	Formed January 1917. Became Garrison Battalion in January 1918
51 Hamps. (Young Soldiers)	Replaced, in 1918, Two Training Reserve Battalions.
52 Hamps.}(Graduated Battalions) 53 Hamps.}	Tasked to train recruits and pass them on to the Young Soldiers Battalion.

Mobilisation

The two regular battalions were on a war footing before the war began. The Telegram ordering mobilisation of the Territorial Force was sent out on 4 August 1914. It said, simply:

"Mobilise. Stop. Acknowledge"

Apparently at least one Depot in the country sent a response:

"I have stopped mobilising"

However, mobilisation went ahead relatively smoothly in Hampshire with almost all reservists reporting for duty and soldiers being equipped and despatched to raise battalions to war establishment.

War Establishments. In 1914 the war establishment of an **Infantry Battalion** was **30 officers** and **977 men** totalling **1,007 all ranks**.

	Officers	Other Ranks
Headquarters	**5**	77
Machine gun section	**1**	**16**
Four Companies (16 Pls)	**24**	**884** (221 per coy.)
Totals	**30**	977

The effect of 300-600 casualties in engagements, therefore, can be imagined. It became the custom as the war progressed to leave 10% of the unit behind in order to help rebuild a battalion if it suffered severe casualties.

An Infantry Brigade consisted of four battalions with a small HQ. This totalled **124 officers** and **3,931 other ranks.**

A Division, with all its supporting units of Infantry, Gunners, Engineers, Medics etc was **585 officers** and **17,488 other ranks** strong. The **bayonet strength** of the three Infantry Brigades in the division was **372 officers** and **11,793 other ranks**.

1914

When war was declared on 4th August 1914 Britain relied upon her Navy to defeat German warships at large, to introduce an economic blockade of Germany, and to provide a safe crossing over the Channel to our Expeditionary Force moving to reinforce the French. The Royal Navy was, in fact well equipped and trained for this and its preparedness was reinforced by the continued mobilisation of the Reserve Fleet which had begun as usual in July, but had not been allowed by Churchill- at the time the First Lord of the Admiralty - to stand down.

The country was nowhere near as well prepared for its military tasks. Two armies actually existed – the Regular army, reinforced by ex-soldiers in the reserves, which could field eight Divisions almost immediately (followed by a further three when units abroad were relieved), and the Territorial Army. The latter comprising 14 Divisions were formed for home defence only and by design needed six months of training before they could be sent abroad. By law there was no obligation for the Territorials to serve outside the United Kingdom, and 60% of a unit needed to volunteer for foreign service before the unit could be made up to strength and sent abroad. Despite deficiencies of their equipment and the poor opinion regulars had of part-time soldiers, 23 Territorial Infantry battalions were on the Western Front before the end of the year. The London Scottish was the first Territorial battalion to launch an attack on 31st October 1914 at Messines-Wytshaete Ridge. In short, the British Expeditionary Force (BEF) would have been badly placed without Territorial units.

Kitchener, however, was not an enthusiast for Territorial formations. Seeing the need to create much larger forces he therefore ignored the existing territorial framework designed for expansion and developed his own "New Armies". This exacerbated existing training and equipment problems but did ensure that there would be significant manpower for the 1916 campaigns.

In Brockenhurst, regulars like **Sergeant Waterman** and the **Large** brothers served in the war in its opening stages. Many locals, however, had been pre-war Territorials. Such men faced the dilemma of staying with their units, e.g. the 5th Battalion of the Hampshire Regiment, against a belief that such units would be retained for Garrison duties allowing Kitchener's New Armies to reach the Front before them. It was seriously perceived that the war would be over by Christmas. Regular reservists – those who had served their time with the colours before 1914, such as **Thomas Moore** and **Charles Tucker** - went straight to Regular battalions.

After three months fighting, the line in France stabilised into roughly the position it would hold until three months before the Armistice in November 1918. The line consisted of muddy trenches with little in the way of a healthy environment, let alone comfort for the fighting soldiers. The German plan to conquer France had been narrowly defeated but at the cost of three Divisions, i.e. 54,000 trained regular soldiers either killed or missing. These losses adversely affected both our training capability as well as the provision of commissioned and non-commissioned leadership for the non-Regular units.

Equipment was in short supply, particularly medium and heavy artillery and also appropriate quantities of high explosive ammunition. The German attack at the First Battle of Ypres in October/November 1914 had been responsible for the draining away of trained manpower and exposed the weakness of our supply and medical systems.

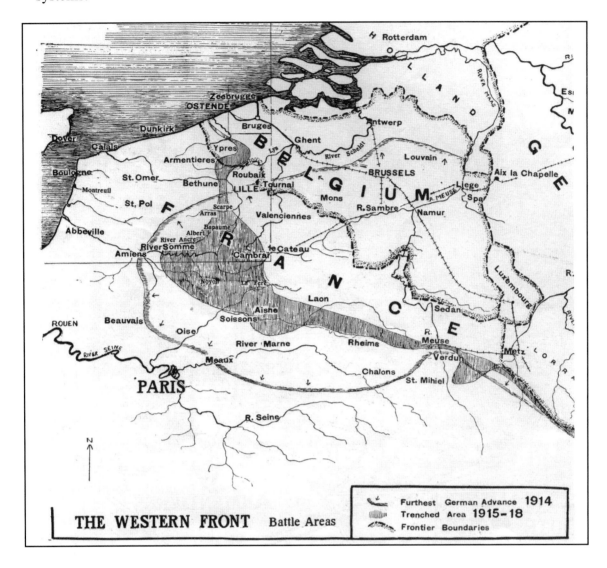

THE WESTERN FRONT Battle Areas

Furthest German Advance **1914**
Trenched Area **1915-18**
Frontier Boundaries

The spirit of patriotism, however, was such that in 1914, at the start of the Great European War, 105 Brockenhurst men - regulars, reservists or Territorials - were serving their King and Country in the Navy (21), Army (80) and Royal Marines (4). Of these 105 names, 20 were to die during the war.

The first casualty in the village was ***Sergeant Harry Waterman*** who was killed at "Plug Street" in Flanders on 7th November 1914.

In the Navy, ***Percy Pope*** was killed on HMS BULWARK on 26th November 1914.

HARRY WATERMAN

Sergeant, 7981

1st Battalion, Hampshire Regiment

Who died on

Saturday 7th November 1914, Aged 27.

According to his grandniece, Sue Lynes, Harry was the second of eleven children born to Fred and Harriet (nee Butt) Waterman. Fred was a carpenter and coffin maker and lived in "Watermans Cottage" in North Road. Harry can be seen as a schoolboy on page 4. His family called him "Midge" because of his small stature. His nephew, born shortly after Harry was killed, was baptised Jesse Midge Waterman.

He enlisted at Lymington, as a regular soldier of the 1st Battalion of the Hampshire Regiment (1 HAMPS) and by the time war was declared was a Sergeant.

He went to France with 11th Brigade, 4th Division of III Corps and is therefore entitled to the 1914 Star and membership of the "Old Contemptibles," whose bravery helped to defeat the Schlieffen Plan and so deflected the German armies from swift victory on the Western Front. This Corps was held back by Kitchener and so did not take part in the Retreat from Mons but joined the British Expeditionary Force by extending the line to the south of the Ypres Salient. Ploegsteert, or "Plug Street" as the troops called it, was never the scene of a set-piece battle but it was an area of continuous trench warfare for the whole of the war. Bruce Bairnsfather first started to draw his "Old Bill" cartoons whilst serving in this sector in late 1914/early 1915. "Plug Street" itself is heavily wooded and with a high water table. The trenches were therefore often flooded and breastworks of sandbags were the natural forms of defence. The casualty rate was both high and continuous, and many bodies were never recovered.

On 7th November 1914 the Germans attacked 4 Division in "Plug Street" Wood. Towards 07.30 a.m., in thick mist, a large group of Germans broke the Worcesters line and spread into the wood. A German officer and 60 men were found behind the line and were promptly dealt with by 1 HAMPS, although at the cost of considerable casualties. Harry Waterman was killed in action on this day and his body was never recovered.

The **Ploegsteert Memorial's** covered circular colonnade records over 1,100 men who have no known grave from fighting in this area. Harry Waterman's name is recorded on:

Panel 6.

PERCY JAMES POPE

Seaman (Signaller), Royal Navy

HMS BULWARK

Who died on

26th November 1914, Aged 19.

Percy's father Percy (Snr.) was born in Brockenhurst but did not go into the family business of wholesale toy makers, which was conducted in the factory behind Clematis Cottage on the Lyndhurst Road. Instead, he became an apprentice blacksmith in the Scammel Factory in Lyndhurst and subsequently joined the army in his trade.

Percy James ("Nip") was born in India on 6th July 1895, where his father was serving as a Farrier Sergeant. Shortly afterwards the family returned to England and lived in Woodlands Road. He attended the village school and on leaving became one of the Telegraph Boys (see page 7) in the village.

This family photograph was taken outside Clematis Cottage with Nip in his grandmother's arms. Nip's mother Fanny, on the right of the picture, died early in 1914 - as did his father - whereupon Nip, when on leave, moved to "River Bank" where he was taken in by his aunt and uncle - Eileen Abbott's parents.

He was always interested in wireless telegraphy and built a radio receiver that worked best with an aerial up the chimney. Eileen Abbot, a cousin now living in Lyndhurst, recalls that this had to be dismantled at the beginning of the war in light of the spy mania of the time.

With this interests it was not surprising that he entered the Navy, as a Boy 2nd Class, on 6th March 1911, initially receiving basic training at IMPREGNABLE. On 24th June he went to GANGES as a Boy 1st Class.

"NIP" POPE AT GANGES

GANGES was a shore-based training establishment for boy ratings founded as a training ship of that name at Shotley, near Harwich, in 1866. The underlying aim was to turn out disciplined, responsible and self-reliant young men possessing confidence, courage, endurance and a sense of service, professionally trained to take their place in the Fleet. Learning to swim was obligatory! He passed out on 8th March 1912 and after further training on VICTORY joined BULWARK on 4th June 1912.

HMS BULWARK

This 15 year old battleship had been refitted at Chatham in 1912 and displaced 15000 tons. It carried 4 x 12" guns and 12 x 6" guns as secondary armaments. It carried a crew of 700-800 all ranks. On it "Nip" progressed to Ordinary signaller and on 8th October 1913 was promoted Signaller. On his Record sheet at this time he was graded "Very Good" for Character and "Satisfactory" for ability.

On the morning of 26 November 1914 the ship was moored at Sheerness and taking on ammunition. At 07.53 an explosion occurred in the forward magazine which rent the ship asunder. The explosion shook buildings in Sheerness and the flash was seen at Southend. When, in the course of two brief minutes the smoke had cleared away the ship had gone down taking all but 12 of its crew with it. As it was a Portsmouth-manned ship four other New Forest men were killed. These were *Alfred Curtis* from Dibden, *William Bricknell* and *William Lowe* from Ealing and *Harry Hyde* from Sway.

Nip was not one of the survivors and his body was never recovered.

His name is therefore recorded on the **Portsmouth Naval Memorial:**

Panel 3

1915

THE HOME FRONT

The mood of the village, reflected from the viewpoint of the Reverend Arthur Chambers writing in the New Forest Magazine, is curious by today's values. After only four months of war, which had seen over 100 village men go off to war, patriotism was intense and the moral justice of it accepted without question.

The Vicar, commenting on the sacrifice of the village's early casualties, writes

> Many of **us are mourning that a dear,** promising lad, Percy James Pope, a **signalman of H.M.S. "Bulwark,"** lost his life in the catastrophe which befell that ship. It has been our privilege to read one or two beautiful **letters** he wrote to his aunt shortly before he died. We confidently **leave his emancipated self in the hands of a loving Father-**God; and **reflect that not one of us who reads these words, has done** as much **as that** sailor lad, in the way of self-sacrifice for National good.
>
> None **of us has given his or her life in the discharge of duty.** We talk and we "fuss" and give our money; and that is *good*; if the end be amelioration of suffering or ill. But oh! let us be honest, and say before God, **that we are infinitely** *less* in the sight of High Heaven, on the point of Self-sacrifice for truth and righteousness, than any humble soldier who dies in the Belgian or French trenches, or any gallant sailor who goes down with his ship. Such a one has given his life for others; we have *not*.

He writes in similar vein in February about Harry Waterman and again in April about Robert Groome.

The *Weekly Dispatch* decided to offer a bronze medallion, designed by a famous sculptor, to be hung forever in a public room of the village deemed to have recruited the greatest percentage of its male population to the Colours before 31st January 1915. Arthur Chambers wrote:

> Wouldn't it be splendid, if Brockenhurst could win **this distinction!** Why not? Let's have **a try, for the cause of** God, Righteousness, King and Country.

The village was certainly behind their Country and their lads. Princess Mary ensured that at Christmas 1914 every soldier in the trenches received a brass box containing tobacco or cigarettes. The village school children raised £4 2s 6d for this cause. The Sunday School children are reported as forsaking their Christmas Tea in order to donate the money saved - £4 4s 5d - to the Belgian Relief Fund.

In September the Ladies of this Parish formed a local branch of the **War Hospitals Supply Depot** to make the bandages and other appliances required for Allied hospitals at home and abroad. A Working Party was formed to make "certain articles of clothing, much needed, for the Wounded Soldiers in the Morant Hospital" (see page 53). In December the Reverend J. E. C. Patterson, whose son was to be killed in the Second World War, appealed for helpers for the **Brockenhurst Sphagnum Moss Depot** to help make wound dressings. The Harvest Festival produce was given to the local Military Hospitals and packages of vegetables were sent weekly to the Fleet in the North Sea

Hospitality to passing units was not unappreciated as the following letter from an officer in the 7th City of London Regiment shows

DEAR VICAR :—May I, on behalf of the N.C. officers and men under my command, ask you to express to the inhabitants of Brockenhurst our great appreciation of the hospitality that they have shown to us during our too short sojourn in the Forest. It was with deep regret that we received our marching orders, and everyone of us came away with a warm corner in our hearts for all the good people of your Parish. Thanking them all.—1 beg to remain, most sincerely yours,

HARRY PARKER.(Lieut.)

Brockenhurst's appetite for lectures continued unabated, with topics during the year covering **"The Organ of Hearing"** and **"Our Mother Tongue"** in February, **"Medical Missionary Work among the Women of India"** in April, and **"Mothers and the War"** in July ("In spite of the rain a good attendance was made".)

Village life continued with school inspections ("Highly Satisfactory"), events to reduce the debt on the Schools Enlargement Fund, excursions organised by the New Forest Natural History Society and the Vicar's worries over meeting the raised contribution of £45 to the Diocesan Fund. The Arts and Crafts Exhibition was held over three days in August and the Vegetable Show in September.

In June the village decided to form the **Brockenhurst Volunteer Training Corps** to assist recruiting for the army as well as providing a training organisation for Home Defence. To motivate men to join the B.V.T.C.

It must also be clearly borne in mind that anyone who declines either to enlist or to join an affiliated Volunteer Corps must not take part as a combatant in the defence of his Country, and in the case of invasion must be prepared to surrender any arms which he may have in his possession. He will also be liable to all non combatant duties such as digging trenches. burying the dead, &c.

Forty-two volunteers had been enrolled by July.

The Memorial. In October the Vicar, concerned by the rising war casualties, wrote

> In view of placing in the Parish Church a permanent Memorial to those Parishioners who have lost their lives in this War, the Vicar is compiling complete and accurate particulars. This will temporarily be placed in the Church Porch, until such time as the permanent Memorial may be erected. Will relatives, or friends of those who have died in action or service kindly send him the following particulars: Name *in full*, age, date of death, Branch of Service, Rank, place of death, cause of death.

THE WAR

Early 1915 saw the B.E.F. reinforced by Canadian and Indian Divisions as well as by an increasing flow of Territorials. The first New Army Division – the 9th (Scottish) - arrived in May. Equipment deficiencies, however, were not made good until later in the year.

Ypres. On 22nd April the Germans initiated the Second Battle of Ypres by releasing its new weapon of poison gas.

They did not, however, follow up their success and the hole in the line was plugged by the amazing bravery of

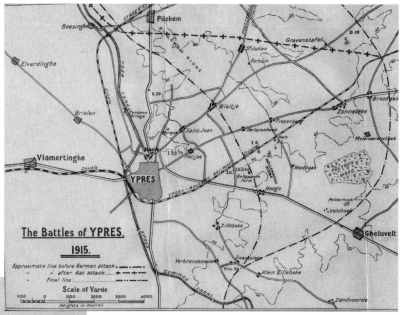

The Battles of YPRES, 1915.

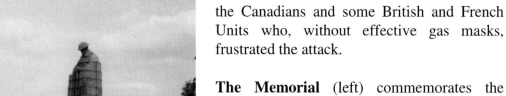

the Canadians and some British and French Units who, without effective gas masks, frustrated the attack.

The Memorial (left) commemorates the Canadian casualties incurred at the site in St Julien of this first gas attack. The trees are deliberately shaped to represent shells exploding.

Herbert and *Philip Large, Robert Groome, Richard Tillyer, Thomas Moore, Charles Tucker* and *Fred Jerrim* all died at Ypres.

The Western Front.. Field Marshal Sir John French, commander of the B.E.F., tried to improve the line with limited results at Aubers Ridge (March – May), Festubert (15-20 May) and later in the year (25 September – 4 October) at Loos. *Harold Large* was killed whilst in reserve for this latter offensive. *Thomas Dove,* not on the Memorial, died of wounds at Bethune in December.

Gallipoli. The need to keep Russia in the war led the Government to favour an attack on the Gallipoli peninsula as a way of defeating the Turks and opening up a southern supply route to Russia. Field Marshal French was against this as it took artillery, ammunition and troops - particularly the Regular 29th Division - away from the main theatre of operations in France.

Three more of the village's recorded casualties, *Charles Christopher, Alan Hinves* and *William Wells* were all incurred in the Gallipoli operation. *John Harris, John Hill* and *Bill Reynard* also died at Gallipoli but are not on the Memorial.

Other Theatres of War. The **Mesopotamian campaign** was in full swing. Private *S. Stokes,* also not on the Memorial, was to die there in December. The occupation of **Salonica** was initiated at the end of the year.

Other Casualties. Finally, not all casualties occurred on the battlefield and two recorded villagers – *Ernest Field* and *William Janes* – died of illness or were accidentally killed. *James Miller,* unrecorded, died at Chichester in November.

RECRUITING IN BROCKENHURST

Before the war the army maintained a recruiting office at Lymington. *Harry Waterman*, who was killed thirteen weeks after the war began - and thereby became the first village casualty - enlisted there, as did **Charles Christopher, George Clark, John Gates, Bill Harrison, Tom Moore, Fred Sibley** and **Jesse Tregunna.**

In Autumn 1914 a recruiting office was opened in Brockenhurst. Tony Johnson believes that the Brockenhurst office was set up at "The Briars" in Avenue Road.

This photograph was taken in 1914 outside what is now Lloyds Bank in Brockenhurst. The photographer was John Martin, whose young son Ken can be seen standing on the running board of the car. A prized possession, his toy plane, is below him on the road.

Jesse Sque is standing above the passenger seat. He worked for the Post Office before enlisting into the Hampshire Regiment. The **New Forest Magazine** for February 1915 reported

---

"Mr. J. Sque, whom many of us know and respect, has been wounded and is a prisoner of war. God protect him! we pray."

22

Recruiting in the New Forest
A days batch from Brockenhurst (15 May 1915)
Photo by
J.W. Martin Brockenhurst

THE RECRUITING OFFICE IN AVENUE ROAD

It would appear that many men preferred to enlist away from home.

Born in village. Statistics taken from **"Soldiers Died"** show that of the twenty-nine men born in the village and who served in the Army, only nine enlisted in Brockenhurst, of whom 4 lived elsewhere and 5 did not offer details of residence.

Born and resident in village. Curiously ten others, who were both born and resident at the time of enlistment in Brockenhurst, enlisted at:

Gosport	***Arthur Rittey.***
Hilsea	***Bill Povey***
Lymington	***George Clark, Bill Harrison, Tom Moore*** and
	Harry Waterman.
Southampton	***Harold Hinves***
Swansea	***Thomas Dove.***
Winchester	***William Waterman.***

Resident in village. Of the 25 village residents who died in the Great War only one man - ***George Christopher*** - declared, on recruitment, Brockenhurst as his place of residence. All of the other 24 residents who died enlisted at other Recruiting Stations - 8 going to Lymington so to do.

ERNEST HENRY HUGH FIELD

Private

Royal Marine Light Infantry

Who died on

6th February 1915, Aged 17.

Ernest Field was born on 30th July 1897 in Lymington. He was brought up in the Wesleyan faith and worked as a clerk. His father later lived at 16 Careys Cottages in Brockenhurst.

Ernest enlisted into the Royal Marine Light Infantry in Southampton on 9th November 1914. He was 17¼ years old on enlistment and his description was given as height 5' 5$^1/_8$", of fresh complexion with grey eyes and brown hair. He also had a scar on his chin. His classification for conduct on enlistment is given as

"First Class."

Interestingly his documents show that he was knowingly enlisted under age and that 263 days of his service would be forfeited before he reached 18 years of age. This would have affected, had he lived, his service towards his engagement, good conduct badges and pension.

He served in the depot with a *"Very Good"* character grading until 6th February 1915 when he was annotated as:

"Discharged Dead".

He actually died from Meningitis which, before penicillin or antibiotics, was difficult to treat successfully. There was a feeling at the time that there was a post-death possibility of cross-infection and this usually meant the funeral was effected quickly. This may account for his local burial in Deal rather than at Brockenhurst.

He is buried in **Deal** Civil Cemetery,

Plot C Row 1 Grave 215.

His name is also commemorated on the **Methodist Church Memorial** (see page 119.)

HERBERT EDWARD LARGE

Captain

3rd Battalion, Middlesex Regiment

Who died on

Tuesday, 16th February 1915, Aged 38.

Robert Emmott Large built Latchmoor in 1911. After Robert died his wife moved to Little Latchmoor on the Lymington – Brockenhurst Road, calling her house after the old home she loved. There were five sons to the marriage. Three sons, all regular soldiers, were killed and the fourth wounded.

Herbert Edward was born on 30th December 1876 at Teddington Middlesex. At some date after 1911 he married Ivy, who came from Mullingar, Co. Westmeath

His Record of Service shows that he joined the Embodiea Militia on 20th December 1899. He took part in the operations against the Boers in Cape Colony from March 1900 until 27th July 1901 when he returned to England to be commissioned into the Middlesex Regiment.

After having passed the Mounted Infantry course at Woolwich he returned to South Africa on 11th March 1902, only to guard Boer prisoners of war on St Helena. He remained in South Africa until 1906 initially as Interpreter and censor, then as Assistant Press Censor, before joining the 6th Mounted Infantry.

On 4th October 1906 the 3rd Battalion of the Middlesex Regiment, with both Herbert and his brother Philip serving together, was posted to China. In 1908 the battalion moved to Singapore until it was posted to India on 19th December 1910. Herbert was promoted Captain on 21st January 1911 and briefly joined the 1st Battalion on 7th July before, as his Record has it, he

> *"Transferred back to 3rd Bn, Aug 1911,*
> *in exchange with Capt Samuel".*

The 3rd Battalion returned from India on Christmas Eve 1914. Commanded by Lieutenant Colonel E.W.R. Stephenson it camped at Mornhill Camp, Winchester, as part of 85 Brigade of 28 Division.

This Division arrived in France on 19th January 1915 and on 7th February moved into the Ypres Salient (St Eloi) , completing its first tour four days later. The next day they were back in the same trenches, but on the 14th of the month "B" Coy. were forced to retire from "O" trench. Due to a misunderstanding they retired too far. "M" trench was also therefore lost and the CO, Adjutant (Herbert Large) and 28 men came forward with the intention of retaking this trench.

During this counter-attack Herbert was killed with two other men.

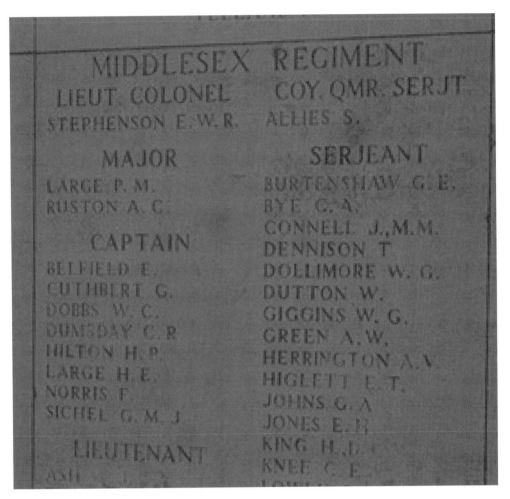

PANEL 49

His body has no known grave and his name therefore appears on the **Menin Gate Memorial** at Ypres on:

Panel 49

His brother, *Major P. M. Large* (see page 32), is also commemorated on the same Panel.

27

ROBERT E. C. GROOME

Second Lieutenant

65th Battery, Royal Field Artillery

Who died on

Thursday 4th March 1915, Aged 19.

Robert Groome was the son of Harry and Marguerite Groome of Brooklands, Brockenhurst.

Whilst his Service Papers have not survived it is known that he entered the Royal Artillery as a 2nd Lieutenant and served with the 65th Battery, RFA. This was a 4.5-inch Howitzer battery in the 28th Artillery Brigade of the 5th Division.

4.5 inch HOWITZER

The War Diary of this unit is interesting as a window into that period.

2nd March. No registration carried out with aeroplanes - weather too cloudy. About 12.30 37 Battery reported that their observer saw Germans massing in O4d08. O.C. 9 Brigade gave orders to Right Group & 1 Belgian battery & one heavy battery were ordered to fire on the spot by HQ. Germans dispersed.

3rd March.

9.15 a.m. 3rd Bde continue the wire entanglement cutting experiment.

2.45 p.m. 366th Battery shelled - two gun wheels broken.

4.00 p.m. 3rd Brigade report being heavily shelled

4.45 p.m. German heavy batteries stopped shelling.

11.30 p.m. **Report received of casualty to Lt Groom of 65th Battery wounded by shrapnel on road - both legs broken. Bombr who accompanied him had right leg broken.**

He was evacuated to the Casualty Clearing Station in Poperinge but later died of his wounds. The **New Forest Magazine** for April 1915 reported

---

Very great sympathy with Mr. and Mrs. Groome is felt by us all in their deep bereavement. Their only son and child, Robert Edward Charles Groome, 2nd Lieut. in the Royal Field Artillery, died of wounds at Poperinghe, France, on March 4th. A letter subsequently received by his Parents from the Colonel of the Regiment shows how heroically and self-denyingly he faced suffering and death. His demand, when fearfully wounded, that a drink of water should first be given to a companion less wounded than himself, makes us think of Sir Philip Sidney. This gallant young Officer, only 21 years of age was no less a hero of the battle-field than Sir Philip of the past.

Robert is buried alongside another Gunner officer in **Poperinge Old Military Cemetery** in:

Plot 2. N. 53

The Groome Trust in Brockenhurst gives help when required to villagers. There is no apparent link, however, between the Trust and the memory of Robert Groome.

RICHARD BATESON BLUNT TILLYER

Lieutenant

1st Battalion, Royal Warwickshire Regiment

Who died on

Sunday 25th April 1915, Aged 22.

Richard Tillyer was born on 27th November 1892 at Cambridge Lodge, Kingston Road, New Malden. He was the son of Richard Henry Tillyer, a farmer (500 acres, 26 men, and 5 boys, in Harmondsworth, Middlesex) of independent means and Florence Anna, formerly Harvey. His uncle, Major C B Harvey, had been killed in South Africa. The family later moved to and lived in Marston Gate, Brockenhurst. For 3 years he went to Haileybury before attending The Army School at Holyport. A report from here records that he was

> *" not a leader, but influence undoubtedly makes for good. Rather shy. Very observant. Above average in common sense and reliability. Best long distance runner in the school."*

Richard was appointed to a Special Reserve Commission in 3rd Battalion The Warwickshire Regiment on 15th October 1912. He received his Commission in March 1913 as a regular officer into the 1st Battalion, The Royal Warwickshire Regiment, and reported to them at Shorncliffe near Dover. The Battalion at this time was commanded by Lieutenant Colonel J F Elkington. It went to France as part of 10th Brigade, 4th Division in what, as the British Expeditionary Force, (BEF) the Kaiser called the "Contemptible little army".

10th Brigade was a curious one with an unlikely combination of 1st Warwicks, 2nd Seaforth Highlanders, 1st Royal Irish Fusiliers and the 2nd Royal Dublin Fusiliers. However, it seemed to work and the Division had a difficult early war serving in the Retreat from Mons, the Battles of Le Cateau, Néry. and the Marne. It was during this retreat from Le Cateau that Colonel Elkington tried to surrender his exhausted unit. Although cashiered for this by court-martial he enlisted in the French Foreign Legion, served heroically for 18 months, was decorated by both the French and British and was subsequently restored to his rank and position in the British Army.

In September the reinforced Battalion was involved in the crossing and the Battle of the Aisne, the Battle of Armentiers and the capture of Metern. There was then a resumption of trench warfare until the 2nd Battle of Ypres began on the 22nd April 1915. This began with the German gas attack at St Julien. It was initially stemmed by the outstanding bravery of the Canadians.

By the 24th, however, they had fallen back and a counter attack was essential. The Warwick's Unit War Diary records:

> ***24 April.*** *".....Brigade came up and orders were received to advance at 4pm via VLAMERTINGHE & halted outside YPRES from 8pm to 12mn. Started to rain. YPRES was heavily shelled and on fire.*
>
> ***25 April.*** *Left YPRES at 12mn for VIELJE where orders were received for the attack. The Brigade attacked at 4.30 am. We attacked wood on the left of the line   with 7th ARG & SUTH HIGHLDRS in support. The SEA. HIGHLDRS, R.IRISH FUS, R. DUB. FUS .attacked on our right on ST JULIEN.   Owing to the German trenches being insufficiently shelled and supports being unable to come up the Line retired at about 7 am to trenches near the farm and consolidated our position.* **Our casualties were very heavy, 17 Officers, 500 other ranks, killed, wounded &Missing.** *Heavy Gunfire all day. About 2.30 pm the NORTHUMBERLAND DIVISION attacked ST JULIEN without success. We opened supporting fire from our trenches. The LAHORE DIVISION attacked on our left but gained very little ground being stopped by gas."*

As the Regimental History says

> ***"The need for a counter attack was imperative, but it was lamentable that it should have been necessary to deliver it without sufficient support from artillery and without a previous thorough reconnaissance of the enemy position."***

The List of Casualties on 25th April 1915 amongst Officers for this unit records that Richard, in "C" Company, was one of the officers wounded in this attack. After the initial entry, however, this document was annotated to show Richard as missing. On 1st June 1915 a letter from C2 Casualties to the War Office about Richard advised:

> ***".... No further news although many enquiries made, so suggest death should be presumed for official reasons as having occurred on or about 26th April 1915."***

His body was never recovered.   His name therefore appears on the **Menin Gate Memorial** on:

Panel 8

PHILIP MARTIN LARGE

Major

Middlesex Regiment

Who died on

Tuesday 27th April 1915.

Philip came from a well known Brockenhurst family.

He was commissioned into the Middlesex Regiment as a regular soldier on 6th June 1896. Promoted to Lieutenant on 26 June 1899 he served in the Boer War, initially taking part in operations in Natal in April to June 1900. On the 11th June he took part in the brilliant little action at Alleman's Nek which caused the Boers to evacuate their strong position at nearby Laing's Nek. He then took part in chasing the Boers in the Transvaal and in the Orange Free State. Towards the end of the war he took part in the operations on the Zululand Frontier of Natal, and in September 1901 was at the defence of Fort Itala when it blocked Botha's last attempt to invade Natal. Philip was awarded both the Queen's and King's South African Medals and was Mentioned in Despatches on 29th July 1902.

In 1903 and 1904 Philip was with the 2nd battalion, firstly in Natal and, later, in Hounslow. From then onwards he served in the 3rd Battalion with his brother Herbert.

When war broke out the battalion was stationed at Cawnpore as part of the 8th (Lucknow) Division. It returned to England on Christmas Eve 1914 to join the 85th Brigade in 28th Division. It landed in France on 19th January 1915, and by 6th February was in the line south of Ypres.

This first spell in the trenches was difficult with the enemy so close and on higher ground that reports could not be sent back in daylight by runner to Battalion Headquarters. When they were relieved on 11th February the Battalion had not only suffered with one officer and 26 other ranks killed (2 and 56 wounded) but also had 80% casualties from frostbite. The Battalion Diary reports that:

> *"Many rifles hopelessly damaged owing to mud, the men standing over their knees in liquid mud practically the whole time, in one trench only 2 rifles able to fire out of 25."*

This particular trench system was untenable and it was in the digging of a new reserve line that Philip's brother Herbert was killed (see page 26).

On 15th February the unit was withdrawn, having suffered in three days of trench warfare 4 officers killed (three wounded), 44 other ranks killed (62 wounded) and 156 other ranks missing. Thankfully March was a quiet month for the unit.

The Second Battle of Ypres began on 22nd April with the Germans initiating poison gas warfare by releasing a dense green cloud of gas late in the afternoon. This caused the attacked French troops to retreat and 3rd Battalion of the Middlesex Regiment had, with other units, to defend St Jean to block the German advance on Ypres. Next day, "A" and "C" Companies of the Middlesex advanced to link up with the Canadians and moved forward under fire to Pilckem Ridge. For most of the day they were heavily shelled and at times almost suffocated by gas fumes, but they hung on until at 4.30 pm another attack was ordered. The Unit War Diary for 23/5/15 reports:

> *"...The Bn. was shelled very heavily for about 4 hours and was nearly suffocated at times with fumes from the shells. During the afternoon reinforcements came up and strengthened the Canadians' position on the left, and some went up on the right of the battalion.*
>
> *The attack then recommenced somewhere about 4.30 p.m..* **The majority of "C" Company under Major Large advanced with (the) first line whilst one platoon of "A" Company under Colonel Stephenson followed in 2nd line, about 150 yards in rear.**
>
> *The advance was conducted by rushing over extremely open country for about 250 yards where 1st line suffered very heavy losses. About 5 maxims swept these companies from right front, and 2 or 3 from left front and practically everybody in that portion of the firing line was killed or wounded within 3 minutes."*

By dusk the two companies had ceased to exist, losing four officers killed, three wounded, one missing and about 200 other rank casualties.

The Regimental History, on page 107, lists the officers killed on 23rd April as being Major P. M. Large, Lieutenant S. Fergusson and 2nd Lieutenants Sharpe and Whitfield. The Commonwealth War Graves Commission, however, records Philip's date of death as 27th April 1915 as does *"Soldiers Died"*, which reports him as killed in action.

His body was never recovered and his name therefore appears on the **Menin Gate Memorial** to the missing, at Ypres on:

Panel 49

THOMAS GEORGE IVEMY MOORE

Fusilier, 12118

3rd Battalion, Royal Fusiliers

Who died on

Monday, 24th May 1915, Aged 26.

Thomas was the son of Fred, an agricultural labourer, and Augusta Moore who subsequently lived in Grape Cottage, Manchester Road, Sway. He, however, was born and bred in Brockenhurst.

He enlisted at Lymington, before the war, into the 3rd Battalion, Royal Fusiliers (City of London Regiment). This unit was in Lucknow (India) when war broke out, and arrived in England on 14th December 1914. It re-embodied at Winchester on 24th December 1914 as part of the 85th Brigade in 28 Division. This regular division, one of the last to be formed, landed in France the following month, and moved directly into the Ypres Salient.

THE MENIN GATE

On 22nd April 1915 the Germans attacked in what came to be called the 2nd Battle of Ypres. The battle lasted for five weeks.

The unit War Diary records:

> *"**May 21**. Moved to trenches - occupying line from Railway 1.11.b to BELLEWAARDE Lake. 2 1/2 Coys in Firing Line - 1 1/2 Coys in support.   Coys 8 DLI (T) attached for instruction -*
> > *3 Officers joined on line of march*
> > *3 men wounded on way to trenches.*
>
> ***May 22.** Slight crumping and rifle fire - casualties 3 killed - 6 wounded.*
>
> ***May 23**. Fairly quiet day. Casualties 12 wounded.*
>
> ***May 24**. 2.30 a.m. - Gassing started by Germans. Trenches on our left vacated by 8 Middlesex and later on in the morning a Coy of East Surreys retired. 1/2 Coy under Lts Sealy and Stollary occupied vacated trenches - several casualties and both Officers killed. The gas used on this occasion was particularly thick and strong and immediately after the gas was emitted heavy and continuous rifle and machine-gun fire was opened by the Germans.*
>
> *By 8 a.m. our fire-trenches were occupied by the Germans - **all the Officers being wounded and the majority of the men gassed or wounded**. A large number of men had only the small old-fashioned respirator, which proved of little use."*

The surviving 150 men of the Royal Fusiliers - out of a battalion strength of 880 - succeeded, with the help of small parties from the Buffs and the Durham Light Infantry, in holding the Third line of trenches until relieved. This was the last action in the Battle of Bellewarde Ridge and finally stopped the German advance. The resultant trench lines remained static for the next two years.

Thomas Moore was not, however, amongst the survivors of the day, and his body was never identified. His name is therefore recorded on the **Menin Gate Memorial** at Ypres on:

Panels 6 and 8.

CHARLES HARRY TUCKER

Private, 11029

1st Battalion, Wiltshire Regiment

Who died on

Thursday 17th June 1915, Aged 28.

Charles Tucker was born in Hendon, Middlesex. The parents and their three children later moved to live in Tattenham Road, Brockenhurst.

He went to the village school with his brothers Fred and Arthur and was a member of the parish church choir. It is not unlikely that he was also a bell-ringer as his father, Charles William Tucker, was both Tower Captain and Choirmaster. Indeed, Charles (Snr.) even taught Jack Hull to ring! His brother Frederick, who also served in the army during the war, certainly rang as his name appears on a Peal Board in the Church tower for ringing a peal on 30th November 1929, which his father conducted.

CHARLES HARRY TUCKER

During the war Charles' sister Hilda met Alfred ("John") Walker, who was a patient in the No. 1 New Zealand Hospital. Alfred was nicknamed "John" by the Tucker family. When he was courting her he used to take Johnnie Walker whisky to Hilda's father Charles!

In time they were married in St Nicholas Church, before settling in New Zealand. Hilda played the organ in Hawkes Bay church there for many years. Three of her children served in the Second World War - Deryck in the Army, Jay in the Women's Auxiliary Army Corps and Dal in the Air Force. Dal and his wife, Ruth laid a wreath at the ANZAC service when they last visited Brockenhurst in 1989.

At the outbreak of the war Charles enlisted in Salisbury as a reservist into the 1st Battalion, The Duke of Edinburgh's Wiltshire Regiment (1 WILTS.).

This regular unit was part of 7 Brigade of 3 Division and had taken part in the retreat from Mons and the Battles of Le Cateau, Ypres and Neuve Chapelle. In this period of 10 weeks the battalion had lost 26 officers and about 1000 men – more than the war establishment of the battalion when it started fighting.

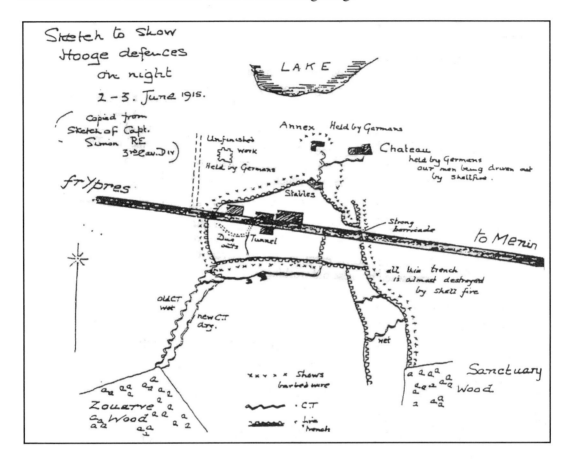

On 5th November 1914, 1 WILTS entered the trenches at Hooge in the Ypres Salient. They remained in the Salient for nine months, taking part in the Second Battle of Ypres as well as defending Hooge and assaulting Spanbroek Molen in support of the Battle of Neuve Chapelle. April and May 1915 were spent in the Dickensbusch Trenches before, in June, they returned to assault the German lines at Hooge Chateau.

At some stage of these actions Charles Tucker was seriously wounded. He subsequently died of his wounds in 3 Division's Casualty Clearing Station at Bailleul.

Charles is buried in **Bailleul Communal Cemetry** in:

Grave 1. E. 94.

WILLIAM JOHN JANES

Private, 2597

1/7th (Territorial Force) Battalion, Hampshire Regiment

Who died on

7th July 1915, Aged 26.

William was the eldest son of Mr & Mrs William Henry and Frances Janes of Martins Road, Brockenhurst. Will was born at Sway. His father, however, being a gardener, followed work around the New Forest - an occurrence reflected in Will's Communion Certificate. This records his baptism in Sway in 1899, his confirmation in Lyndhurst in 1904 and his first communion in Brockenhurst.

WILL AS A CHAUFFER TO MONTAGUE ELLIS, OF CULVERLY, BEFORE THE WAR.

He enlisted at Bournemouth and joined the Hampshire Regiment's 7th Territorial Battalion (7 HAMPS) before the war and was at camp at Burford when war was declared. (See Moses House). One brother also joined the Hampshire Regiment, whilst the other enlisted into the Veterinary Corps.

Will embarked on 9th October 1914 with the battalion for India. A month later the battalion relieved 2 HAMPS at Colaba.

He was a member of "D" Company. With his driving skills he was attached as an assistant driver to the Maxim gun troop of three armoured cars.

The battalion carried out its normal round of garrison duties and was also put through challenging "Kitchener tests" to determine fitness for active service. These included field-firing exercises during one of which William was accidentally killed by a gunshot wound.

WILL IN INDIA

In reporting the accident the **HYDERABAD BULLETIN** *noted:*

" The three cars were being used on 22 Cavalry Range at Bolaram. Janes was in his usual place in the assistant driver's seat, which is in the front, protected from gunfire by a hood. The Maxim inside, capable of discharging about 400 shots a minute, is fired over the heads of the driver (Corporal Bartlett) and his assistant.

About 8 o'clock the car was advancing at a slow pace while the gun was being used. The ground was uneven, a sudden jolt of the car gave the gun such a jerk that a bullet, instead of passing over the protection hood, struck the edge and was diverted downwards. It struck the unfortunate Janes in the back of the head, and killed him instantaneously.

The funeral took place the same evening in Trinulgherry Cantonment Cemetery.

Full military honours were paid to the deceased and every available man in his Company paraded. Ted Blachford, a fellow villager, was the main wreath-bearer.

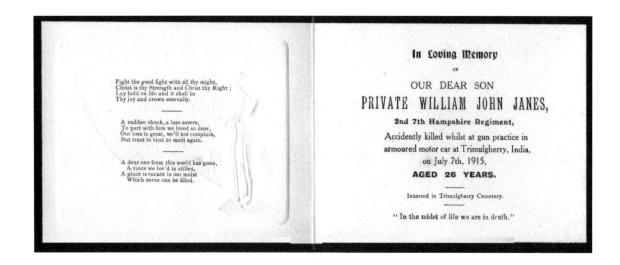

His name is recorded, as one of the 1000 servicemen who served in garrisons and died in India in the 1914-18 war, on the **Madras War Memorial** Chennai on:

Face 17.

BRONZE MEMORIAL PLAQUE AND WAR MEDAL FOR PTE WILLIAM JOHN JANES

FRED HENRY JERRIM

Private, 3/3417

1st Battalion, Hampshire Regiment

Who died on

Wednesday 7th July 1915.

Fred Jerrim was the son of Thomas and Mary Jerrim who lived in Woodlands Road. He had a sister who is remembered as being a teacher at Sway School in the 1930s.

He either enlisted into the 1st Battalion of the Hampshire Regiment (1 HAMPS) or was a reservist recalled to the colours and had returned to the battalion. 1 HAMPS, in 4 Division, had had a difficult war having been involved on the Western Front since Mons. They were heavily involved in the Second Battle of Ypres, that started on 22nd April 1915. By 3rd May 116 had been killed in the battalion and 208 wounded, with a further 60 killed and 109 men killed by 14 May 1915.

The Second battle of Ypres ended in the last week of May and the month of June was a quieter time for the unit. As the British Army grew in size so French trenches to the south of Ypres were taken over and much time was spent in co-ordinating and improving them as well as aggressive patrolling of No Mans Land. This cost another 29 casualties.

On 6th July 1915 1 HAMPS were ordered to support an attack by the Rifle Brigade on the International Trench, a 300 yard feature lost by the French before we took over their line. The attack succeeded but cost the brigade 450 casualties.

Fred was one of the eleven Hampshire men killed in this action.

His body was never recovered and he is therefore recorded on the **Menin Gate Memorial** at Ypres on:

Panel 35.

HAROLD E LARGE

Captain

10th Battalion, Rifle Brigade

Who died on

Friday 8th October 1915, Aged 35.

Harold Emmot Large was born on 31st March 1880. His Service Records, curiously, have apparently only survived because they were amongst correspondence sent to his solicitor for remission of death duties.

Harold was commissioned as a Second Lieutenant into the 6th Battalion The Rifle Brigade on 10th April 1900. He successfully attended Riding Courses at the Curragh in 1901 and at Aldershot in 1904 and attained the rank of Captain before resigning his commission on 4th April 1908, when the battalion was disbanded.

He rejoined the army on 30th September 1914 and was posted to the 10th Battalion The Rifle Brigade (10 RB) as a Temporary Captain. From the time war was declared until its disbandment on 14th April 1918 10 RB was part of 59th Brigade of 20th (Light) Division. This New Army Division had no existence before the outbreak of the war but during September 1914 this junior Division of the 2nd New Army began to assemble in the Aldershot area. After problems with equipment were resolved the Division was inspected by the King, on 20th June 1915, before embarking for France four days later.

On 15th September it took part in the attack towards Fromelles as part of III Corps of Second Army. The Front soon stabilised, however, and from 20-27th September only 3 were killed and 7 wounded.

On the 27th the Battalion moved into billets in Levantie as Brigade reserve. During the following 10 days 10 RB suffered a number of casualties whilst training with grenades, on working parties at night to the line and in attempting to clear enemy wire to assist the attack of another unit. On 9th October the unit War Diary records

> *"Capt H E Large, whilst walking along the Rue Tilleloy, was wounded by a stray bullet and died the same day."*

Harold was medically evacuated back to 60 Field Ambulance where he almost immediately died of his wounds.

He is buried in the Royal Irish Cemetery at **Laventie in:**

Plot 1.H. 13.

Fanny Speedy, a Matron with the No. 1 New Zealand Hospital, visited Latchmore House on 13th December 1916. She wrote in her diary for that day:

> *"...Had tea with Mrs Large and spent a pleasant 2 hours in a comfortable well-built house and before an open fire. The entrance door is like a stable door. The Larges are an elderly couple with plenty of money, but they do the work themselves as all their men servants are at the war. Mrs Large was Matron of a London hospital at one time. She is his second wife.*
>
> *He has lost three sons in the war and the only remaining one is in France."*

GALLIPOLI

The Gallipoli Campaign was originally conceived by Winston Churchill. The immediate purpose was to force the Straights and deal Turkey such a blow that it would withdraw from the War. Bulgaria would similarly be deterred from co-operating with Germany and pressure on Russia reduced with improved Allied supplies. Had the initial attack been successful these objectives could arguably have been achieved and the war significantly shortened.

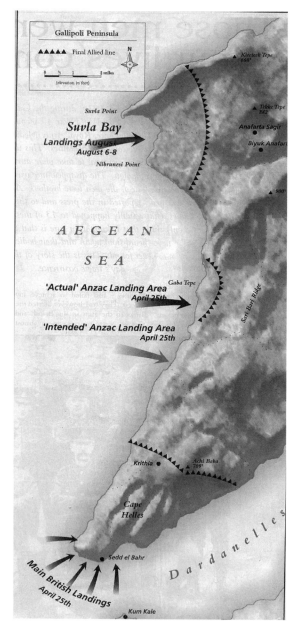

THE GALLIPOLI PENINSULA

The initial assault by the British and French Navies was not successful. In the last week of April 1915, therefore, two ANZAC Divisions and the 29 Division effected a landing at Helles on the Southern tip of the peninsula. The subsequent Battles for Krithia and Achi Baba were not a success. Turkish reinforcements, freed by Russia's inability to co-ordinate attacks in the Black Sea, helped by German "advisers" frustrated attempts at the Second (where ***Charles Christopher*** and ***John Hill*** were killed) and Third battles for these locations.

More troops were sent out and on 6th August 1915 landings were made at Sari Bair and Suvla. Confusion, lack of urgency by senior commanders, shortages of water and strong Turkish counter attacks negated early successes.

John Harris of the 2nd Battalion (killed on 6th August), and ***Alan Hinves, Walter Reynard*** and ***William Wells,*** all serving in 10th Battalion the Hampshire Regiment, were killed in this phase of the campaign. The loss of four villagers in five days can be imagined. None of these six bodies were ever recovered.

The principal aim of the operation unachieved, the Peninsula was finally successfully evacuated on 8th January 1916.

CHARLES RICHARD CHRISTOPHER

Private, 10543

2nd Battalion, Hampshire Regiment

Who died on

Saturday 8th May 1915, Aged 18.

Charles was born in the autumn of 1896 in Christchurch, Hampshire, lived in Brockenhurst (see page 113) and enlisted at Lymington into the 2nd Battalion, Hampshire Regiment.

After training, 2nd Hampshire (2 HAMPS) were sent to Gallipoli as part of 88 Brigade, itself part of the "Immortal" 29th Division. The 29th Division had taken part in the landings at Helles on 25th April 1915 and experienced such a very difficult first five days ashore that its effective strength was down to 149 officers and 6746 men. With some reinforcements, however, the Division was earmarked to spearhead the next attack on the Turks.

The 2nd Battle of Krithia began on 6th May. 2 HAMPS, like the other units of 88 Brigade, had lost its commander as well as most of its company, platoon and section leaders. Not a man had had a real night's sleep for a fortnight. Both attacks on 6th and 7th May were disastrous failures from which the unit emerged yet further weakened. Reduced artillery ammunition supplies caused the attack scheduled for mid-morning on 8th May to fail. At 5.30 p.m. all reserves, including 2 HAMPS, were thrown in for another advance on Krithia which again failed, with a third of all troops used killed or wounded. The **New Forest Magazine** for December 1915 records:

> *"Missing since last May, killed, his body was found in the early part of May and was buried. The Alexandra Enquiry Office apologised for the delay due to the heavy fighting in Gallipoli. Our deepest sympathy to the family for one who was only 18."*

Charles has, however, no grave. His name is therefore recorded on the **Helles Memorial** in Turkey on:

Panel 128

John Philip Godwin Hill, who was born and enlisted in Brockenhurst into the same battalion, was also killed in this action. He is not recorded on the village Memorial but his name is to be found at **Helles** on

Panel 130

ALAN HINVES

Private, 14645

and

WILLIAM CHARLES WELLS

Private, 10547

Both of 10th Battalion, Hampshire Regiment

both of whom died on

Tuesday 10th August 1915.

Alan Hinves was baptised in Brockenhurst on 7th July 1895. He was a son of Charles, a gardener, and Harriet Hinves of Tattenham Road, Brockenhurst. He enlisted in the village into the 10th Battalion of the Hampshire Regiment.

William Wells was the son of Charles and Harriet Wells of Partridge Road. He also enlisted into the same battalion.

10th Hampshires (10 HAMPS) was a Kitchener battalion which curiously was the only non-Irish formation in what was otherwise the Territorial 10 (Irish) Division. Alan and William therefore found themselves serving in 29th Brigade alongside 6 Royal Irish Rifles, 5 Connaught Rangers and 6 Leinsters under the Divisional command of Lieutenant General Sir Bryan Mahon KCVO. This Division was part of the XI Corps that landed at Suvla Bay on 7th August 1915.

ALAN HINVES

Whilst the initial landings on the evening of 6th August had gone quite well lack of control soon allowed reinforcing units to become confused and muddled, with instances of troops firing on friendly forces in the dark.

Both soldiers landed at Suvla at daybreak of 7th August. Of the three Brigades in 10 Division one was landed correctly, one put ashore well to the South and one had been detached at the last minute to what is now known as Anzac Cove to help the main assault there. Units were, however, thrown piecemeal into the action, initially under other Divisional control. In short, in the first 24 hours ashore IX Corps achieved very little but lost 100 officers and 1,600 men either killed or wounded. The Sari Bair Ridge, the key to the position remained in Turkish hands.

Dawn on 10th August found part of 10 HAMPS on the left flank of the attack, in the area of "The Farm", intermixed with elements of 39 and 40 Brigades. The other half of 10 HAMPS were on the opposite side of the Aghyl Dere with elements of the 38th Brigade. In between were Gurkhas, Australians and Midlanders. All were tired, hungry and thirsty. The Turks then counter attacked and by sheer weight of numbers overwhelmed the defence. There were so few survivors at "The Farm" that no clear account was ever given of what happened. Alan and William (aged 21) were two of the 12,000 casualties of this battle. With the failure to gain the ridge at Chunuk Bair the last real hope of victory went at Gallipoli.

THE HELLES MEMORIAL

Both soldiers have their names recorded on the **Helles Memorial**:

Alan Hinves' name is on **Panel 130**
William Wells' name is on **Panel 138**

Lance Corporal Walter Reynard, who lived in Brockenhurst but whose name does not appear on its War Memorial, was also killed in this action. His name is recorded on the **Helles Memorial** on:

Panel 227

THE VILLAGE AND ITS HOSPITALS

THE LADY HARDINGE HOSPITAL

In September 1914 India sent the 3rd (Lahore) and 7th (Meerut) Divisions and a cavalry division to France. This Indian Corps landed at Marseilles and, by 23rd October the Lahore Division had begun to concentrate at Estaires. Within a week it had incurred 1565 casualties from the fighting at Neuve Chapelle. It remained in the La Bassee area during the First Battle of Ypres and suffered badly from the winter.

In 1915 a hospital was set up for Indian troops in Brockenhurst under the patronage of Lady Hardinge, the wife of the Viceroy of India. Located in Church Lane, with wards also at Balmer Lawn and Forest Park, it cared for nearly 3000 patients resulting from the Indian Corps involvement in the battles of Second Ypres, Festubert, Aubers Ridge and Loos.

KING GEORGE V AND QUEEN MARY VISITING THE LADY HARDINGE HOSPITAL IN 1914

Convalescent Indian troops were located in a tented camp opposite the Forest Park Hotel in Brockenhurst. The King is seen here accompanied by Lieutenant Colonel Robert Archer Lloyd of the Indian Medical Service, who was in command of the hospital.

Eileen Abbott (see page 2) recalls being told that when King George and Queen Mary visited wounded Indian soldiers in the Forest Park Hospital, they drove to it up a road which was then given its present name of Meerut Road.

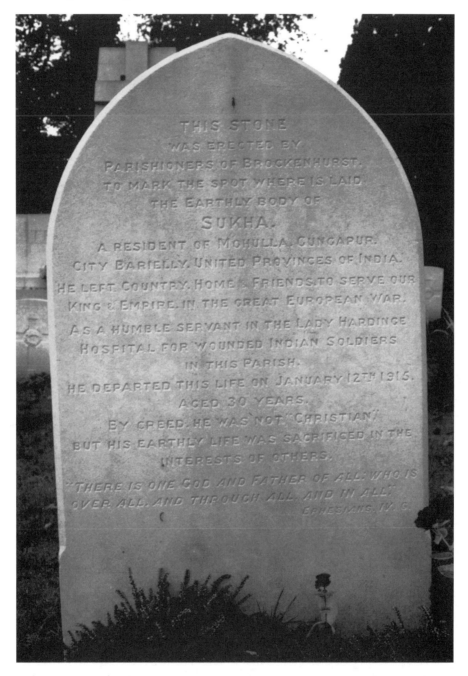

THIS STONE MARKS THE SPOT WHERE IS LAID THE EARTHLY BODY OF SUKHA

Other reminders of this time are the graves of three of the Indian medical staff who are buried in the churchyard. One of these graves is to **Sukha**. This Indian so impressed the villagers that The Reverend Chambers organised a collection to provide his headstone. The necessary £5.2s.0d was duly raised.

The Indian Divisions incurred a total of 34,252 casualties before they were moved to the Middle East in November 1915.

NO. 1 NEW ZEALAND GENERAL HOSPITAL

In 1916 the Indian hospital was taken over for the care of New Zealand Troops. The New Zealanders fought in all the major actions in France from May 1916 to the end of the war.

THE ENTRANCE IN CHURCH LANE

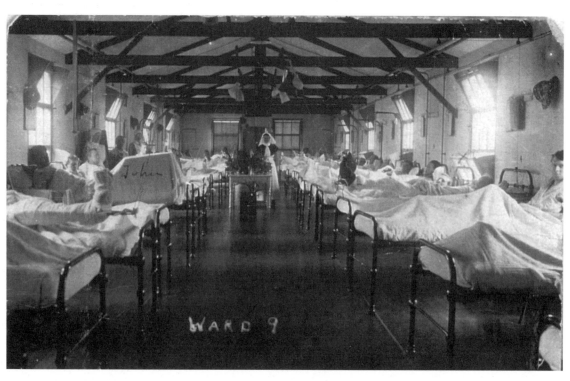

ALFRED "JOHN" WALKER (SEE PAGE 36) IN BED ON LEFT OF WARD 9

THE VICTORIOUS TEAM.

Whilst they were very professional at their job the nurses clearly enjoyed themselves whenever possible.

The story behind the photograph (left) is unknown but Hilda Tucker (see page 36) is kneeling on the right of the middle row.

New Zealand and Colonial Soldiers Corner. In 1919 a Guild appears to have been set up to look after the ANZAC graves.

THE BROCKENHURST BULLETIN - - - Page 27

Brockenhurst Activities—*continued.*

Roll of Honour Guild. *For Brockenhurst Parish Churchyard, New Zealand & Colonial Soldiers Corner.* President, The Hon. Sir T. M. Wilford, K.C., *High Commisioner for New Zealand, London, 1930.* Patrons and Subscribers :—The Hon. James Parr, K.C.B., The Hon. Sir James Allen, K.C.B., Col. P. Clennell Fenwick, G.M.G., M.S.M.G., New Zealand., Sir Hercules Read, London. Mrs. Baring, Mrs. and Miss Alexander, "The Old Mansion," Lady Blanche Thornycroft, Isle of Wight, Mr. and Mrs. Charles Tatham, Grey Town, S. Africa, Mrs. Mary Cooper, Auckland, New Zealand, and others many of whom send donations for the up-keep of the Graves. Mrs. C. M. Salwey, Life Member of the Red Cross Society of Japan, Lady Guardian by appointment since 1919.

The hospital treated over 21,000 casualties before it closed in February 1919.

In 1924 the 94 graves of those who died in the hospital were formally reorganised and headstones erected.

The Great War Cross was erected and the present headstones put in place in 1927.

The ANZAC Day Ceremony is believed to have begun about this time. In 1934 the vicar trenchantly writes:

THE BROCKENHURST BULLETIN - • - Page 31

[Vicar's Supplement.

ANZAC SUNDAY. The annual service of Commemoration was held in beautiful weather at the New Zealand War Memorial in the Parish Church Graveyard on Sunday, April 22nd, at 3 p.m.

There was a very good attendance by the Village folk, Boy Scouts, Girl Guides, Cubs, Brownies and Life Brigade, but as it was so fine, and those we were specially remembering had come and died 10,000 miles and more from their own homes, one was a little surprised not to see a larger number of other folk, on whose behalf, just as much as any one else's the supreme sacrifice of these men was made. Especially were absent those few who spend so much of their time and waste so much of their breath, and, writing materials on letters (of course unsigned) in making mountains out of mole hills, of generally things that are not done, or if they are done, they are not as they should be done. Next year we are going to invite at their own request members of the Bournemouth and Southampton branches of the Old Contemptibles' Association, I shall also send an invitation to the High Commissioner for New Zealand. But should he or any other person of even higher position be able to be present, the honour we try and pay is still the same. Whoever may be present merely joins with us in our little but reverent act of simple remembrance.

The Service consisted of three hymns, a short passage of Scripture, some prayers and a short address, and before the final prayers, and during the last hymn flowers were laid on the memorial.

I should like to thank the Scout and Guide organisations for the orderly way they took up their positions. It really should not be such a difficult matter to make our larger National Memorial Service on November 11th as orderly and reverent.

Representatives of the New Zealand High Commission continue to regularly attend

the annual ANZAC service, organised by the Brockenhurst Branch of The Royal British Legion and held on the Sunday nearest to St Georges Day. At this service the New Zealand flag is paraded, posies are laid at each grave and the No. 4 bell, presented in 1924 by relatives of those New Zealanders who died, is tolled 94 times. This 2-cwt. 1-qtr. bell was cast with the inscription:

"In remembrance of the New Zealand Soldiers who served during the Great War, 1914-1918, and were buried in this Churchyard."

THE MORANT WAR HOSPITAL

The Morant War Hospital was a convalescent facility in Morant Hall, organised by a committee of villagers.

CONVALESCENT SERVICEMEN IN THEIR DISTINCTIVE UNIFORM OF BLUE SUITS AND RED TIE

The Prime Minister of New Zealand, the Right Hon. W. F. Massey visited the Morant Hospital on Sunday 15th October 1916 and expressed

> *"In the highest terms my admiration of the building, the Nursing Staff and the splendid arrangements made for the care and comfort of the Wounded Soldiers."*

THE CHRONICLE of Thursday, July 5 1917 also reports

The following is a list of gifts received at the Morant War Hospital, Brockenhurst, for the week ending June 28th: - cake, vegetables Mr. Arderne; cake Mrs. Groom; flowers and vegetables, Mr. Bobman, Hillcroft; flowers, Mr. Henshawe; vegetables Mr. Falcon-Stewart, Sway; cake, Mrs. Cox; cake, Mrs. Keppel Poultney; strawberries, Mr. Hooker; vegetables, Mrs. Bishop; cake and scones, Mrs. Pigott; swabs, bandages and cushions, War Supply Depot, Brockenhurst Branch. Owing to an increase of beds the following articles are required: - towels, socks, pyjama suits, and vegetables.

1916

THE HOME FRONT

By 1916 most of the village activities were geared up to support the war effort.

In January Miss Curtis declared that the **Working Party**, which met on Wednesday afternoon in the Church room, "would be pleased to give shirts and socks to any of our men and boys who are serving at the front." About a hundred articles had already been given away. In February the Working Party received a letter written on 22nd December 1915 from Corporal Walls, 6th Royal Scots Fusiliers:

> " Dear Miss Curtis,
> Thanks ever so much for parcel of shirts, socks, and mittens received. I have to convey my men's heartfelt thanks for your kindness to both me and them. Your gifts could not have come at a better time, as we were just out of the trenches, after being in them 13 days, without a change, and wet to the skin. I divided them as well as I could, and gave them all something. I gave the shirts to the most deserving cases, &c."

On 16th February a well attended meeting, chaired by Cecil Sutton, was held to promote the cause of **Women's help in Agricultural Work** *"In view of the shortage of male labour in consequence of the war."* A village branch of the **War Supplies Depot** was set up to provide medical necessities such as surgeons' operating coats, bandages and other necessities.

During the year **fund-raising activities** took place to procure seats for wounded soldiers, crutches and walking sticks for the wounded soldiers of the Morant Hospital, presents for soldiers and sailors and in support of the Star and Garter Hospital for Totally Disabled Soldiers and Sailors, as well as for the extension of the school and the Nursing Association. In September it was decided to set up a scheme *"To mitigate the sufferings of the Men of Hampshire who are Prisoners of War, by periodically sending them Parcels of Food."* This was to become a major cause in the village with a target, in the first few months, of £18 being contributed each month.

Normal activities continued, however, with the **Natural History and Antiquarian Society** enjoying a lecture in January on *"The Men of the Old Stone Age"* for which the Rev. G. C. Williams both "lent and manipulated his lantern." In the same month The **New Forest Natural History Society** listened to a lecture on *"Vegetable Physiology,"* although *"The very wet evening considerably affected the attendance."* During the year, however, the **Brockenhurst Horticultural Society** decided not to hold its annual show due to *"Conditions arising from the War."* In July a Committee was formed to promote a **Band of Hope** in the village as a branch of the Church of England Temperance Society.

Gerald Gandy. Individuals do not feature as prominently in the Brockenhurst reports in the New Forest magazine as for other villages. In January, however, it does report that **Gerard Gandy, RN** had been appointed acting First-Lieutenant of H. M. Minesweeper ARABIS. In March ARABIS was torpedoed in the North Sea and his mother wrote that *"I have no news as yet about him."* The following month he was known to be *"Alive and well, though a prisoner at Osnabruck, in Germany."*

The Curate, George Combe Williams, surely did his bit. Apart from being Chaplain to the military hospitals and giving communion to all that asked, he organised writing paper and other comforts for the men. He never forgot their need for the solace of tobacco, which the War Office did not supply in Home Hospitals. He somehow purchased this duty-free and distributed pipe tobacco and cigarettes in vast quantities from his "Smokes" Fund. Clearly a passionate believer in the weed he wrote:

> I cannot resist telling you a funny incident which came to me years ago. I had been inspecting a Church School, and had had six or more hours of continuous work. As I seated myself at Kingston in the train, I lighted a cigarette and was enjoying it. A very tall, lank individual with a very big top hat got into the same compartment, and as I was reading the newspaper I saw him "eye-ing" me up and down. I was of course dressed like a clergyman. I saw he was mentally on "the move" about something; and at last he evidently thought I was very wicked for smoking that soothing cigarette. He turned to me and said: "Would your Master have smoked a cigarette?" My answer was: "Would the Master have worn a top hat?" He got out at the next station.

Military Graves and Proposed Memorial. Due to increased usage the Morant Trustees were approached with a view to a possible extension of the churchyard to enlarge the plot for soldiers graves.

> Mr. Alexander has written to the Vicar to say that the Trustees will *give* the piece of land required for the enlargement of the plot for the soldiers' graves, and will grant to us an extension of land for Parish needs, equivalent to what has been used for Military burials. This kind offer we have, of course, most gratefully accepted.
>
> It has been proposed, and we think all our people will heartily approve of it—that we should erect in the Parish a Memorial Shrine in honour of those from among us who have given their life for King and Country, and for those who are serving in the Navy and Army. We have taken the matter in hand, and Captain Ashmore, The Rosary, Brockenhurst, has most kindly consented to act as Hon. Secretary. We cannot, at the moment, say what the cost will be: but it will not be such as to make the proposal impracticable. We must raise the funds by subscription. Will those who may like to contribute, kindly send their subscriptions to Captain Ashmore, or to the Vicar. The shillings and sixpences of our poorer friends will be no less appreciated than the larger donations of those who are "better off."

THE WAR

On the 19th December 1915 Field Marshal Sir Douglas Haig took command of the BEF and in so doing inherited the plans agreed for 1916 by Sir John French with the French Army. These centred on a major assault on the Somme where the two armies joined.

The Somme. The bulk of the assault was planned to be carried out by the French but as the Germans attacked Verdun in early 1916, in what became an increasingly attritional battle, so French involvement was scaled down. British participation therefore increased, with additional French-manned trenches being taken over up to a month before the battle. Objectives and tactics therefore changed significantly as the date of the battle approached.

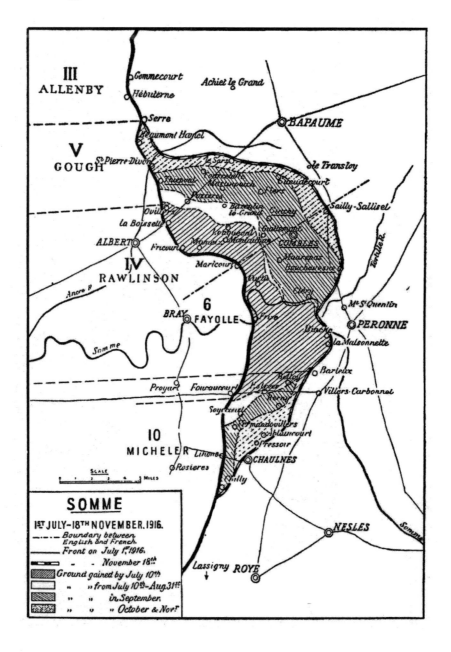

By 1916, the British army had learnt some hard lessons. Equipment and ammunition provision had been reorganised and railways now allowed the rapid concentration of large bodies of troops. The Kitchener armies were arriving in France in large numbers but their training, perforce, had been rushed. Progress on the battlefield was still dictated by the pace of the Infantryman or the horse. These factors led, on the Somme, to the policy of a simple assault after a seven-day artillery barrage against limited objectives. The more difficult objectives were given to the better-trained Regular Divisions e.g. the assault on Beaumont Hamel, which was entrusted to 4 and 29 Divisions. Medical and Engineering services – including the provision of water on the battlefield - were well thought out and the prospects for success were considered good.

Surprise, however, had been sacrificed during the pre-battle preparations and the first day of the Somme (1st July) resulted in nearly 20,000 deaths of which two – *Alfred Hayter, William Harrison* and – were from the village. Other deaths – *Harold Hinves* and *Harold Burton* - were experienced at the end of the battle. Five other villagers, unrecorded on the War Memorial, also died on the build-up (*John Legg* and *Alex Mac'Intosh*), or during the battle of, the Somme (*David Kitcher, Samson Holman* and *Reginald Bew*).

Ypres. Meanwhile, the attrition of trench warfare in other parts of the line went on. Whilst 1916 was the only year in the war when there were no set-piece battles by either side in the Ypres Salient. *George Clark* and *Albert King* were both killed there during the year.

Mesopotamia. *Christian Patterson* was killed at the very end of the year with the Force that was sent to relieve Kut in Mesopotamia.

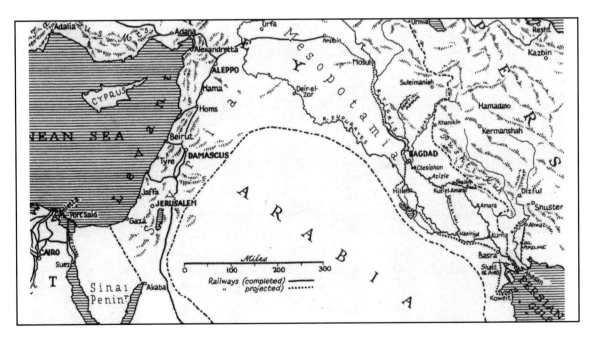

Joseph Rickman and *Sidney Stokes* also died in the Mesopotamian campaign . Both were Privates in the 2nd Battalion the Dorsetshire Regiment who lived in Brockenhurst, but neither name is recorded on the War Memorial.

ALFRED TOM HAYTER

Private, S/1992

14th Battalion, London Regiment (London Scottish)

Who died on

Saturday 1st July 1916, Aged 19.

Alfred was the son of Tom, a farmer, and Ellen Hayter of Sway Road, Brockenhurst

In 1914 he was living in Kew.

ALFRED TOM HAYTER

On the outbreak of war he enlisted into the 14th Battalion (The London Scottish) of the London Regiment. After initial training in England the Battalion, which was part of 168 Brigade of the 56th (1st London) Division, sailed to France in November 1915.

On 30th June 1916 the Division moved up to Bayencourt in preparation for the Somme battle.

The 46th and 56th Divisions were given the task on the 1st July of staging a diversionary attack on Gommecourt to the North of the battlefield. The aim of this was to draw German resources away from the main real attack further south.

At 7.30 am on 1st July the London Scottish attacked on the right of the Division, close to the Hebuterne-Puisieux Road. The attack was over a slightly downhill slope covered with some still uncut barbed wire and under enemy observation. Whilst the German Front Line was reached under cover of smoke the battalion suffered serious casualties.

Reserves sent to reinforce and exploit the initial success suffered badly in the German artillery barrages and counter-attacks. It soon became clear that the position was untenable. During the evening the Battalion therefore withdrew back to the British Front Line having lost 590 killed and wounded.

Alfred Hayter was one of these fatal casualties.

He is buried **in Gommecourt British Cemetery No. 2** at **Hebuterne** in:

Plot III, K7.

The family had the gravestone inscribed simply:

"AT REST"

59

WILLIAM HARRISON

Private, 6999

2nd Battalion, Hampshire Regiment

Who died on

5th July 1916, Aged 30.

BILL HARRISON

William Harrison was born on 21st February, 1886. His parents, Charles - a labourer - and Susan lived in Brockenhurst.

His twin sister, Rose, died in infancy. Brother Charles, however, had been born in 1880, and Edith in 1885. They all went to the local school. This picture shows him, before the First World War, as a member of the village Quoits team.

Before the war he enlisted in Lymington as a Regular Soldier into the 2nd Battalion of the Hampshire Regiment (2 HAMPS) where he served with several other villagers.

At the beginning of the war this battalion was serving in India. They returned to the UK where they were embodied into 88 Brigade, along with 4th Worcesters, 1st Essex and the 1st Battalion of the Royal Newfoundland Regiment.

This brigade joined the 86th and 87th Brigades to form the 29th Division. This Division had already served in the Gallipoli campaign (see p 45) and at the time of the battle of the Somme was considered as one of the best fighting formations. Being well trained with regular battle-seasoned troops, it was given the difficult task of capturing Beaumont Hamel.

The Battle of the Somme opened at 7.30 a.m. on 1st July 1916, after the heaviest preparatory barrage experienced in the war.

The Hawthorne Ridge mine, however, was blown 10 minutes earlier to enable the resultant crater to be captured in order to support the attack on Beaumont Hamel.

THE HAWTHORNE RIDGE MINE

The mine went off only 600 yards away from where Bill was waiting in reserve to advance from his trench. The attack failed so disastrously that the two assaulting battalions of 1 Essex and (later) the Newfoundlanders were almost totally destroyed.

2 HAMPS were in next in line for this attack but it was called off, and in the afternoon they moved forward to hold the front line at St John's Road. Bill Harrison was seriously wounded during this time. The Battalion's War Diary records that the Germans permitted parties to go out into No-mans-land to bring in the wounded. Trenches were repaired, equipment salvaged and the dead buried.

Bill Harrison died of his wounds close to the front line and is buried in **Knightsbridge Cemetery**, Mesnil-Martinsart, Somme, named after the communications trench, close to Newfoundland Park. Today this battlefield, over which the Division fought on 1st July, has been preserved as a memorial to the Newfoundlanders.

He is buried in:

Grave D 44.

GEORGE HENRY CLARK

Private, 10518

2nd Battalion, Hampshire Regiment

Who died on

Wednesday 9 August 1916, Aged 19.

George was born on 6 December 1896, the son of Harry - a platelayer on the railway - and his wife Susan. The family lived at 2 Northbrook Cottage, Martin's Road, Brockenhurst.

He enlisted into the 2nd Battalion, The Hampshire Regiment (2 HAMPS.) as Bill Harrison and many of his other friends had also done. In 1916 this battalion was part of the 88th Brigade in 29 Division. This Regular Division ("The Immortal") was a fighting Division of high repute having done well in Gallipoli.

WILLIAM   *GEORGE*
WALTER   SUSAN (MOTHER)

They returned to France and on the first day of the Somme battle had taken a heavy part in trying to capture Beaumont Hamel. They remained there until, on 27 July, they were rotated to the quieter Ypres section to recover before returning to the Somme in early October.

Whilst there were no set piece battles at Ypres at this time, the Salient continued to be an area of heavy attritional trench warfare.

2 HAMPS. had gone into trenches near Potijze, near Ypres, on 30 July and had spent the time improving them and consolidating a new mine crater into the position.

GEORGE CLARK

On 8 August 1916 the enemy released gas on nearly the whole Ypres front. The slowly moving mainly phosgene gas cloud descended on the trenches.

As the troops were donning their respirators and manning the Fire Step of the trenches a heavy German artillery barrage descended.

This enemy attack cost the Battalion 240 casualties, 129 of whom were fatal.

George Clark was one of the soldiers killed in this action.

He is buried alongside many other Hampshire casualties of that attack in **Potijze Burial Ground Cemetery** Ypres. His grave is to be found at:

Plot T.2.

His parents had the following inscription placed on his headstone:

"A PLACE IS VACANT
IN OUR HOME
WHICH NEVER CAN BE FILLED"

HAROLD HINVES

Rifleman, R/16787

7th Battalion, King's Royal Rifles Corps.

Who died on

Friday 18th August 1916.

Harold Hinves was born and lived in Tattenham Road, Brockenhurst. The family had an interest in music (see pages 7 and 46) and were keen members of the village band.

HAROLD HINVES

He enlisted at Southampton into the 7th (Service) Battalion, the King's Royal Rifles Corps. (7 KRRC). After training, the Battalion was incorporated into the 41st Brigade, part of the 14th (Light) Division.

At the time of the opening of the Battle of the Somme 14 Division was in the (quieter) Arras area. They left here on the 29th July 1916 for the Somme battle and arrived at Dernancourt on 8th August. Four days later they occupied Pommiers Redoubt, which overlooked the enemy in Orchard Trench. They came out of the line on 15th August, being relieved by 8 KRRC. On 17th August, however, they returned to Pommiers Redoubt and attacked Orchard Trench at 2.45 pm the following day.

The German front line was almost totally destroyed by the British artillery barrage, and 7 KRRC advanced 100 yards beyond it, digging in under heavy rifle and machine gun fire. They also successfully repulsed several enemy counter-attacks.

7 KRRC incurred 272 casualties in this attack. Harold was not amongst those of the Battalion who were relieved that evening.

His body was never recovered and his name therefore appears on the **Thiepval Memorial** on:

Pier and Face 13 A and 13 B

Harold's name also appears, with that of his brother, on the **Methodist Church Memorial** (see page 119).

ALBERT KING

Private, 33446

8th Battalion, Devonshire Regiment

Who died on

Saturday 21st October 1916.

Bert King was born in Wimborne to Albert Tom, a market gardener, and Mary King. When he was twenty years old Bert married Lucy Waterman - the wedding taking place in St Nicholas Church on 17th April 1912. They lived in Brockenhurst. Their daughter later lived in Waters Green and played the organ in the Baptist Chapel.

Early in the war he enlisted into the 8th (Service) Battalion of the Devonshire Regiment. On 4th August 1915, on completion of its UK training, this unit joined 20th Brigade, which formed part of 7th Division commanded by Major General sir Tom Capper, K.C.M.G. Seven weeks later it took part in the Battle of Loos.

The Battalion then fought on the Somme almost continuously from 1st July 1916 until 7th September. On 1st July the 8th and 9th Battalions of the Devonshire Regiment attacked from Mansell Copse. One hundred and sixty of them died. Some of them were buried where they fell in the forward trenches of Mansell Copse. A portion of this trench is now a small cemetery with the following inscription at its entrance:

"The Devonshires held this trench
The Devonshires hold it still"

Later in July it attacked Mametz Wood incurring 207 casualties and then took part in the successful attack against Bazentin-le-Grand Wood where they crept forward to within 25 yards of the enemy trenches during the pre-attack bombardment. This attack cost the battalion 171 casualties with a further 201 casualties being suffered from a subsequent attack on High Wood. After refitting they returned to the Somme for operations around Ginchy before being withdrawn to the (quieter) Ypres salient.

Sadly, after having survived the Somme, Albert was killed in action on 21st October 1916 in the attritional warfare of the Plug Street/Armentiers trenches near Ypres. Bert Freeman, who lived in Sway and was in the Duke of Cornwall's Light Infantry, was with Bert King in France. When next on home leave Freeman went to see Albert's wife. Apparently Bert King ignored a warning not to look "over the top" and was, presumably, killed by an enemy sniper. Bert Freeman was himself to be killed in action on 24th April 1918 whilst serving with the Machine Gun Corps.

Bert King is buried in **Tancrez Farm Cemetery** in:

Plot 1 J. 4

HAROLD BURT BURTON

Gunner, 17202

11th Brigade, Royal Field Artillery

Who died on

Monday 20 November 1916, Aged 22.

Harold, nicknamed "Bertie", was born on 20 May 1894, being the son of Richard and Eveline Burton of Brockenhurst. He married Emily Waterman in St. Nicholas Church on 18th June 1915 and they subsequently lived in the family home in North Road, Brockenhurst.

Bertie was well known to the entire village, as he was a very promising young athlete. He took a leading part in village cricket and football and at 12 captained his School's 1st football team (see page 5), which played undefeated throughout the season. In 1906/7 the same team under his captaincy won the New Forest Schools League. In 1913/4 he "won the ball" at cricket for the best bowling average in the village side.

At the outbreak of war he enlisted into the Gunners and served in "B" Battery, 11th Brigade, Royal Field Artillery. This Brigade was part of 4 Division – a regular division and therefore one that tended to get the more difficult attacks. At the opening of the Battle of the Somme 4 Division was tasked with taking the Ridge to the North of Beaumont Hamel. This it succeeded to do but the failure of the flanking division's attacks made the gains impossible to hold.

Bertie was killed on the last day of the Somme battle - after 14 months continuous active service in the field and without any home leave. His Commanding Officer wrote:

> *"About 8 p.m. on the 20th November a shell struck our telephone dugout. Your husband, who was next for guard, had just entered to ask the time when the dugout was struck. He was killed instantly, and four others with him. We all, officers and men, offer you our heartfelt sympathy in your terrible loss. He was a first-rate Gunner and his work never left anything to be desired. He was most cheerful and willing and his loss will be greatly felt by us all. He lived and died a good soldier. We again assure you of our heartfelt sympathy."*

Bertie left a widow and a small son. Only a month before a brother- in-law, *Albert King*, had been killed, whilst Mrs Burton's elder brother, *Harry Waterman*, was killed early in the war.

He was initially buried in Mouquet Farm Cemetery Grandcourt, immediately north of the Farm.

Later in the war his body was re-interred, along with the other 35 graves of this cemetery, into the present location at **Courcelette British Cemetery.**

Whilst it is known to have been buried there the exact location of the grave was lost in the shellfire of the German advance in 1918.

His grave is therefore recorded on:

Special Memorial B

His family have had inscribed on the base of the headstone

"MIZPAH
HYMN 595."

This reads:

"The Lord watch between me and thee, when we are absent one from another."

His name is also recorded on the family grave in **St. Nicholas Churchyard.**

CHRISTIAN BINGLEY PATTERSON

Lieutenant

Indian Army Reserve of Officers

Who died on

30th December 1916, Aged 30.

Christian was born on 12th November 1886, the son of the Reverend J. E. C. and Mrs F. A. Patterson of Broadlands Gate, Brockenhurst. Reverend Patterson had served for some years in India, and during the war, was the Resident Vicar to the Indian hospital housed in the Forest Park Hotel. He later lived in Overbrook, Brockenhurst.

After graduating from Oxford Christian went to India to join the Imperial Forest Service. On 30th December 1911 he became an Assistant Conservator of Forests in the United Provinces of Northern India, being attached to the Siwalh District in the Western Circuit based on Dera Dun. Here he joined the Provinces' Light Horse Volunteers. He later moved to the Chakrata District before returning to Siwalh in December 1912. A letter from the Lieutenant Governor of the United Provinces noted his promise

"...having passed first in his year. He was placed in charge of a Heavy Division, very early in his service, and managed it with distinct success."

After training with the 39th Garwalis he was commissioned into the Indian Army Reserve of Officers on 19th February 1916 and joined the Depot of the 1st Battalion the Gurkha Rifles at Dharmsala - a curious choice as he spoke German and Urdu. He was passed as "fit for service" on 20th March.

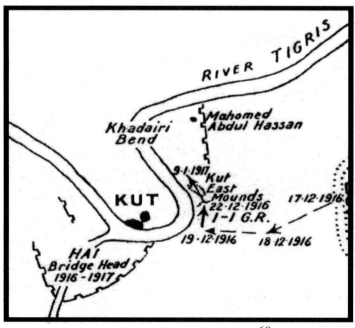

On 25th July 1st/1st Gurkha Rifles moved to Mesopotamia where they joined the 9th Brigade of the Lahore Division under the command of Brigadier L. W. Campbell. British Forces, under Major-General C.V.F. Townsend, had reached to within 30 miles of Baghdad when a Turkish stand at Ctesiphon forced him to retreat to Kut.

After nearly five months siege Townsend surrendered on 29th April 1916.

In August 1916 Sir Stanley Maude took over and reorganised the weary Anglo Indian forces on the Tigris Front. On 13th December his revitalised forces attacked and secured positions covering the Hai bridgehead. Christian was, at this stage, with 1st/1st GURKHAS in trenches near to the Kut East Mounds (see map). Heavy rains and the flooding of the Tigris then caused the attack to stall. By Christmas 1916 the battalion was occupied in advancing their trenches by sapping forward towards the enemy. The ground, however, was of the very hardest and all ranks had badly blistered hands. On 22nd December Christian led out a daylight patrol 600 yards from the Turkish trenches. By "trailing his shirt" for about a mile and attracting enemy fire he brought back useful information on which trenches were occupied and unoccupied.

The Unit War Diary for the period 25-28th December records the continuous digging of trenches and the improving of their defensive positions. It then goes on:

December 29th. *"Digging trenches most of night. Heavy rain for 1 hour. Strong posts connected up and line occupied 1/1 GR on left - 105 Mahrattas Light Infantry on right".*

December 30th. *"As above. After dark communication trenches 300 yards to be dug out by the Bn towards enemy and "T" head to be made at end of each by Sappers and Pioneers. 1/1 GR dug 200 yards out from MOUNDS strong post. Covering party of two platoons under **2/Lt C. B. Patterson** I.A.R.O. and working party of 200 O.R.s under Temporary Captain F. Williamson I.A.R.O. detailed. Covering party were heavily fired on and **2/Lt C. B. PATTERSON I.A.R.O. was killed** - Temporary Capt. F. Williamson I.A.R.O., both attd 1/1 GR, wounded - also 3 O.R.s killed and 5 O.R.s wounded. The trench was completed and "T" head wired in by Sappers".*

The Regimental History records that it was a "vivid flash of lightning" that revealed to the Turks the presence of the covering party moving forward to take up its position.

The advance was resumed in January. Kut was recaptured on 23rd of February and Bagdad was finally captured on 11th March 1917.

Christian is buried in **Amara War Cemetery**, Iraq. In 1933 all of the headstones were removed from this cemetery as salts in the soil caused a rapid deterioration of the stone used. Instead a screen wall was erected with all of the names engraved upon it. His name is recorded on:

Panel X. D.4.

1917

THE HOME FRONT

Despite the nine deaths in the village from the Somme battles and the twenty-five other deaths from the war to date, the mood of the village, from its 1917 records, appears to have remained fairly positive.

The Reverend Chambers continued to exhort parishioners to share his beliefs in the power of God, to rail against the Hun and to worry about reducing the School Extension Debt. He clearly had a very good sense of humour, publishing as an erratum to a previous report

> *"By a curious mistake in the last number of the magazine, Mrs. Wyndham Cook's kind gift was acknowledged as being that of "Mrs Wyndham Goose." We hope this lady will excuse the blunder. We write fairly clearly."*

He was also keenly interested in the paranormal. He wrote that when farmer William Bennett was dying he knew his son was returning from Canada, but had heard no word of his passage. A few hours before he died he said

"He will be here by half-past four, but it will be too late."

The father died before the son arrived at half-past four precisely. Indeed, on 8th May the vicar, by invitation, addressed the Clergy of Southampton on **Psychic Research and its Relationship to Christian Truth.**"

He was also very concerned about the progress of the proposed War "Shrine." At the start of the year only £10.10.0d had been subscribed. Construction of the "Shrine" began in April. In May he wrote that

> Our object is that the Memorial shall represent the action of the Parishioners *as a whole*. Thus the gifts of the shillings and sixpences of our poorer friends will be no less appreciated than larger gifts from others who may be able to afford more. The substantial building which will enshrine the Memorial will effectually preserve the latter from the effects of the weather; and moreover, if at any future date the Parishioners should elect to put up a perpetual Memoral in *stone*, we can foresee how this could be suitably done, by facing the brick-wall on which the present Memorial will rest with stone or marble, and inscribing the names thereon.

In June he again appealed for contributions and observed

> We are told that one or two persons object to the erection of this War Memorial, on the ground that it savours of superstition. We wonder what they would say if we objected to their putting up a tombstone to the memory of a departed friend, and alleged the same reason ! *Silly*—isn't it ?

It is, of course, conceivable that some locals were not comfortable with the idea of the names of living villagers being displayed alongside those who had died as, in a peculiar way, it could be seen as tempting providence.

The "Shrine" (see page 80) was dedicated on 27th June, with contributions still being solicited on the day!

In the magazine for July the Vicar, in his individualistic way, wrote:

> The Trustees of the Morant Estate have most kindly promised to supply the oak for the fencing which will be placed around the War Memorial. We shall need some more funds, please, to enable us to meet the cost of completing the Memorial; which, when finished, will undoubtedly be a worthy representation of those who have made "the great sacrifice " in fighting against the greatest system of military tyranny, blasphemous pride and barbarity which the world has ever seen.

Earlier in the year Lady Morant, in order to encourage the keeping of rabbits and so increase the food supply, very kindly offered six rabbits to the elder scholars of the school for the best essays on rabbit keeping. Some good papers were handed in and the rabbits awarded to Dorothy Minchinton, Phillip Andress, Keturah Burden, Basil Davey, Violet White and Harriet Hobart.

In December the vicar was glad to be able to report that

> **"We have succeeded in securing direct from the colliery over 50 tons of coal at 32s .6d. per ton for the 71 members of our coal club. We have to pay 3s. per ton for cartage from the railway station to the houses of the members, so that the price paid by them is 35s. 6d. per ton, a very big saving on the price paid through the ordinary channels of supply."**

This was clearly needed as an address, given in the Church Room on "The War and Religious Education at Home and Overseas" was received by a small number of people

> *" ...the weather being, well! about as bad as it could be.*

71

THE WAR

1917 was a year of mixed blessings for the Allies.

On the negative side the French offensive under Nivelle failed and some units mutinied. Russia was knocked out of the war allowing German divisions to be transferred to the Western Front. Their submarine offensive against allied merchant shipping was causing serious concern and the Italian Army had collapsed at Capporetto.

Positively, however, America was now in the war – with all that that meant for 1918 and 1919. The assaults on Vimy Ridge, where **George White** was killed, and at Arras had been successful, although the latter cost the lives of **Frederick Burton** and **Joseph Wells** The Battle of Cambrai in November had also, initially, very encouraging results although **John Gates** and **Bertram Payne** were both killed there.

Passchendaele. Above all, however, for the British, 1917 was dominated by the Third Battle of Ypres, otherwise known as Passchendaele. The aim, to attack northwards and capture Dunkirk and Ostend before turning the German front more significantly was frustrated by stubborn resistance, and awful weather. **Thomas Lucas** and **Lionel Salmon** were killed in the Messines phase of this battle.

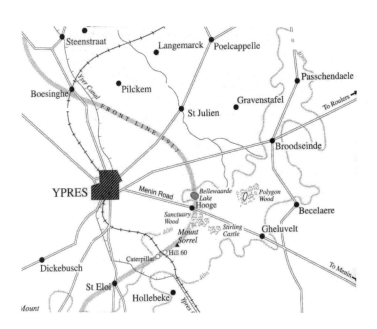

In the second phase of Passchendaele four months fighting cost over 300,000 British casualties including **Albert Murch, William Povey, William Waterman. Edward Moores, William Durnford** and **Charles Baker** were also killed in this battle but are not recorded on the Memorial.

As a result of the casualties of Passchendaele the end of 1917 saw a change in the composition of the British armies. The volunteers – "the flower of British Manhood" in the Kitchener units – would be replaced by conscripts called up under new legislation. Lloyd-George also restricted the flow of reinforcements to France to limit the scope for further offensive action.

Other Deaths. **Bill Cleveland** died of wounds received some months earlier in the Battle of the Somme. and **Frederick Raisey** (not on Memorial) was killed there in March. **Dan Broomfield**, also unrecorded, died in hospital in Etaples. **Sidney Payne** died of wounds in Palestine, **Herbert Pope** was torpedoed off Egypt, and **Frederick William Burton** died during recruit training.

WILLIAM HAROLD CLEVELAND

Private, 3/7243

5th Battalion, Dorsetshire Regiment

Who died on

Friday 26 January 1917, Aged 22.

William Cleveland was the son of Charles and Lily "Queenie" Cleveland who lived at Shalfleet on the Isle of Wight. William, however, is recorded as living at Setley, Brockenhurst.

He enlisted at Poole into the 5th (Service) Battalion of the Dorsetshire Regiment. This Kitchener Battalion was part of the 34th Brigade of 11 (Northern) Division for the whole war. Its first bout of active service was in Gallipoli when on 15 August 1915 it landed at Suvla Bay.

It returned via Egypt in time for the Somme where it was part of the Thiepval Ridge battles in September 1916. From 16th - 21st September the battalion was opposite "Mucky Farm" on Theipval Ridge. Mouquet Farm had 3 groups of buildings- one in British hands, one in German occupancy and the third group in no-mans-land. They had once formed part of the same German redoubt and so were all interconnected by tunnels. The Germans therefore had a habit of popping up behind the Dorsets' lines, until sentries were posted on their exits.

The unit returned to these trenches on the 25th and at 12.35 p.m. attacked the Farm. Heavy German shellfire killed or wounded all the Company Commanders and their Sergeant Majors before the objective was reached. The Dorsets, however, moved through the farm and attacked the Zollen Redoubt beyond - at a cost of 423 casualties, amongst whom was William.

Being badly wounded he was sent to No. 8 General Hospital, which was accommodated in Boisguillaume near Rouen in a large private house and grounds. Recovering from this he had been sent to work at a local quarry. It was whilst working here he suffered a serious accident from which he subsequently died. The Hospital Chaplain wrote saying that full military honours had been accorded, and a beautiful wreath placed upon the coffin.

He is buried in a double plot in **Boisguillaume Communal Cemetery** in:

Plot II, C 10A.

FREDERICK BURTON

Private, 26592

2nd Battalion, Wiltshire Regiment

Who died on

Monday 9 April 1917, Aged 31.

Frederick Burton (not to be confused with Frederick William Burton, see page 76) was born in Brockenhurst in 1886, the son of John and Harriet Burton.

FREDERICK BURTON

He married Olive Rose of Lower Road, Winterslow, Salisbury. Whilst they were living in Eastleigh, he enlisted in Southampton, into the 2nd Battalion of the Wiltshire Regiment (2 WILTS.).

This battalion originally went to France in October 1914 as part of the 21st Brigade in the all-regular 7th Division.

In December 1915, however, this brigade was transferred to 30th Division. This was a new Army Division and the policy was followed of putting one regular battalion into a New Army Brigade to "stiffen" the unit.

One of the results of the Somme battles in 1916 was the German withdrawal to the Hindenburg Line. On 9th April 1917, 2 WILTS. attacked part of this position. They started at 5.30 am. The advance was made over 2000 yards, crossing two sunken roads containing German machine gun outposts and swept by shellfire, before they could pass through the wire and assault the objective. Amazingly, the wire covering the Hindenburg Line was reached - but was found to be uncut. The survivors returned to hold the first sunken road position until relieved that evening. A blizzard covered the recovery of wounded from the battlefield, one of whom was Frederick Burton. This attack cost 16 officers and 363 other ranks killed and wounded.

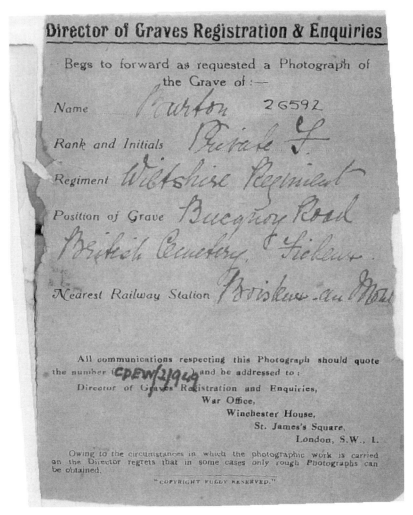

He died of his wounds on 9th April 1917 aged 31.

He is buried in **Bucquoy Road Cemetery, Ficheux**, which was the site of VII Corps Main Dressing Station.

The grave is grouped with four others of the Regiment and is to be found in:

Plot 1.A.17.

THE ORIGINAL GRAVE IN 1920

THE PRESENT GRAVE

FREDERICK WILLIAM BURTON

Private, 7/7021

94th Training Reserve

Who died on

Tuesday 10th April 1917, Aged 18.

Fred Burton was born in Boldre and later baptised in St. Nicholas church on 4th September 1898. His father, William, was born locally in Dilton and worked on the railway as a platelayer. His mother, Elizabeth, came from Ryde in the Isle of Wight.

Before he enlisted Fred was living with his mother in 18 Carey's Cottages, Brockenhurst. He sang in the church choir for several years and was described by the vicar as a

"Good and conscientious lad"

In February 1917 he joined the 16th (Reserve) Battalion of the Gloucestershire Regiment as a Private.

Whilst under basic training with the 94th Training Reserve he was stricken down by fever and after a little more than a week's illness, died in hospital in Swindon.

His funeral took place in **Whitworth Cemetery**, near Swindon, on 14th April.

Two beautiful wreaths were sent, one by the officers of the Company and one by the NCOs and men.

He is buried in:

Grave M, 650.

LIONEL JOSHUA SALMON

Corporal, 306650

5th Battalion, Hampshire Regiment
attached
8th Battalion, Royal Inniskilling Fusiliers

Who died on

Thursday 16th April 1917, Aged 22.

Lionel Salmon was born on 7th July 1895, the son of Victor (a carpenter) and Mina Salmon of The Nook, Middle Road, Highfield, Lymington.

He enlisted in Bournemouth and served in the 5th Territorial Battalion of the Hampshire Regiment attaining the rank of Corporal.

At the time of his death he was attached to the 8th Battalion, Royal Inniskilling Fusiliers (8RIF) in 49th Brigade of the 16th (Irish) Division commanded by Major-General W. B. Hickie. At this distance in time it is not possible to say why he was serving with "The Irish." He may have had some specialist skill e g in signalling, or it may just have been the need for urgent reinforcements that led to the unpopular expedient of posting the most readily available drafts of men from the reinforcement depots at Etaples in France. It may also be of relevance that the Pioneer Battalion for this Division was 11 Hampshires.

In April the battalion was taking its normal turn in the trenches of the Ypres Salient when Lionel Salmon was killed.

The rain, shellfire and the resultant quagmire made the recovery of bodies impossible.

His name is therefore recorded on the **Tyne Cot Memorial** to the Missing on:

PANEL 89

GEORGE WILLIAM WHITE

Private, 766518

20th Battalion, Canadian Infantry (Central Ontario Regiment)

Who died on

13th May 1917, Aged 26.

George was born in February 1891 and baptised on 16th August in St Nicholas Church Brockenhurst. He was the second son of John and Ellen (Flora) White, being preceded - three years earlier by brother Walter. A younger brother, William, (see page 102) was to be born in 1894. At this time John was aged 26 and a general labourer living at Pear Tree Cottage, South Weirs. The White family, however, were commoners and their main livelihood, was keeping cattle and ponies on the forest and running a smallholding.

FAMILY GRAVE AT BROCKENHURST

George went to the village school and was subsequently employed by the Monroes at Rhinefield House as a gardener. Nothing is known of his interests. He did, however, emigrate with his brother and some other village lads before the First World War to Canada and lived and worked there. Apparently he never married.

He enlisted in Toronto into the Central Ontario Regiment of the Canadian Army and went to France with the 123rd Pioneer Battalion (Royal Grenadiers Overseas Battalion). This unit was involved in the capture of Vimy Ridge on 9/10th April 1917 and continued to serve in the area. He was killed in action there on 13th May 1917.

He is buried in **Aubigny Cemetery**, France in:

Grave III. J. II.

His name is also recorded on the family gravestone in **St. Nicholas Churchyard**.

THOMAS FARQUHAR LUCAS

Lieutenant

3rd Battalion, Royal Warwickshire Regiment
Attached
20th Balloon Company, Royal Flying Corps

Who died on

Saturday 16th June 1917, Aged 30.

Thomas F Lucas was the eldest son of Sir Edward L. Lucas, Bart. of 5, The Avenue, Newmarket, Cambridgeshire. A memorial plaque in St Nicholas Church, however, records that the family also lived at Whitley Ridge.

Regrettably no War Diary appears to have survived for the 20th Balloon Company. Tom's own records, severely weeded, have survived - mainly, perhaps, because of repeated requests from his father for information .

In answer to a questionnaire completed in February 1920, his father thought that Thomas had been a Private in the Ceylon (Tea Planters) Rifles around 1912. He was commissioned from an Officer Cadet Unit and appointed to the Royal Warwickshire Supplementary Reserve on 14th February 1915. He was attached to the Royal Flying Corps (RFC) in October of that year.

He was killed in action on Saturday, 16th June 1917 whilst serving with 20 Balloon Company. RFC. This unit was commanded by Captain R W Bruce. It consisted of 22 and 34 Sections, each of four Officers, providing one balloon. In his will Thomas left everything - money and possessions - to Captain Arthur Dove Vaughan and his wife Kate.

There is a memorial to him in the Parish Church of **St Nicholas**, in Brockenhurst, but he is buried in **Brandhoek Military Cemetery**, Vlamertinghe, Ypres in

Plot I. L. 1

THE "SHRINE"

The "Shrine" as the first memorial was called was erected in 1917, on the site of the present war Memorial, at the initiative of the then Vicar - Arthur Chambers.

THE SHRINE

"Will the relatives of them kindly examine the list as it now appears in writing and should there be any inaccuracy inform the vicar of the same.

The Shrine was built on manorial wasteland to house lists of those from the village who were **serving King and Country,** as well as those who had already died in the war.

The Rural District Council and the Morant Trustees both gave consent - the latter on the undertaking that the Reverend Chambers paid a nominal peppercorn rent of one shilling per annum.

The cost of the shrine, however, was met by the subscriptions of the parishioners. As the vicar was at pains to stress[1]:

"It is entirely a Parochial Memorial."

In March 1918 the vicar wrote in the **New Forest Magazine** informing villagers that the names of Brockenhurst men who have **given their lives** in the war are to be painted on the panels of the War Memorial.

Arthur Chambers died suddenly in 1918, but before his death had persuaded the Parish Council to Assume the guardianship of the Memorial. This it did, being duly approached by the Morant Trustees for the said shilling rent[2].

---

[1] Letter from A Chambers to the Parish Clerk dated 10th September 1917.

[2] Letter from Estate Office to the Parish Clerk dated 11th September 1919.

THE CHRONICLE, THURSDAY, JULY 5, 1917.

WAR SHRINE DEDICATED AT BROCKENHURST

The dedication of the war memorial at Brockenhurst on Wednesday evening was an impressive scene. At the unveiling of the memorial, every man in the assembly stood with head bared, soldiers present saluted and every woman stood with bowed head as a silent token of respect to those brave men from Brockenhurst who have made the supreme sacrifice on the battlefield of honour. Commencing at six p.m., the Vicar (the Rev. A. Chambers) announced the opening hymn, " O God, our help in ages past." This was sung reverently by all the assembly of some five hundred, including a large number of wounded New Zealand soldiers attired in hospital blue.

The Vicar, addressing the gathering, said they had met there that evening with three great feelings. Firstly, a religious feeling, as they had just shown in the opening of the ceremony with praise and prayer. Secondly, a feeling of patriotism for the tremendous work undertaken by the British nation and her colonies in the cause of honour and humanity. And, thirdly, with the feeling of intense gratification. Behind the veil of the Union Jack (which covered the wooden part of the memorial) there were inscribed the names of those who had left home and loved ones in order to protect those who remained behind from the ravages of the Hun. Surely that was a cause for a feeling of gratitude. Continuing, he said there might be one or two facts with regard to the memorial that would be of interest to the public. The memorial had been erected by the people of Brockenhurst. The parishioners felt that the least thing they could do to show their respect for all those who had laid down their lives for their country, would be to put up something that would stand as a permanent memorial to those who had made "the great sacrifice."

It was also proposed to raise a cross in the Parish Church with the names of those who had fallen inscribed thereon. It was intended after the war to paint the names of the men on the memorial, but at present, when the numbers were increasing, the names would be written on parchment. There were 316 names on the memorial, 65 of whom were dead and two missing. Three Indian, one British, one Australian and 31 New Zealanders who had died in hospital here, and who had been buried in the churchyard, were included in the list of those killed.

THE BROCKENHURST MEMORIAL.

The names were inscribed of 249 men whose homes were at Brockenhurst, and considering that the population was only just over 2,000, he thought it was very creditable. That number was made up of 31 in the Navy, 12 in the Royal Marines and 206 serving in the Army; but that was not all for he was sure that there were a number more to be added to that by the end of the week.

He wished to express on behalf of the parishioners thanks to the Morant Trustees for having allowed the memorial to be erected on their land; to the Rural District Council for having sanctioned the erection; and to Captain Ashmore for having acted as hon. secretary.

In closing, he said that £14 was needed to completely extinguish the debt on the memorial and that boxes were in the hands of some of the young ladies present to receive donations towards that amount. He also stated that the wood with which the inner part of the memorial was made was the teakwood from H.M.S. BRITANNIA.

The New Forest Magazine for August reports:

"The Roll of Honour." The postcard reproduced on page 80 showing the Shrine is titled "The Roll of Honour." This term was first used by Stevens the printers for its roll of all those **serving** in the Armed Forces in 1914. The manuscript lists by the cross in the Shrine on page 82 therefore reported both the living and the dead of Brockenhurst and were to be continuously updated. This may be confusing as the modern meaning of the term is retained exclusively for the names of those who died.

ALBERT E MURCH

Private, 260124

6th (Service) Battalion, Duke of Cornwall's Light Infantry

Who died on

Thursday 23rd August 1917, Aged 20.

Albert was born and lived at The Weirs in Brockenhurst. His father, Samuel was a general labourer who had been born in Ashburton, Devon. His mother, Rosina, came from Lymington. The Census of 1891 shows three sons in the family. Albert himself was baptised in St Nicholas Church on 7th February 1897.

He enlisted into The Hampshire Regiment, but later transferred to the 6th Battalion, The Duke of Cornwall's Light Infantry (6 DCLI). 6 DCLI were, at the start of the war, part of 43 Brigade in 14 (Light) Division and had arrived in France on 25th May 1915. This was the first Kitchener Battalion formed in Cornwall and the men, responding to Kitchener's call for the "first hundred thousand" were, according to the Regimental history

"The Very Cream of the Male Civilian Population of the County."

By August 1917 6 DCLI were involved in the Battle of Langemarck which was the second phase of 3rd Ypres, otherwise known as Passchendaele. On 14th August the Unit provided a 500 strong working party to carry gas cylinders up to the front. The party was caught by shellfire near Sanctuary Wood and suffered 12 casualties.

On 22nd August 6 DCLI attacked Inverness Copse.

The plan involved 6 DCLI forming up by 6.00 a.m., covered by the thick mist experienced the previous evening. "B" Company were tasked with drawing water and rations for the whole attacking force but lost their way in the "sinking darkness". The attacking forces therefore occupied their assault positions, without rations, in clear visibility and were observed by a German aeroplane which fired on them.

At 7.00 am, the assault began. It was initially checked by German machine gun fire but the appearance of a British tank (the only one of the four detailed to support the attack that was effective) helped the advance to continue and its machine guns assisted in the breaking up of a German counter attack. In the confusion of battle, however, reinforcements from other battalions did not arrive and German resistance solidified.

A German counter attack that evening, using flamethrowers, recovered some of their lost ground.

By 24th August, when the unit was relieved, British gains of 200-400 yards only were retained at a cost to 6 DCLI of 350 killed, wounded and missing.

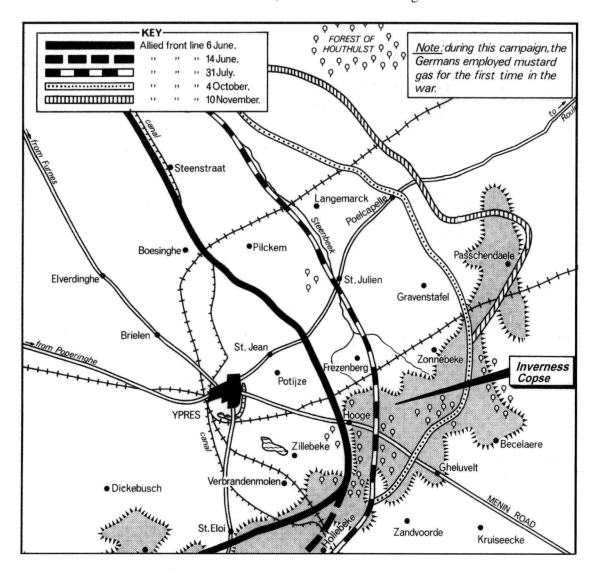

Albert Murch was one of the wounded in this action. He was evacuated back to a Casualty Clearing Station in Lijssenthoek near Poperinge were he died.

He is buried in **Lijssenthoek Military Cemetery**. This is the second largest British War Cemetery with nearly 10,000 1914-18 deaths commemorated on the site.

Albert Murch's grave is in:

Plot XVIII, D.3.

The **New Forest Magazine** for November 1917 noted that

> *"Albert is the youngest son of Mr. and Mrs. Murch, and our sympathy with the parents deepened by the fact that four of their other sons are serving in the Army, two of whom have been seriously wounded."*

WILLIAM POVEY

Private, 54292

12th Battalion, Durham Light Infantry

Who died on

Thursday 20th September 1917, Aged 35.

William was one of the six children of Frederick, a stonemason, and Rosina Povey. He lived at Norton Cottage, Brockenhurst, (see page 3) with his wife Harriet Eliza.

As an older man he responded to Kitchener's call for volunteers, initially joining the Royal Field Artillery (No. 164396). He then transferred to the 12th Battalion of the Durham Light Infantry. (12 DLI).

WILLIAM POVEY

On 20th September 1917 the Battalion was part of 68th Brigade, 23rd Division taking part in the Passchendaele offensive.

Earlier in the year General Plummer, Second Army Commander, had secured the right-hand flank of the Ypres salient by his successful attack of the Messines ridge. Now he had the task of attacking the German lines in the centre of the salient. By retaking the central Gheluvelt Plateau, lost in the 2nd battle of Ypres, it would make it easier for Gough to capture Passchendaele on the left.

On the night of 19th September 65,000 troops moved into their assault positions. The preliminary bombardment was a great success against the enemy trenches, but not so successful against the German artillery to the rear.

At midnight it began to rain heavily. Nevertheless, 12 DLI advanced with their brigade against Inverness Copse and by midday were 1500 yards into the enemy lines. They then successfully repelled the inevitable German counter-attacks made to recover the position. The British attack was successful, but at the cost of heavy casualties to 12 DLI.

William Povey was amongst those missing from the attack.

The **New Forest Magazine** reported:

> *"Private William Herbert Povey, esteemed by so many of us as an upright and good man, was killed in action in France on 20th September.*
>
> *Mr Povey, in conjunction with his late father, did some of the beautiful stonework in connection with the new church.*
>
> *We extend our deepest sympathy to the widow and four children, who mourn the loss of a good parent,"*

His name is recorded on the **Tyne Cot Memorial** of the Missing

TYNE COT MEMORIAL

It can be found on

Panels 128-131 and 162-162A.

WILLIAM WATERMAN

Private, 32570

14th Battalion, Hampshire Regiment

Who died on

Thursday 27th September 1917, Aged 27.

Bill Waterman was the seventh child of Fred and Harriet Waterman, who lived in what is now known as Waterman's cottage in North Road. He was born in 1890, being a younger brother to Harry Waterman (see page 14). Bill was, by trade, a fishmonger and lived with his wife, Rose, in a cottage that has now been absorbed into the Cloud Hotel. They had two children - Bob and Madge. Rose later remarried to become Rose Tucker and had another son called Tommy.

Bill was brought up in the village, attending the local school and singing in the Parish Church Choir. He was known for his cheerful disposition, his energy and his perseverance in all matters. The Vicar summed him up by saying that

> *"His invariable way of always looking at the bright side of things and his consistent life will cause many of us to long remember the bright young spirit removed from our midst by the debased and degenerate Huns."*

Bill enlisted into the 14th (Service) Battalion of the Hampshire Regiment. This unit had been raised and equipped at Portsmouth at the beginning of the war by a local committee.

It reached France in March 1916 and moved to the Somme in late August. On 3rd September it incurred 457 casualties in its attack on Hamel. It then continued to serve on the Somme and on 17th October occupied Schwaben Redoubt where the wet, cold and muddy conditions were worse than the enemy activity. Cut off from supplies they foraged food, ammunition and equipment from the enemy dead and held the position despite fierce counter attacks.

They finally reverted to the Ypres sector on 18th November. spending the winter in and out of the trenches and suffering continual casualties. The unit needed continuous drafts of replacements to maintain itself at fighting strength.

On 31st July 1917 the unit attacked Pilckem in the Battle of Passchendaele, capturing over 200 prisoners, 3 guns and 17 machine guns. In this action Second Lieutenant Hewitt of 14 HAMPS was awarded a posthumous VC.

In the August edition of the **New Forest Magazine** the Vicar reports:

> We have received a very interesting letter from the Front from Captain James Bradford, who forwards ten shillings for our War Memorial Fund. He was mentioned in the list of Sir D. Haig's despatches of May 23rd last, and was promoted on the field. Lieut.-General Sir Aylmer Hunter-Weston writes to Captain J. Bradford, "I heartily congratulate you on the honour done by His Majesty the King, in mentioning you in his recent birthday honours despatch." Captain Bradford writes very cheerily; speaks of our chairman, Mr. Willie Waterman, as being "a smart little soldier who works hard."

On 26th September 1917 the Battalion was back into the battle attacking Tower Hamlets, an enemy position by the Menin Road. Despite enemy fire and boggy ground the battalion gained most of its objectives, although their Commanding Officer Major Goldsmith – who had given up his leave to command the attack – was killed along with three other officers and 75 men killed or missing. A further 122 all ranks were wounded in this action, one of whom was William Waterman.

William died of his wounds the following day in a British Field Ambulance at Westoutre, 8 miles southwest of Ypres.

He is buried in **Westoutre Churchyard** Extension,

Grave II. F. 8.

His death is also recorded on his son's grave in **St. Nicholas churchyard.**

The Waterman family suffered badly through the war. They lost two sons, two sons-in-law and a third son, Wilfred, was badly wounded.

SYDNEY RICHARD PAYNE

Private, 260121

2/5th (Territorial Force) Battalion, Hampshire Regiment

Who died on

20th November 1917, Aged 40

According to "**Soldiers Died**" there is only one S. R. Payne who died in the war. Sydney Richard Payne does, indeed, have a tenuous connection with the area through the territorial affiliation of his unit. There the trail ends, as there is no cross-referencing evidence of a Brockenhurst connection.

According to documents Sidney was the son of James and Emily Payne. He was born in Clewer, Berkshire, lived in Windsor and enlisted in Reading. In 1934 **The Brockenhurst Bulletin** shows a Mrs E Payne (Mr E Payne was on the Council in 1918 - see page 100) living at Park Close and an A Payne living at 4 Railway Terrace. **Was Mrs E Payne his mother? If so she might have wanted his name on the Memorial?** But this is surmise! At some stage Sydney married a girl called Mary. She subsequently remarried and, after the war, lived at 104 Lavender Hill, Tonbridge, Kent. **Was Mary a local girl? Was another S. R. Payne discharged before the end of the war, dying locally as a civilian? What, indeed, was his relationship - if any - with Bertram Payne (see page 91)?** Sadly, despite much research by several very able people the answers to these questions have not yet materialised, but they must be there somewhere. Perhaps YOU can help?

The following details are accurate but are only of relevance if Sydney Richard is our man. It is therefore offered in that conditional spirit.

On 19th November 1917 2/5th Hampshire were part of 232 Brigade of 75 Division. This Brigade led the attack to cross the **Nablus** Road, north of the city to avoid a direct attack on Jerusalem. Initially the opposition was light but Turkish troops on the hills either side of the road had to be dislodged and "C" Coy. of 2/5th Hampshire helped in this task. The following day this battalion concentrated on clearing the hills south of the road to Saris. "D" Coy. incurred some casualties in this action. Whilst it is not known which Company Sidney belonged to, his wounds proved fatal. He died on 20th November 1917 in one of the Field Ambulances in Ramleh.

He is buried in **Ramleh War Cemetery**, Israel, in

Plot H. 47.

Another villager, *Roger Ash*, who died on 23rd September 1943 (see page 230), is also buried here.

BERTRAM JOSEPH PAYNE

Sapper, 221680

55th Divisional Signal Company, Royal Engineers

Who died on

Friday 30th November 1917, Aged 31

Bertram Payne was born at Emery Down, Lyndhurst, being the son of George Payne - an agricultural labourer - and his wife, Rose. Bert lived at Bank, Lyndhurst, and enlisted at Brockenhurst into the Royal Engineers.

He was posted to the Signal Company of the 55th (West Lancashire) Division. This was a pre-war Territorial unit raised mainly in the area between the Lune and the Mersey with its Headquarters in Liverpool. In 1915 it was absorbed piecemeal as reinforcements for the 2/1 (West Lancashire) Division, but it was re-formed in France in January 1916. The Signals Company had been retained in England and rejoined the Division on 14th January 1916.

Unfortunately there appears to be no evidence as to when Bert himself joined his unit. The Division fought in the second part of the Somme battles, at Passchendaele and at Cambrai, where it was commanded by Major General H. S. Jeudwine.

Bert was killed in action at Cambrai on 30th November 1917.

As his body was never recovered he is commemorated on the **Cambrai Memorial**, Louverval, Nord, France on:

Panels 1 and 2

JOHN FRANCIS GATES

Driver, 94247

Royal Field Artillery

who died on

3rd December 1917.

According to "**Soldiers Died**" John Gates was born in Lymington. He was, however, baptised in Brockenhurst on 3rd May 1896 and lived with his parents and two brothers in Waters Green. His father, James, was an estate labourer. One of his brothers, Frank, became a carter and specialised in collecting village rubbish to take to the tip in Hollands Wood. Frank was known to

"enjoy his glass!" .

John enlisted at Lymington as a driver into the Royal Field Artillery and was killed on the last day of the Battle of Cambrai on 3rd December 1917.

THE CAMBRAI MEMORIAL

As his body was never found his name is commemorated on **the Cambrai Memorial** on:

Panel 1.

HERBERT GEORGE POPE

Private, 533090

15th Battalion, London Regiment
(Prince of Wales' Own Civil Service Rifles)

Who died on

Sunday, 30th December 1917, Aged 37.

George was born in March 1881 to George and Julia Pope. The family later grew with two further sons. George (Snr.) was by trade a wood turner. He was also the youngest brother of James Pope (who was "Nip's" - see Page 15 - Grandfather) and worked in the family toy business. He retired after the fire (see page 6), however, and lived in Ringwood Terrace, later moving to Restormal House in Southbourne.

One of the sons, Charles, became clerk to the local firm of Jackman and Masters, the Estate Agents shown on page 146. He later became a member of the firm, married, and had several children. The other two sons both died - George in the war and the other son being killed in a cricket match on a pitch near Lymington.

George enlisted at Chelmsford into the 15th Battalion of the London Regiment. This was a Kitchener battalion and both 1/15th and 2/15th Battalions had fought on the Somme before the latter unit had, on 15th November 1916, been ordered to Macedonia.

On 10th December the battalion boarded the Hired Transport "Aragon" (Captain Francis Bateman in command) at Marseilles for transport to the Mediterranean. The ship was fully loaded carrying 2700 troops including 150 nurses. It finally sailed on 20th December for Alexandria in Egypt.

At 10.00 a.m. on 30th December 1917 this ship was approaching the harbour of Alexandria. As it waited in the offing whilst mines were being cleared its destroyer escort, ATTACK, ordered "Aragon" to make to sea to avoid possible floating mines.

As "Aragon" cleared to seaward she was torpedoed.

THE SINKING OF H.M.T. "Aragon" ON 30th DECEMBER 1917

The nurses, in lifeboats, got clear of the sinking ship. ATTACK then came in to rescue the hundreds of men in the water. This was all but completed when ATTACK was, herself, torpedoed. The Master of "Aragon" and 18 of his crew lost their lives, and the bodies of 591 soldiers were not recovered. Herbert was one such.

Curiously his Death Certificate, which would appear to be in error, shows him as being 39 years old.

Herbert's name is recorded on the **Chatby Memorial, Alexandria,** Egypt on:

Memorial Index Number M.R. 41.

1918

THE WAR

After Passchendaele, Lloyd-George was determined to limit Haig's capability to initiate costly offensives and so restricted the flow of reinforcements to France.

The mutinies in the French army in 1917 led to the requirement for British forces to take over yet more of the French-held line. Starved of troops, therefore, with additional commitments and knowing that a German offensive was imminent, Haig had to make his troops go farther.

Advances in firepower and communications enabled him to reorganise Infantry divisions into smaller formations. Whilst the 3 Brigade structure was retained, its constituent parts of 12 infantry battalions (with 16 Lewis guns each) was reduced to 9 battalions, although each battalion was issued with 36 Lewis guns (an effective light machine gun). Each division, therefore, was reduced from 18,825 to 16,035 in strength. The 5th Army under Gough was created to take over the extra trench line with the "extra" divisions "saved." Divisional efficiency, however, had been sapped by four years of heavy losses, although the "colonial" divisions from Canada and the Dominions were in much better standing.

The lack of troops had led Gough to adopt the concept of a thinly held outpost line supported in depth by the main defensive line, in turn reinforced by reserve formations as necessary.

The defensive line, however, was - in some parts - still being dug and reserves were largely notional. Specially trained German assault troops attacked under cover of thick fog.

They captured or bypassed outposts and drove on to the main defences before Gough's men even knew they were there. This successful assault took the town of Albert, wiped out the gains of our 1916 Somme successes and threatened Amiens.

Fierce German pressure on the Somme and Armentieres Fronts following up the success of the initial enemy attack led Haig to issue his famous - and effective - "Backs to the Wall" order of the day on 11th April 1918.

The threat posed to the allies by this determined German action forced Haig and Petain, at Doullens on 26th March, to finally agree to accept the control of Foch as coordinator - later Commander in Chief - of the Allied Armies. This resultant unity of command led to the successful defence of Amiens, where the British and French Armies joined. Allied units were thrown into the battle piecemeal and the German assault was held.

Over the next four months it was followed up by further serious German assaults across the whole Front, the defeat of which could be described as a close run thing. *Jesse Tregunna* and *Harry Hunt* were both killed in containing these German offensives as were *Sidney White* and *Alfred Beard* - neither of whom appear on the Memorial. *Fred Johnson* was killed in the attritional warfare of the Ypres Salient.

THE HOME FRONT

Despite the deaths of twenty-one villagers in the war in 1918 village life continued on an apparently even keel.

On 12th January the bells of the parish church were rung to celebrate the entry of General Allenby into Jerusalem.

Food production was encouraged. On 15th February a lecture on "Potato Spraying," illustrated by Lantern, was given in the Church Room by S. H. Melbourne, Esq., of the Board of Agriculture. Extra allotments were rented by the Council to encourage self-sufficiency.

War Savings were taken seriously. The contribution to The National War Funds in "Businessmen's Week" in April was £4332. In August this Association had 287 members who had subscribed over £1200. Over half of this sum had resulted from the public 6d Coupon Subscription, while £166 represented the 6d coupons of the school children alone, collected by **"the indefatigable Mr Quinn."**

Coal Club. In September this club ceased operations due to the shortage of coal!

Brockenhurst Evening School Classes recommenced on 30th September with the following classes:

Monday	7.15 to 8.15 - Physical Drill
Tuesday	6.45 to 8.45 - Rural Arithmetic
Wednesday	5.00 to 7.00 - Needlework
	6.45 to 8.45 - Scale Drawing and Mensuration

The Hampshire Prisoner of War Fund was keenly supported in the village. An entertainment, organised by the committee, was held at the Pupil Teachers' Centre School on 22nd December 1917 and the proceeds raised £30. 10. 5d. Mrs Bell, the Hon. Sec., sent a cheque for £60 in February, £50 in March and achieved similar sums thereafter. Subsequent months also showed additional small donations to the Ladies Emergency Royal Navy Fund and the Royal Navy Division Comforts Fund.

THE WAR

Haig was one of the few allied commanders who recognised that at the end of these offensives Germany had shot its bolt and that the war could be won in 1918 - rather than extending the campaign to 1919 with its implicitly larger casualty bill. His policy of counter-attack in the summer of 1918 led directly to the retreat of German forces and the subsequent armistice in November of that year.

The "Big Push" began south of the Somme on 8th August, led by Canadian and ANZAC troops. Two weeks later Byng's Third Army attacked north of the Somme and Horne's First Army added to the offensive by attacking the Germans at Vimy on 26th August. In late September Foch initiated four attacks - by the British at Ypres and at Cambrai, by the Americans at Mezieres and by the French in the Argonne. *Fred Sibley*, *George Christopher* and *Moses House* all died in these operations. The advance from Cambrai cost the life of *Albert Kitcher*. *James Hewlett*, *James Elford*, *Walter Middleton* and *William Phillpott* all died in these attacks but their names do not appear on the Memorial.

Six weeks later the war was over.

```
B.M.672.


11th. November 1918.



        Following received from 9th. Division :-


   "Hostilities cease at 11.00 to-day   aaa   Troops
   have been ordered to stand fast on the line
   reached at that hour   aaa   Defensive precautions
   will be maintained. "



                                            Captain,
                                    a/Brigade Major,
                              27th.(Lowland) Brigade.
```

In matters Naval, *John Hibbs* died when his ship ran aground, *William Stride* was killed when his ship HMS BRITANNIA was sunk by a German submarine and *Victor Bowden-Smith* was killed in an accident in the North Sea whilst recovering a German torpedo.

Finally, *Edwin Pullen*, *Edmund Fisher*, *Arthur Cole* and *Leonard House* all died of illness during the year. *William White* died of his wounds in Canada.

JOHN HIBBS

Leading Stoker, Royal Navy

HMS OPAL

Who died on

Saturday 12th January 1918, Aged 30.

John Hibbs was the youngest son of George and Harriet Hibbs who lived in Meerut Road. He joined the Royal Navy at the beginning of the war, and in 1917 was part of the Ships Company of OPAL.

OPAL was a modern three-funnelled destroyer of about 1000 tons displacement, armed with three 4" guns and four 21" torpedo tubes in two pairs of two. The class was a popular one with the continuous building of 85 of them between 1914 and 1917. The names ran through "Ms", "Ns" and "Os" to "Ps". OPAL was built in 1916 by Doxford.

H.M.S. OPAL

On 12th January 1918 OPAL and NARBOROUGH were part of the Escort Force "P" taking a convoy from Peterhead to Lerwick.

A gale suddenly got up and the Convoy Commodore ordered the two destroyers to take shelter. Both ships ran aground in Windwick Bay on the East Coast of South Ronaldsay while making for Scapa Flow.

The Admiralty Enquiry into the loss of OPAL found that the ships had missed the entrance channel and, in the blinding snowstorm, had struck the rocks at the Clett of Crura. OPAL initially remained upright but the following seas soon broke her up. NARBOROUGH capsized immediately and broke in two. There was only one survivor from the two ships - Able Seaman (Gunlayer) William Sissons (Ports. J 16486).

In his evidence to the Enquiry he remembered that the ship was doing eight knots while the lead was used to check the depth.

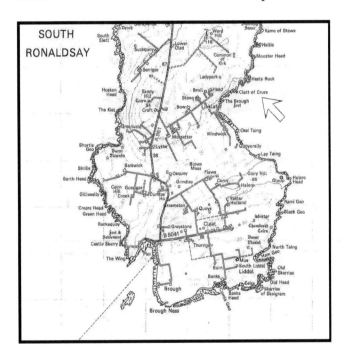

"**Suddenly the cliffs appeared. OPAL sounded three blasts on her siren to indicate going astern, but the seas carried her onto the rocks.**"

He described how he climbed one of the funnels as the ship broke up and then somehow managed to struggle ashore. He was found the next day, sheltering in a small cave above the Clett of Crura. Rescue parties had not been able to reach the scene earlier because of the blizzard conditions.

The Enquiry found that the Captain of OPAL was probably inaccurate with his position and had not allowed sufficiently for the set of the storm in his course. It was noted that he was relatively inexperienced in these waters. The Enquiry also questioned the wisdom of sending these ships for shelter, given that it would involve them navigating a restricted passage in difficult conditions.

John Hibbs was one of the 179 men lost that night. Their names are recorded on the **Portsmouth Naval Memorial:**

Panel 30

John is also recorded on the family gravestone in **St. Nicholas Churchyard**.

EDMUND MONTAGU PRINCEP FISHER

2nd Lieutenant,

Royal Field Artillery

Who died on

31st March 1918, Aged 46.

Edmund Fisher was born on 13th January 1872 in Onslow Square London. His father was a Barrister and a J.P for the county of Sussex. The family lived at 8 Swan Walk, Chelsea but hailed from Whitley Ridge Brockenhurst which served as the country home.

The four daughters and seven sons of the family grew-up happily in Brockenhurst. One brother joined the Royal Navy, and became the Commander-in-Chief of the Mediterranean Fleet. Another became Chairman of Barclay's Bank. A third went down in INVINCIBLE at the Battle of Jutland in 1916. Yet another brother, Arthur, who was a professional soldier, died from illness whilst serving in the Boer War.

Edmund was educated at Haileybury College and went on to practice as an architect. He married Janice Freshfield on 6th June 1899 and in the next 14 years they raised a family of five sons and two daughters.

Edmund's brother HAL Fisher, the historian, writes of his brother as being

> *"a naturalist, a sportsman and an architect. He had an extraordinary sympathy with animals, a virtuoso's discernment of porcelain and painting, and a rare and individual taste in the exercise of his profession. The Hall of Somerville College, Oxford and the Protestant Church in Rome were among his most important buildings. He died for his country. Although he was the father of seven children and well over military age, he volunteered for military service, received a Commission, and succumbed to a malady contracted in the trenches after the exertions of the battle of Cambrai."*

Edmund joined the Army as an Officer Cadet at Exeter on 29th December 1916 at the relatively elderly age of 44. His medical examination at Topham Barracks reported that he was 5 foot 10.5 inches tall, weighed 151 lbs, had a chest expansion between 31 and 37 inches and enjoyed good physical development.

He rode well and this skill would have helped him in being commissioned on 15th May 1917 as a 2nd Lieutenant to the Royal Field Artillery. His initial appointment is not known but whilst attached to the 36th (Irish) Divisional Artillery Column he fell ill to a malady contracted in the trenches after the exertions of the battle of Cambrai.

A report from No 8 General Hospital at Rouen dated 21st January 1918 was sent to his wife by the Military Secretary's branch of the War Office stating that he was seriously ill. Mrs Fisher applied for permission and visited Edmund in Rouen on 9th February 1918. Pyrexia of unknown origin (PXO) and subsequently appendicitis then caused him to be evacuated back to Lady Inchape's Military Hospital at 7, Seymour Place, Mayfair. After an operation for an appendisecular abscess, however, he died from complications and pleurisy on 31st March 1918.

He is buried in **St Nicholas's Churchyard**, Brockenhurst in

Plot 2.2.

WILLIAM HENRY WHITE

Staff Sergeant, Canadian Army

Who died on

20th April 1918, Aged 23.

William was baptised in Brockenhurst on 19th August 1894. He was the son of John and Ellen (Flora) White, and the younger brother to George, (see page 78), all of whom lived at Pear Tree Cottage, South Weirs, Brockenhurst. The family grave is shown below. Pear Tree Cottage has since been demolished and "Huntsgreen" has been built on its site. This home is presently occupied by Mrs Weeks, a niece of George and William, who has kindly provided information on the two brothers.

William, like his elder brother, also attended the village school and went on to work

THE FAMILY HEADSTONE AT BROCKENHURST

for the Monroes at Rhinefield House as a gardener. His family still remembers that he was something of an artist and was keen on fretwork. Indeed, one of the family still has a wooden fretwork box that he made.

He emigrated to Canada with other young men of the village some time before the First World War. He lived and worked in Canada, married a Canadian Girl and had a daughter who, in later life, qualified and practised as a doctor.

He joined the Canadian Army and, as family memory has it, became a Staff Sergeant. At some stage he became ill or was wounded and was repatriated to Canada and discharged.

He subsequently died on 20th April 1918.

He is commemorated on the family grave in **St. Nicholas Churchyard**.

He is buried in:

Woodlawn Cemetery, Ontario, Canada.

JESSE TREGUNNA

Private, 25298

1st Battalion, Hampshire Regiment

Who died on

Monday 22nd April 1918, Aged 32.

Jesse was born in Brockenhurst in 1886, one of four sons born to James Tregunna, a railway labourer from Cornwall, and Annie - a London girl. They lived in Lower Buckland, Lymington.

Jesse enlisted in the army at Lymington and served in the Regular 1st Battalion of the Hampshire Regiment. 1 HAMPS was part of the 11th Brigade in 4th Division in the 4th Army Corps. This Corps had born the brunt of, and then checked, the German offensive when it attacked Arras in April 1918.

On 22nd April 1 HAMPS were tasked with the capture of Pacaut Wood, as the opening phase of the British counter-attack. This was just across the canal opposite Gonnehem and was a wooded position of considerable tactical importance. Three companies were used for the attack, which had to cross the canal over footbridges laid for the purpose. The attack went in at 05.15 am and the German counter barrage fell three minutes later. Within 30 minutes the objective was captured. Seventy prisoners and several machine guns were taken at a cost of the Commanding Officer, Colonel Armitage, four other officers and 43 other ranks killed, of which Jesse was one. Three other officers and 148 men were wounded out of the battalion's strength in action of 14 officers and 650 other ranks.

He is buried in **Mont-Bernanchon British Cemetery**, Gonnehem in:

Plot I. C. 4.

His name is also recorded on the **War Memorials** of **Lymington** and **Sway.**

FREDERICK CHARLES JOHNSON

Lance Corporal, 37433

15th (Service) Battalion, The Hampshire Regiment
Attached
122nd Trench Mortar Battery

Who died on

6th May 1918, Aged 38.

Frederick Johnson was born in Southampton in 1880. He worked for most of his adult life as a carter in Brockenhurst.

His grandson, Tony Johnson, recalls that Fred had the reputation of being a very fit man. Apparently he frequently used to win the impromptu races held when local carters went for loads at Brockenhurst railway station. This involved each carter racing with a sack of corn over a shoulder from the station, over the footbridge, and back to the carts.

FRED JOHNSON STANDING BY HIS HORSE WITH THE BLERIOT AEROPLANE

He is also remembered for towing a Bleriot aircraft from the station to Beaulieu aerodrome. It was then assembled and flew to take part in the Bournemouth Airshow in the summer of 1910.

He occasionally worked for local coal merchants and the gasworks. It was whilst working at Rhinefield House, however, that Tony believes Fred may have met Lucy House, a Brockenhurst lass, whom he subsequently married. They later lived in Ober Road.

FRED JOHNSON

Frederick Johnson enlisted in Brockenhurst into the 15th (Service) Battalion of the Hampshire Regiment.

15 Hampshires, a Kitchener Service Battalion, had gone to France on 1st May 1916 as part of 122 Brigade. It had taken part in the Somme battles of Fricourt, Flers and Mametz Wood.

Two years later, as part of the 123 Brigade 41st Division, out of its 850 strength only 80 of its original members still served with the Battalion.

In April 1918 it had come from Bucquoy and gone into trenches at the very apex of the Ypres salient.

The 3rd Battle of Ypres (Passchendaele) had resulted in the destruction of both drainage and vegetation in the salient. Although the weather was fair the line held was really just a series of connected-up shell holes, with very few creature comforts. Under such circumstances the battalion moved in and out of its trenches for two months.

Fred was , by this time, attached to a trench mortar battery. Family memory has it that on 6th May 1918 he was killed in action on the Menin Road going up to the line. The lorry in which he and eight others were travelling received a direct hit from a shell. There were no survivors.

His body was, however, recovered and he is buried in **Ypres Town Cemetery** Extension near the Menin Gate in:

Grave 3. H. 1.

In November 1917 Fred sent this postcard back to his wife:

No. 32. Menton — Une allée de Palmiers

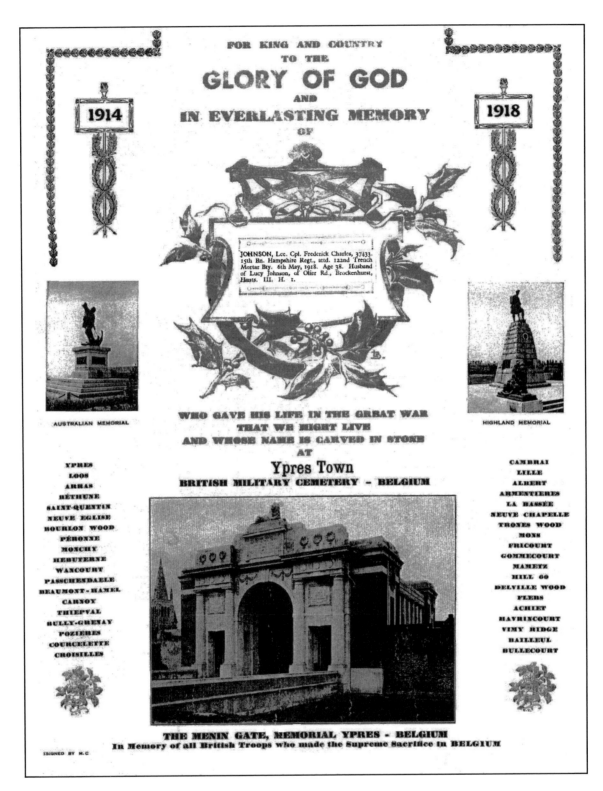

THIS CERTIFICATE WAS SENT TO FRED JOHNSON'S FAMILY AFTER HIS DEATH

HARRY GEORGE HUNT

Corporal, 8185

1st Battalion, Wiltshire Regiment

Who died on

Monday 27th May 1918, Aged 27.

Harry was born in Chippenham but lived with his wife Frances in Oak Tree Cottage, The Weirs, Brockenhurst. They appear to have shared this cottage with the Cole family (see page 116).

Harry enlisted, in Devizes, into the 1st Battalion, the Duke of Edinburgh's Wiltshire Regiment (1 WILTS). This regular battalion belonged to 7th Brigade in 3 Division.

The German assault on 21st March 1918 found 1 WILTS defending Bapaume. Four days later the battalion was reduced to three officers and 54 other ranks having incurred over 400 casualties in that time. In this action Captain R F W Henry-Ward won the VC. In early April, after receiving heavy reinforcements, they were defending the Ypres Salient and were again reduced to three officers and 100 men.

On 23rd April the Battalion was reinforced from 6 WILTS. and was back up to strength of 850 all ranks. Their losses in early May, defending Kemmel Hill at Ypres, were thankfully fairly light. Harry was serving in "B" Company of the battalion at this time.

On 27th May, however, the Germans attacked on the Marne and 1 WILTS was ordered to help cover the withdrawal of 8 Division. The enemy attacked in great strength that evening at Boufignereau and the battalion was pushed back, splitting up into small parties to fight rearguard actions as necessary. The Commanding Officer died of wounds and losses were heavy.

Corporal Hunt was killed in this action.

His body was not recovered but his name is recorded on the:

Soissons Memorial, Aisne, France,

There is also a gravestone in **St. Nicholas Churchyard**, Brockenhurst for both Private Cole and Corporal Hunt.

The two families were clearly great friends and shared the same house. The impact of the loss of both men in less than five months of each other can be imagined.

Frances had inscribed on the gravestone:

"NOT GONE FROM MEMORY, NOT GONE FROM LOVE,
GONE TO OUR FATHER'S HOME ABOVE."

VICTOR JAMES BOWDEN-SMITH

Lieutenant-Commander, Royal Navy

H.M.M.L. No. 403,

Who died on

Thursday 22nd August 1918, Aged 31.

The Bowden-Smiths were a well-known local family, the origins of which appear to lie in the marriage of Robert Smith with Ann Bowden about 1790. In 1817 they bought Carey's Manor which was originally the property of John Carey the riding forester to Charles II. The original building was demolished in the 19th Century and the present Carey's Manor was rebuilt on a nearby site in 1877.

Victor was born in 1887 to the Reverend Frederick Herman Bowden-Smith and his wife in the Rectory at Weston Patrick in Hampshire.

In the 1881 Census Frederick's father, the Reverend Philip Bowden-Smith was described as being a "Clergyman without Cure of Souls". He was, in fact, a Housemaster at Rugby School. His boarding House was shown as housing his family of 3 daughters and 7 sons, 46 boarders and 8 servants. By 1915, however, the family were living in Carey's Croft, as the Reverend Frederick had become the Rural Dean for Lyndhurst.

Victor was, not surprisingly, educated at Rugby from whence he joined the Navy. He was appointed midshipman on 29th February 1904 to QUEEN a battleship in the Mediterranean Fleet. By April 1907 he was a Sub-Lieutenant in KINSHA, a river steamer for service on the Yangtsze in China.

1916 saw him as a Lieutenant and torpedo specialist on board EURYALUS, a heavy cruiser built in 1898. He was promoted Lieutenant-Commander whilst still in the ship in January 1917.

He later commanded the HMML No. 403. This 37-ton motor launch was built in 1915 and armed with a 3 pdr. gun and depth charges. These were sea-going wooden - hulled ships designed to work in the North Sea patrolling mine barrages and to act against light enemy vessels and submarines.

On 22nd August 1918, only three weeks before the war ended, a German torpedo was found floating in the North Sea. This was a hazard to shipping. Victor was killed when the torpedo accidentally detonated whilst it was being recovered from the sea.

There is a memorial tablet for him, erected by his family, in St. Nicholas Church.

THE PLAQUE IN ST. NICHOLAS PARISH CHURCH BROCKENHURST

His name is recorded on the **Portsmouth Naval Memorial** on

Panel 28

Interestingly, another member of the family who died in the war was

Walter Adrian Carnegie Bowden-Smith.

He was the only son of that part of the family at Vernalls, Lyndhurst. He entered Rugby in 1894 and in 1899 went to Sandhurst, being commissioned into the Royal Fusiliers in 1900.

He was wounded on the Tibet Expedition of 1903-4. He was wounded again on 23rd August 1914 at the opening battle of Mons. Whilst bringing up reinforcements under a fierce fire he was hit in the right arm and abdomen. Of his 50 reinforcements 47 were shot down.

He died on 27th August at the convent of St Joseph Maisières, aged 32.

FREDERICK JOHN SIBLEY

Corporal, 10541

2nd/4th Battalion, Hampshire Regiment

Who died on

Wednesday 28th August 1918, Aged 26.

Frederick Sibley was born on the 29th May 1892 at Melbourne Cottage, Lyndhurst. He later married Maude and lived at Northbrook Cottages, Brockenhurst.

He joined the Territorial Army and served with 2nd/4th Battalion of the Hampshire Regiment, rising to the rank of Corporal. The Battalion had had an interesting war (see Moses House page 114). It had returned from Egypt on 1st June 1918 and after helping to frustrate the German attack at the Chemin des Dames, had moved to Rheims to repeat the process. In doing so it had taken a full part in operations on the Ardre under 62 Division from 20th-29th July. This involved the loss of two officers and 172 men killed or missing with a further nine officers and 170 men wounded. However, real progress had been made and the enemy defeated.

Two weeks later the Battalion was moved on 24th August to Ayette on the Somme. On 25th August, 5 Brigade attacked Sapignies with 186 Brigade in reserve. Piles of equipment indicated the rapid withdrawal of the Germans whose counter attacks were also contained. The next day the advance continued against increasing opposition. An assault by the Battalion to come up level with its flanking brigade was successful at a cost of 50 casualties and an officer and 16 men killed or missing.

Whilst the units poised themselves for an assault on the Hindenburg Line, fighting patrols were sent out to determine enemy opposition. On 28th August "B" and "C" Companies incurred casualties in patrolling. They were also heavily shelled and incurred over 30 casualties.

Frederick was wounded at some stage and was evacuated back to a Casualty Clearing Station at Frevent, where he died of his wounds on 28th August 1918.

He is buried in **Ligny-sur-Canche British Cemetery** in

Plot A. 34.

On his gravestone is inscribed:

> "FROM HIS LOVING WIFE AND MOTHER
> GONE TO BE WITH JESUS
> WHICH IS FAR BETTER."

GEORGE THOMAS ANSTEY CHRISTOPHER

Lance Corporal, 20185

2nd Battalion, Wiltshire Regiment

Who died on

Saturday 14 September 1918, Aged 23.

George Christopher was born in 1895 in Christchurch, Hampshire to George and Kate Christopher. The family, including another son - Charles, (see page 45) - later moved to 2 Railway Terrace in Avenue Road, Brockenhurst.

He enlisted into the Royal Field Artillery (17203) but later transferred to the 2nd Battalion The Wiltshire Regiment (2 WILTS.). On 21st March 1918 at St Quentin 2 WILTS. lost 22 officers and more than 600 other ranks to the German Offensive. Reconstructed in May the unit needed to absorb 20 officers and 509 men to bring it back up to strength.

This unit moved from 30 Division (see Frederick Burton page 74) on 13th May 1918 to 58th Brigade 19th (Western) Division. They went, at the end of the month, under French command to attempt to stop another German breakthrough between Soissons and Rheims. By early June, however, the 3 battalions in the brigade of 2,500 men were reduced in total to half a battalion – about 350 men. 2 Wilts reformed again in late June and moved to the Loos sector.

In August the unit took part in the beginning of the final assault against the German lines. On 3rd September they successfully assaulted the German lines at Neuve Chapelle, but on 14th September their CO was killed by a shell and other members of the party killed or wounded on the way up to the lines.

George was seriously wounded at this time and died in the Field Ambulance Station on 14th September 1918.

He is buried in **Chocques Military Cemetery**, France in:

Plot III B 2.

The family had the following dedication engraved on his headstone.

**"LOVE, JOY, PEACE,
LONG SUFFERING, GENTLENESS,
GOODNESS, FAITH."**

MOSES HOUSE

Private, 25468

2nd/4th Battalion, Hampshire Regiment

Who died on

Sunday 29th September 1918, Aged 35.

Moses was born on 9th November 1882, one of the 16 sons and daughters of William and Emma House of Latchmoor, Brockenhurst. Father and son(s) all worked at some time in the gravel pits at Setley. Emma came from Salisbury. They were married in Sway Church.

MOSES HOUSE AND HIS FAMILY

Moses married Daisy Young from Boldre on 8th June 1912 at St Nicholas Church. They had three children, Frank, Fred and Daisy - who was known as "Tuppence". The eldest son, Frank, lived, until recently, in the family home in North Weirs, Brockenhurst. Before he died Frank - along with a great cousin, Mrs James - provided the following history.

Just as many villagers did, Moses joined the Hampshire Regiment. After training he was drafted to the 12th Battalion, formed as part of the 26th Division in Kitchener's Third New Army, "K 3." It moved to France in September 1915 but, after a brief two-month spell of training in the trenches, it was sent to Salonica, in Northern Greece.

The Salonican Front was a joint Anglo-French operation designed to help the Serbians from being defeated by Austrian and Bulgarian attacks. It is not known when Moses arrived but we do know, from a letter sent home dated 16th December 1916, that he was there, serving in B Company.

Another letter exactly a year later reported that he was in the Military Hospital at Cottoncia, Malta, having been evacuated from Salonica with an injured leg. He left Malta on Boxing Day, but did not have an easy journey to England as the ship he was on was torpedoed. Moses was rescued after 5 hours in a lifeboat and finally arrived in England on 5th January 1918. He spent the next two months hospitalised in Bristol and in Wells.

On 31st March he wrote to say he was back in Winchester. He would have been attached to the 3rd (Special Reserve) Battalion. This was a holding unit that fed drafts of reinforcements to active service battalions. After six months of training - including another spell in hospital during May - he was granted home leave before being sent to France. His son, Frank, (see page 274) before he died in 2001, said he remembered his father, Moses, going down the garden path and off to war at the end of his last leave in August 1918.

By September 1918 the German attacks had been defeated and Haig, recognising that the war could be won in 1918, furiously attacked the German Hindenburg Line.

Moses was sent to "B" Company 2nd/4th Hampshires, part of 186 Brigade of the 62nd Division in Third Army. On 12th September 2/4 HAMPS were tasked to attack Havrincourt. This they successfully did but in so doing incurred over 200 casualties. This assault was, however, an essential preliminary to the major attack on the Hindenburg line.

The battalion joined the battle on 28th September by attacking Marcoing, near Cambrai. "B" Company, under Captain Cottam, took over the advance on the outskirts of the town. Despite fierce opposition its leading platoons reached the canal beyond; some of the Company even crossing and consolidating beyond it. Further attacks by the unit the following day to exploit this success were unsuccessful.

Moses was seriously wounded at this time. A fellow villager, Alf Foster, was with him when he died of his wounds in a Casualty Clearing Station in Grevillers on 29th September 1918.

He is buried at **Grevillers British Cemetery** in:

Plot E 12.

The following inscription is engraved on his headstone:

"NOT GONE FROM MEMORY,
NOT GONE FROM LOVE,"
DAISY AND CHILDREN, ENGLAND."

ARTHUR COLE

Private, 69588

Royal Defence Corps

Who died on

Saturday 19th October 1918, Aged 29.

Arthur Cole was born in Ardingly, Sussex but later moved into the village. On 26th October 1916 he married Edith May Harrison. They lived at Oak Tree Cottage in the Weirs sharing the house with the Hunt family (see p 108).

He originally enlisted at Brighton into the Royal Sussex Regiment as a Private (No. 2870). His service with the Royal Sussex is unknown but at some stage he transferred into the 268th Protection Company Royal Defence Corps.

Not a lot is remembered today about this Corps. The **Lineage Book of British Land Forces** records that it came into existence by being formed into a separate category of the Army on 17th March 1916. It remained in existence until 1936 when its role was taken over by the National Defence Companies of the Territorial Army.

The Corps was divided into 19 battalions, each of which had several numbered companies. Its task was to be responsible for guarding local "Vulnerable Points" such as railway stations, bridges and pumping stations against possible enemy attack. This freed regular and territorial units for service overseas.

From its formation in 1916 until the end of the war 632 of its members died in Home Command, with a further 31 soldiers dying at sea when their ship was sunk on 10th October 1918.

Arthur died of Spanish influenza, which swept Europe at the time, on 19th October 1918 in South Tidworth Military Hospital.

Arthur Cole is commemorated on two headstones in **St. Nicholas Churchyard**.

Details of The family headstone is in the background of the picture below. A close-up, with its details, can be seen on page 109 (see Harry Hunt).

He is buried in **St Nicholas's Churchyard**, Brockenhurst in a military grave with the inscription:

**"THERE IS NO DEATH
UNTO CHRIST HE STILL LIVETH."**

ALBERT THOMAS KITCHER

Private, 44541

8th Battalion, Gloucestershire Regiment

Who died on

Sunday, 20th October 1918, Aged 19.

Albert was baptised on 7th May 1899 a son of George, a dairyman, and Sarah Kitcher of Setley, Brockenhurst. An older brother George had been born on 6th January 1895 and younger siblings included Mabel, Bert and James. Mabel was a nurse during the Great War at "Tin Town," the New Zealand Hospital in Church Lane.

Albert, or "Tom," as he was known in the family, went to the old school in the village and then went on to work at Tile Barn Farm with his father. His sister-in-law, Mrs. Minerva Kitcher, recalls that he sometimes had to walk cows to Ringwood market for sale. William George Gearey, Minnie's father, served in the Royal Navy as a Chief Petty Officer, and she attributes her name to his commission on HMS MINERVA.

TOM KITCHER (BACK ROW)

Tom enlisted in Brockenhurst into the Royal North Devon Hussars but later transferred into the 8th (Service) Battalion of the Gloucestershire Regiment. The 8th Battalion served throughout the war as part of the 57th Brigade in 19th (Western) Division, and, given his age, Albert would probably have joined the Battalion during 1918.

118

The Battalion took part in the holding battles of St Quentin and Bapaume in March 1918 and the Battles of the Lys in the following month against the German attempts at breakthrough on the Western Front. They were also at the Battle of the Aisne from 29th May to 6th June 1918 when the Division was attached to the 5th (French) Army, which successfully frustrated the final German attack.

Albert was a member of "C" Company of the Battalion in the final advance to victory in Picardy. The Battle of the Selle raged from 18-23rd October during which the Battalion captured Haussy.

Albert was killed in action on 20th October 1918 and was buried by his unit in **Haussy Communal Cemetery** in:

Grave B. 2.

After the war the original wooden cross from his grave in France was brought back and placed on his parent's grave. Family memory recalls that it was, regrettably, later destroyed by vandals.

THE METHODIST CHURCH MEMORIAL

WILLIAM CHARLES STRIDE

Private, PO/14254,

Royal Marine Light Infantry

HMS BRITANNIA,

Who died on

Saturday 9th November 1918, Aged 31.

William Stride was baptised in Brockenhurst on 20th February 1887. He was a son of Charles, a railway platelayer, and Ellen Stride.

After attending the village school he joined the Royal Marine Light Infantry and by 1918 was serving on BRITANNIA.

This was a Pre-Dreadnought battleship of the King Edward Class, which had been built at Portsmouth in 1906. It had undergone a refit in May 1917 at Bermuda and was flagship for the 9th Cruiser Squadron, which was tasked with Atlantic patrol and convoy duties, being based mainly at Sierra Leone. William Stride's task on board is likely to have been the manning of "X" Turret of her 9.2" guns which, traditionally, was manned by the Royals.

GIBRALTAR NORTH FRONT CEMETERY

On 9th November 1918 she was torpedoed by U50 en route to Gibraltar, causing her to list 10 degrees. A second internal explosion after the torpedoing started a fire in a 9.2" magazine, which caused a quantity of cordite to ignite.

This, surprisingly, did not increase the list and the ship remained afloat for nearly three hours before sinking. Most of her crew were therefore saved but 50 men were killed and 80 injured out of a ship's company of 777 souls.

BRITANNIA was the last British warship to be sunk by enemy action in the Great War.

William Stride is buried with 22 of his shipmates in **Gibraltar (North Front) Cemetery** in:

Plot B 4215.

William's wife Flora later lived at Upper Pikes Hill, Lyndhurst. On his gravestone Flora had inscribed:

" **IN MY LONELY HOURS**
OF THINKING
THOUGHTS OF YOU
ARE OFTEN NEAR."

LEONARD BADEN HOUSE

Private, TR/8/30480

51st (Garrison) Battalion, Hampshire Regiment

Who died on

Sunday 24th November 1918, Aged 18.

Leonard was baptised on 26th August 1900. He was the son of Frederick James and Elizabeth (nee Husker) House, of 17 Carey's Cottages, Brockenhurst.

Born in 1900 one could venture to suggest that, with many other babies of the time, his middle name possibly reflects the public esteem in which the hero of Mafeking was held.

The 51st (Garrison) Battalion was a Young Soldier's battalion formed towards the end of the war as a replacement for the former Training Reserve Battalions. For the Hampshire Regiment two Graduated Battalions (52nd and 53rd) provided basic training for recruits and then passed them onto the 51st which, after further training, sent them as trained soldiers to the operational battalions of the Regiment.

Whilst under training, however, Leonard died of influenza in the Military Hospital at Colchester. This great Spanish Flue epidemic of 1918/20 swept across Europe and was reportedly said to have killed more people than the fighting in the war.

On 29th November 1918 he was buried in **St Nicholas's Churchyard**, Brockenhurst in:

Plot C. 23.5.

The inscription reads:

**"IN LOVING MEMORY
OF OUR DEAR SON
IN THE MIDST OF LIFE
WE ARE IN DEATH"**

He is also commemorated on the **Methodist Church Memorial** (see page 119).

THE HOME FRONT: THE ARMISTICE

From the written evidence that remains the village seems to have been unprepared for the sudden ending of the war.

In November, before the war was known to have ended the vicar, the Reverend George Combe Williams, wrote in the **New Forest Magazine**:

In connection with the Hampshire Regiment Prisoners of War Fund the following announcement ought to stir up a desire on the part of all to do as much as possible for the upkeep of the Fund. Contributions will be gratefully accepted by Mrs. Bell, the Hon. Sec. for the Brockenhurst Branch of the Fund.

"There are now in Germany about 340 prisoners belonging to the various Battalions of the Regiment, besides those in Bulgaria and Turkey, who bring the total up to about 550. These men are dependent for their actual existence on the food sent to them from home, and this food has to be provided for by voluntary subscriptions.

During the past year each man in Germany has been sent six parcels per month and the men in Bulgaria and Turkey provided for by sending them money and when possible parcels.

Owing to the high price of food, it is calculated that during the ensuing year, parcels cannot cost less than 10/- each, so that allowing a little extra for bread and small comforts, such as tobacco, the cost of providing for one man for one year will amount to £40—or to £22,000 for 550 prisoners of the Regiment without allowing for any possible increase in their numbers.

As far as this Committee can judge, unless a serious effort is made, there is no prospect of more than £7,000 being raised in Hampshire to meet the required £22,000 and it is felt that in spite of the many other calls that may be made upon them for charitable purposes, the people of Hampshire will wish, if possible, to provide for those who have gone out at the risk of their lives to represent them in the great war."

Happily these endeavours were not to be needed.

Whilst the Great War ended on 11th November, no mention of this momentous occasion is to be found in the minutes of the Parish Council held two days later - although the supply of seed potatoes to small growers was debated.

On the 27th November the minutes note that it was unanimously agreed:

> *"That in view of the necessity of more cottages and allotments in Brockenhurst on the men's return from military service the Parish Council of Brockenhurst with Rhinefield would be glad that the question of taking up another site for allotments should be postponed for a year, for which the Parish Council are prepared to rent as hitherto."*

The Church was quicker off the mark.

> The good news of the signing of the armistice which we received in Brockenhurst before midday on the 11th, came as an almost non-understandable condition after the four years of war. It was celebrated by a thanksgiving service in the old Parish Church at 5 p.m., when the church was full. A thanksgiving celebration of Holy Communion on Tuesday morning and a thanksgiving service in the evening of the same day, began a week of thanksgiving which will remain in the memories of many people of Brockenhurst. The offertories at the celebrations of Holy Communion on Tuesday and Thursday are to be forwarded to the Lord Roberts Memorial Workshop Extension Fund, which is doing so much for the crippled soldiers and sailors in giving them a chance of becoming useful citizens and ready to take their part in the economic war with their late enemies of the battlefields of Europe.

The War Memorial. In December the Vicar asked parishioners who had lost relatives in the war to let him know rank and regiment to which they were attached, for inclusion on the permanent Role of Honour on the War Memorial.

Peace Celebrations. Finally, in the minutes of the Parish Council for January 1919 it is noted that:

> *"The question of Peace Celebration was brought up forward by Mr A. Keeping, who suggested that a public meeting should be called to appoint a representative committee of the Parish and that also a circular letter should be drawn up and forwarded to prominent residents of the village inviting them to take part in the movement, so that when the time did come round Brockenhurst would not be behindhand in this respect. These suggestions consequently formed the resolution, which was seconded by Mr E. Payne and unanimously agreed. The proposed date was the first Wednesday in February at 6.0 p.m. in the schools."*

Regrettably the Minute Book has no record of this meeting.

The village, in common with the rest of the country, seems to have experienced a period of being "in limbo" at the end of the year. Casualties continued to impact on the village with **William Stride** being killed two days before the end of the war and **Len House** dying two weeks later from the Spanish Flu epidemic. The village was full of the patients from the two hospitals, who were now keen on going home to New Zealand and local men who had been wounded and discharged. Demobilisation of men serving in the forces would not occur for some months yet to come. The reported gap in perception of those at home who could not always grasp the realities of war and those who were only too well versed in it was yet to be fully experienced. Meanwhile both factions wrote letters and sent Christmas cards. Those from France reflected continued military alertness mingled with nostalgia for a past home life.

This Christmas Card, printed for the 9th (Scottish) Division, was sent home by Ted Brown's father at the end of the war.

Inside, the actions in which the 9th Division fought are listed as:

Loos 1915	Longueval 1916	Somme 1916
Arras 1917	Passchendaele 1917	Somme 1918
Wytschaete 1918	Meteren 1918	Hoegenacker 1918

This was the record of but one of the sixty-three divisions in existence at this time.

The Soldier

If I should die, think only this of me:
That there's some corner of a foreign field
That is forever England. There shall be
In that rich earth a richer dust conceal'd;
A dust whom England bore, shaped, made aware,
Gave, once, her flowers to love, her ways to roam
A body of England's, breathing English air.
Wash'd by the rivers, blessed by suns of home.
And think, this heart, all evil shed away,
A pulse in the eternal mind, no less
gives somewhere back the thoughts by England given;
Her sights and sounds; dreams happy as her day;
And laughter, learnt of friends; and gentleness,
In hearts at peace, under an English heaven.

RUPERT BROOKE
1877-1915

Brockenhurst
between
The Wars

1919-1924: ADJUSTMENT

The village gradually adjusted to the aftermath of the war.

1919 saw the return to Brockenhurst of servicemen on demobilisation. Some of the seriously wounded, like Len Smith, Frank Perkins and Jo Clare, had already been discharged and were living in the village, a visual reminder of the human cost of the war. This was reinforced by the large number of widows and orphans of the village.

The children in this photograph of two classes of the village school, taken in 1919, are a bridge between the two wars. Born before 1914 many of them, identified in the photograph below, had lost fathers, uncles or cousins in the recent conflict. Most of them were to experience the forthcoming Second World War, with its attendant losses.

1919 STANDARD FORMS 4 AND 5

Mr White is the teacher on the left and Mr Quinn, the Headmaster, on the right.

Back Row   Edith or Winnie Stride (3rd from right).
Eileen Pope (2nd from Right)

Third Row   John Hibbs (Left/below Mr White)
Hilda Clarke (4th from left)
Peg Humphreys (4th from right)

Second Row   Lily Povey (3rd Left)
Phyllis Smith (7th from left)

Front Row   Harry Lancaster (left)
Bert Harrison (Right of Harry Lancaster)
Syd Stride (3rd from right)

128

Patients recovering or convalescing in the New Zealand Hospital were an everyday sight in the village in their distinctive blue and red uniforms. A number of friendships were made with village girls, which resulted in marriage. Hilda Tucker married "Johnnie" Walker in this way (see pages 36, 50 and 51) and after the war emigrated to New Zealand .

Prisoners-of-war returned from Germany, amongst whom were:

> **Len Hinves**. His niece, Bliss Phillips, remembers it being said that he had had a rough time with very little food in the closing months of the war. He returned to the village to work as a painter and decorator. He died on 10th May 1959.

> **Jesse Sque**. His grandson, Tony Johnson, never heard him talk about his experiences as a prisoner of war. Captured in early 1915 he spent several years as a prisoner in Munster where they were paid in camp money, bringing this example back as a souvenir. He lived in the village, working as a postman. He died in 1964.

Casualties. Debilitation from war service and the Spanish Flu epidemic would take the following ex-servicemen in 1919.

> *Selim Chandler*
> *William Harrison*
> *David Humphries*
> *John Lancaster*

1921. Interestingly, the population of the village in the 1921 Census showed that it had increased by 111 people. The number of men, however, had only increased by four, whilst women had increased by 107. The number of families had increased by 66. Some of these, like the House family, must have been single-parent homes, reduced to that status by the war.

Len Smith is remembered, by Arthur Stevens, to have died from the long-term effects of his wounds about 1921. This is reasonable as the inclusion of his name on the memorial predicates his death before April 1921.

JOHN HENRY LANCASTER

Lance-Corporal

Hampshire Regiment

who died on

26th January 1919, Aged 28.

In the 1891 British Census conducted in April of that year Frank Lancaster, a gardener, and his wife Janet are shown as living in Brockenhurst Road. There were two sons to the marriage - Frank, who was 10 years old, and John, who was 9 months. The latter was baptised on 17th August 1890. Brother Frank, "Jigger" to villagers, later lived in Setley and worked as a gardener looking after the Morant's Pleasure Garden. John was a house painter and journeyman.

At some stage he joined either the 2nd or 10th Battalion of the Hampshire Regiment both of which fought in Gallipoli. As the **New Forest Magazine** of March 1916 records that:

> *John Lancaster, son of Mr and Mrs Frank Lancaster, is dangerously ill with diphtheria in the Far East.*

The **RINGWOOD AND NEW FOREST CHRONICLE** of 31st August 1916 states, under "Wounded," that:

> *"Private "Jack" Lancaster of Brockenhurst Park Gardens and of the Hampshire Regiment who is now in hospital in England and whom we are glad to say is well on the road to recovery, has certainly received his share of mans misfortunes having been wounded during the Gallipoli Campaign and whilst recovering from his wound, while in hospital abroad, having suffered from diphtheria, pleurisy and enteric concurrently."*

Jack is not recorded on the databases of either **"Soldiers Died"** or the Commonwealth War Graves Registry. It must therefore be presumed that he was discharged from the army before the end of the war.

He lived with his parents in The Gardeners Cottage Brockenhurst Park but despite the promising tone of the CHRONICLE's report Jack's health deteriorated during 1918.

There came a stage where he was admitted, as an

"Ex-Lance-Corporal the Hampshire Regiment,"

into the No. 1 New Zealand hospital in Brockenhurst. Here he was found to be suffering from cancer and general exhaustion. His Death Certificate records that he died in the hospital on 26th of January 1919.

The funeral took place on 30th January, the Priest in Charge being the Reverend Geoffrey Combs-Williams. Jack is buried in **St Nicholas Churchyard** Brockenhurst.

"I HAVE FOUGHT THE GOOD FIGHT"

WILLIAM ALFRED HARRISON

Private, 10513

Depot, Hampshire Regiment

Who died on

Wednesday 29th January 1919, Aged 25.

William was baptised on 17th September 1895, the son of William, a sawyer, and Annie Harrison who lived at The Weirs in Brockenhurst.

The details of his service with the Hampshire Regiment are unknown. Clearly, however, from the War Graves headstone, he was still serving in the army when he died.

He died of double pneumonia and malaria, on 29th January 1919 at the University College War Hospital at Highfield, Southampton. This College had been built to replace the Institute in the town centre, but was commandeered from the start as a war hospital for the duration. In 1952 it gained University status.

His funeral took place on the 3rd February and was conducted by the Reverend Geoffrey Combs-Williams.

He is buried in **St Nicholas Churchyard, Brockenhurst** in:

Plot C 12.8.

The inscription reads:

**"HE HAS GONE FROM OUR HOME,
BUT NOT FROM OUR HEARTS. "**

DAVID ARTHUR HUMPHREYS

Private, 85073

Royal Defence Corps

Who died on

Friday 7th March 1919, Aged 19.

Arthur was born at home on 12th August 1899, to David and Mary Humphreys who lived in Brookley Road, Brockenhurst. A daughter was also born to them in 1905. David Humphreys (Senior) kept an ironmongers shop in Brookley Road which, amongst other things, also sold paraffin. The father was an ardent Baptist and was known as "Sniffer" to the village children. After the war the family moved to 38 Lodge Road, Southampton.

David (Junior), or Arthur as he was known in the family, started working as an

assistant in his father's shop. He was called up towards the war's end and appears to have been still serving with the 63rd Protection Company of the Royal Defence Corps when he died on 7th March 1919 as his name is held in the records of the C. W. G. C.

His Death Certificate, however, describes him as an

"Ex Private Royal Defence Corps."

He died at his home in Brookley Road after six days suffering from broncho-pneumonia. His mother's sister, Fanny Spencer, was present at his death.

His funeral took place on 12th March at **St Nicholas Church** and was conducted by the Baptist minister, the Reverend D. D. Bennett.

He is buried under a family headstone in the Churchyard in:

Plot A.7.3.

SELIM CHANDLER DSM

Petty Officer, Royal Navy

Who died on

2nd September 1919, Aged 37

Selim Chandler was born on the 19th May 1883. He was a son of Alfred and Mary Chandler who farmed at Boldre. Alfred was also an agister. The family consisted of another brother and three sisters.

Selim was a smallish man, 5ft 2" tall with a dark fresh complexion who worked as a farm boy before enlistment.

He joined HMS ST VINCENT as a Boy Seaman on 27th February 1899.

After further training afloat he was rated an Ordinary Seaman on 19th May 1901 and an Able Bodied Seaman 7 months later. He was an efficient man with

"Very Good"

ratings throughout his career.

For the last 2 years of his service he was appointed to H M Submarine Depot ships ARROGANT and DOLPHIN. All told he served in 25 ships and shore stations before completing his 12 years and transferring to the Royal Fleet Reserve.

HMS ADAMANT

On being called up on the 2nd August 1914 for war service he again served on Submarine Depot Ships and it was serving as a Leading Seaman aboard ADAMANT, that he was awarded the Distinguished Service Medal (DSM). Regrettably, no details are forthcoming of this award from the London Gazette announcement in 1915.

He subsequently served out the war in more depot ships (TITANIA, AMBROSE and again ADAMANT) as well as being on two of the operational steam driven "Fleet Submarines" K8 and K10.

K 8

He was promoted to Petty Officer in July 1917, but was invalided out of the Royal Navy on 24th October 1918 with an ulcerated heart attributed to his naval service.

Selim died on 2nd September 1919 with his brother Leroy Chandler, of Pikes Hill, Lyndhurst, present at the death. The Reverend C. Hope-Gill officiated at his funeral on the 4th September.

He is buried next to other graves of his family in **St Nicholas Churchyard**, Brockenhurst in:

Grave B.7.4.

A simple inscription on the War Graves headstone reads:

"THY WILL BE DONE"

LEONARD E SMITH

who is believed to have died in 1921.

Before the war "Soldier" Smith lived at Wide Lane Cottage and kept a number of cows. He was considered to have a working knowledge of animal illnesses that was widely called upon to advise on matters veterinary by other villagers. His military service was clearly not without influence as, at the beginning of the war, the following villagers of that name were serving their King and Country:

Royal Navy:	Smith F. T. (Petty Officer).		Smith H. A
Army:	Smith L.E.	Smith P. E. (Sergt.).	Smith W.
Royal Marines:	Smith G. A. (Sergt.).		

In 1991 Arthur Stevens, who lives in Lymington, met Leonard's daughter Susan again after a gap of 75 years. They remained in contact until her death three years ago. He remembers that Leonard, who had a younger brother, was of small stature, and was

"One of the first to go out there."

In 1915 Leonard was, apparently, very badly wounded at Ypres, having half his face shot away. After extensive hospitalisation he was discharged from the army. Whilst they had

"done a good job on him"

he always had to wear a mask over the lower part of his face. He was, however, a cheerful, jovial man who walked all over the place from his home in North Weirs. The mask, happily, had an appropriate hole that enabled him to enjoy a smoke. He also visited the Foresters Arms where he frequently was to be seen having a pint with his friends.

Arthur recalls Leonard's wife as being a very homely person. She bore Leonard two sons, Bill and Ted, and daughter Susan. Both boys became engine drivers - Bill driving mainline King Arthur Class engines, whilst Ted drove Lymington trains. Susan married and became Mrs Rickman.

Arthur believes that Leonard died from the long-term effects of his wounds in 1921. It is not known where he is buried, but the present Parish Clerk Mary Pattison has confirmed that the appropriate Register of Burials shows no entry for an L. E. Smith's interment in **St Nicholas Churchyard**, Brockenhurst.

THE PRESENT WAR MEMORIAL

The original Shrine was demolished and replaced by the present Memorial in 1921.

THE PRESENT WAR MEMORIAL

When the present Memorial in Sway Road was erected in 1921 the site was open to the road - hence the handsome railings. At some stage these railings were removed - perhaps to help the war effort in a later conflict. Their passing is not now remembered.

In 1921 the following article was published in the Parish magazine: -

VILLAGE WAR MEMORIAL

ADDITIONAL NOTES
By the present Vicar, The REV C. HOPE-GILL, MA

This Monument stands in the heart of the Village on the site of the former War Shrine.

The Memorial is a handsome obelisk of Portland Stone, about 18 ft. in height. On the front apex is a cross in relief. In the centre is engraved

"To Our Glorious Dead"

On the lower plinth is a bronze tablet bearing the following inscription: -

"In ever-grateful Memory of the Men of Brockenhurst who gave their lives for their Country during the Great War 1914-1919."

Here follow the names of 50 men. The inscription closes with the words

"Their Name liveth for evermore"

The Monument is suitably fenced around; and the site, which forms part of a wayside green, with a fine spreading oak as a background, has been conveyed to the parish by the Morant trustees. The site is on the Sway Road, near Lloyds Bank.

The Memorial, which has been erected by public subscription, was formally unveiled on Sunday Evening, June 26th, 1921, by one of the Ex-service men who was crippled in the war. It was a touching and memorable ceremony and was attended by a large crowd of Parishioners.

Mr. W. Ravenscroft, of Milford-on-Sea, was the architect for the memorial and gave his valuable services free of charge.

138

The timber memorial and cross of the old **Shrine**, however, is now appropriately to be seen in the porch of St. Nicholas Church.

THE BOARD FROM THE OLD SHRINE

Despite Arthur Chamber's plea for accuracy of detail this board is at variance with the Memorial in that it does not include the names of *A. Cole, E. Fisher* or *W. Janes* but does include a *W. Jones*.

Forgotten and not recorded on the memorial are the names of twenty-five men who were born in Brockenhurst or were resident in the village at the time of the war and who died whilst serving in the Army. These include:

Hill J	Pte	2 Hamps	08/05/15	KIA	Galllipoli
Harris J	Pte	2 Hamps	06/08/15	KIA	Gallipoli
Reynard W	L/Cpl	10 Hamps	10/08/15	KIA	Gallipoli
Miller J W	Pte	10 Hamps	01/11/15	Died	Chichester
Dove T L	L/Cpl	1/6 Welsh	16/12/15	DOW	Bethune
Stokes S D	Pte	2 Dorsets	25/12/15	DOW	Mesopotamia
Legg J W	Cpl	1 Hamps	02/01/16	KIA	Somme
Macintosh J	Pte	7 Leic	30/01/16	KIA	Somme
Kitcher D	Pte	1 E Yorks	01/07/16	KIA	Somme
Holman S	A/Cpl	2 Hamps	13/07/16	KIA	Somme
Rickman J A	Pte	2 Dorsets	18/08/16	Died	Mesopotamia
Bew R	Pte	15 Hamps	07/10/16	KIA	Somme
Raisey F	Pte	2 Berks	04/03/17	KIA	Somme
Wells J	Gnr	RGA	08/04/17	DOW	Arras
Moores E W	Pte	14 Hamps	31/07/17	KIA	Passchendaele
Dunford W	Gnr	RGA	18/09/17	KIA	Passchendaele
Baker C J H	Pte	9 Devons	06/10/17	KIA	Passchendaele
Broomfield D	Pte	Lab Corps	31/12/17	Died	Etaples
Pullen E G	S.S.M.	RASC	18/01/18	Died	Fulford, York
White S L B	Pte	8 Berks	09/04/18	KIA	1918 Retreat
Beard A H	Sgt	2 Ox & Bucks	20/04/18	DOW	1918 Retreat
Elford J F	Pte	2 S Staff	23/08/18	KIA	1918 Advance
Middleton W	L/Cpl	14 Welsh	27/08/18	KIA	1918 Advance
Phillpott W T	Pte	13 Lond	10/09/18	DOW	1918 Advance
Hewlett J E	Pte	2/4 Berks	28/10/18	DOW	1918 Advance

The reasons that led to the omission of the names of these twenty-five Brockenhurst men can only be guessed. Of these men twenty-one were from fighting units, with fifteen of them being killed in action, with a further six dying of wounds. Four died from illness or accident in Mesopotamia, France or in England. Their inclusion here may go some way towards the restoration of their memory.

The village therefore suffered in;

1914-2 deaths	1915-19 deaths	1916-13 deaths
1917-19 deaths	1918-21 deaths	1919/21-5 deaths

The loss of seventy-nine men, with twenty-one deaths in the last year of war alone - would have had a severe economic and emotional impact on many village families.

The British Legion Club was opened in 1924. It soon became the centre of village social life with dances, whist drives, concerts and all manner of other social activity.

THE BRITISH LEGION CLUB HALL

The two posters by the stage advertise forthcoming concerts. The two oval mirrors on the right commemorate links with Auckland and Wellington in New Zealand. The club was bombed in 1940, rebuilt, but closed after a fire in the 1960's.

Disabled servicemen were taught skills by many charitable organisations.

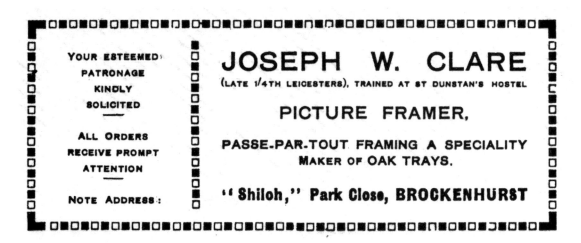

YOUR ESTEEMED
PATRONAGE
KINDLY
SOLICITED

ALL ORDERS
RECEIVE PROMPT
ATTENTION

NOTE ADDRESS:

JOSEPH W. CLARE
(LATE 1/4TH LEICESTERS), TRAINED AT ST DUNSTAN'S HOSTEL

PICTURE FRAMER,

PASSE-PAR-TOUT FRAMING A SPECIALITY
MAKER OF OAK TRAYS.

"Shiloh," Park Close, BROCKENHURST

The Emergency Help Fund. This fund was a much-needed safety net at the time.

> "This organisation helps ex-servicemen (except officers) and their dependents. The term ex-servicemen means ex-servicemen suffering from *disabilities accepted by the Ministry of Pensions as attributable to the war*. Applications, accompanied by all necessary evidence should be made to Lt-Col H. W. Russell, Moor Cottage, Setley."

1925-1934: THE INTERIM

THEIR FATHERS' SONS

1929 SENIOR CLASS

Most of the children of this class were destined to experience the Second World War at first hand. Many of the boys served in the Forces and three were killed:

Back Row   *Alfred Shilleto* (Left)
                 Leslie Dukes (Middle)

Third Row   *Harold Cleveland*
                 (2nd from left)

Another link between the generations can be seen in this photograph.

Wilfrid ("Jack") Waterman, who was wounded at Ypres towards the end of the war, is sitting with his wife, Annie, and three sons - Wilfred (left), Jack and Midge (right).

Jack returned to his job in the Post Office and worked there until after the Second World War.

His son, Wilfred, worked for the village firm of Tractors and Motors and was in the Home Guard. Both other sons served in the Second World War.

142

Jack's father, Frederick, was clearly a local character, as this very sensitive obituary - written in 1934 by the vicar - admits:

JACK (Jnr.)   FREDERICK   WILFRID "JACK" (Snr.)

FREDERICK WATERMAN. One of the real human " land marks " of our Village disappeared in the passing of Frederick Waterman, who was suddenly called to his rest on Saturday, March 30th. His record of 70 years as a chorister in church choirs is one that cannot be allowed to pass without this short note of recognition. We shall indeed miss him in the vestry of the Parish Church, as there was always a note of cheer for most of us before we went into church. Like many others of his generation he did not always approve of changes, but unlike many others his disapproval was always tempered with good humour, even when the choir stalls were placed a little further back and he found some difficulty in accomodating himself to the more confined space, perhaps I may say so now, that is why he always sat at the end of the row. But I for one, and I know I speak for the rest of the choir, will indeed miss him in his usual place on Sundays. But we are glad to have in his son Jack another regular chorister, and sometimes a grandson who will always remind us of the one now entered into his rest.

The Waterman family is still represented in the church choir today.

BROCKENHURST ACTIVITIES

With a much smaller population than today the village had more organised activities then, than now. Some still continue. Some of the more interesting are given below.

Ancient Order of Foresters.
Life Boys. 1st Brockenhurst Team for Boys 9 to 12. Parades on Mondays and Fridays at the Wesleyan Schoolroom. Officer, Mr L. J. Ashlett, New Park Cottages.
Boy Scouts Association.
British Legion Club.
British Red Cross Society.
Brockenhurst Cricket Club and Brockenhurst Football Club.
Brockenhurst Infant Welfare Centre. 1st & 3rd Tuesdays at the Morant Hall. Health clinic for babies and young children. Tea and biscuits provided in the supper room.

1929: THE BROCKENHURST WELFARE GROUP IN THE MORANT FAMILY GARDENS IN THE PARK

1st Brockenhurst Girl Guides.
Brockenhurst Horticultural Society.
Brockenhurst Hospitals Committee
Brockenhurst Lawn Tennis Club.
Brockenhurst Manor Golf Club Limited.
Brockenhurst Manor Artisan Golf Society.
Brockenhurst Mother's Union
Brockenhurst & Rhinefield Conservative & Unionist Association.
Brockenhurst Slate Club. The Club meets in the Church Room, Sway Road, every alternate Friday, from 6.45 p.m. till 7.30 p.m., and has a membership of 107. All men between the ages of 16 and 60, if in good health, are eligible to join. Treasurer, Mr H. Young. Steward, Mr F. Emms, Secretary, Mr E. G. White.
Brockenhurst Women's' Institute.
Burley & District New Forest Pony & Cattle Society.
Church Working Party. Meet every Thursday, except 3rd in the month, in the Church Room, from 2.30 till 5. Orders for needlework taken.

144

"Crown" Slate Club. Rose and Crown Hotel alternate Mondays between 7 - 9 p.m.

Gas Company. Manager Mr. C. O. Vicary, Gasworks, Brockenhurst.

Girls Friendly Society.

Guardians' Committee (of the County Council).

Ladies' Linen League - Royal South Hants Hospital.

Le Petit Orchestra, Brockenhurst. Dance Orchestra, Hon. Sec. Miss B. Wingate.

Medical Practitioners.

    Mr Reginald Stilwel Freeland, Harting, Brockenhurst.

    Mr D. K. Gaitskell, Waters Green house, Brockenhurst. Telephone 72.

    Mr G. B. Henley-Jones, Partridge Road, Brockenhurst. Telephone 81.

Missions to Seamen. Hon Sec. Brockenhurst Branch, Mrs Philip Stopford, Soundings.

National Deposit Friendly Society.

New Forest Commoners Defence Association. Chairman Capt. Cecil Sutton MBE.

New Forest Motor Ambulance. The Garage, Sway Road. Tel. 37.

Penny Bank and Coal Club.

Places of Worship

    Parish Churches of St Nicholas and St Saviour.

    Weseylan Methodist Church

    Baptist Church

    Roman Catholic Church. Mass is held at the Morant Hall once a month.

Police. Constable in Charge, Mr James, "Pretoria", Waters Green, Brockenhurst.

Schools.

    National School. Built in 1863 and since enlarged for 240 children.

VILLAGE SCHOOL PANTOMIME "SANTA CLAUS IN JAPAN" 1933
PEARL BURTON, MARY EMM, POPPY HAYTER, RUTH BURTON, KAY SHERARD.

    Brockenhurst County School. Head Mistress Miss E. C. Ward.

    Glenholm School Brockenhurst. Kindergarten and Preparatory for pupils from 4 to 11 years of age. Principal, Miss B. Wingate.

Southern Railway station. Station Master Mr F. W. Brockman, Woodside.

Unity Slate Club Men's and Women's Sections meet on alternate Mondays at the Foresters Arms at 7.45 p.m.

HOUSING IN BROCKENHURST

Property. By the mid-1930s, recovery from the Depression Years began to be experienced across the country. Whilst many of the villagers lived in rented accommodation more houses were being bought privately as prices in Brockenhurst were still "reasonable".

July 15 1934

No. 2, The Laurels, Tattenham Road, BROCKENHURST.

FOR SALE

SIX-ROOMED COTTAGE (Semi-detached) with Garden. Ample Room for Garage. Water & Main Drainage connected. FREEHOLD—Possession August.   PRICE, £485.

Apply: I. M. INGS, or Messrs. Jackman & Masters, Estate Agents, Lymington.

Captain Cecil Sutton MBE came to the village in 1906 as agent to the Morant Estate. He served in the First World War with the Royal Engineers, mainly engaged in surveying training camps for troops in the Weymouth area. As agent he was largely responsible for the Morant Hall being used as a wartime convalescent hospital. It was for his work in connection with this hospital that the Captain was appointed to his MBE.

In the half century he lived here the village grew from 1000 to over 2500 inhabitants. Believing that improvements to the village and the Estate were mutually beneficial he negotiated the supply of piped water from Southampton Corporation. This was followed by the introduction of modern sanitation and the building of the sewage disposal plant. He was one of the directors of the Brockenhurst Gas Company and in the early 1930s succeeded in getting electricity brought into the village. The introduction of these amenities ensured the ready sale of building plots by the Estate and significantly determined the character of Brockenhurst today. He was also President of the Land Agents Society - entitled P (Past) P.L.A.S.

His daughter, Primrose, recalls that one of his favourite expressions was *"What fun,"* be it concerning some recent battle he'd had with opposing authority - or, of course, all the "monkey-tricks" of the young who he loved so dearly - as they loved him.

He is still remembered by the older villagers for his skill at playing the banjo at village concerts. He was also very instrumental in the donation and transfer of Morant land for the site of the War Memorial. His name is commemorated in **SUTTON PLACE**, the site of the old Estate Office, off the Lyndhurst Road.

Brokenhurst Estate

"Heart of the New Forest."

HOUSES

and

BUILDING SITES

(FREEHOLD, or 99 YEARS' LEASE, with option to Purchase)

Special Terms to Builders.

The Brokenhurst Estate is surrounded by the glorious New Forest, and is one of the most beautifully situated Estates in England. The subsoil is chiefly gravel. Building sites of every size are available for large or small houses. There are also many excellent Sites for Shops and Business Premises near the Station and in the Village.

COMPANY'S WATER, GAS and ELECTRIC LIGHT,
PERFECT DRAINAGE SYSTEM.

The following are some of the materials which can be purchased from the Estate :—
TIMBER (Oak, Ash, Beech, Birch, Alder, Fir), OAK FENCING MATERIAL,
FIREWOOD LOGS, PEASTICKS, BEAN RODS, GRAVEL, SAND.

The Brokenhurst Estate is known as the centre for Sport in the New Forest.

NEW FOREST LAWN TENNIS & CROQUET CLUB
(13 Grass, 3 Hard Courts, 2 Squash Racquets Courts).
BROKENHURST MANOR GOLF CLUB (18 Holes).
HUNTING—Foxhounds, Staghounds, Otter Hounds, Beagles.
YACHTING and SEA BATHING within easy reach.
FISHING ON THE ESTATE BY DAILY TICKET.

For all particulars apply :—

CAPT. CECIL SUTTON, M.B.E., P.P.L.A.S., F.S.I.
CHARTERED LAND AGENT, CHARTERED SURVEYOR and VALUER,
THE ESTATE OFFICES, BROCKENHURST.

YOUTH

Culverly Green and Waters Green were the main areas for cricket, football and golf. The absence of cars meant that cycling was not a problem. Rides to Southampton cinemas in the summer and over to Hythe to look at the Empire Flying boats and watch the first Pan Am Clipper were normal adventures. The HINDENBURG airship was eagerly observed flying over the village. When old enough, children caddied at the Golf Club for pocket money, 2d of which often went on deposit at Merriotts General Stores to be redeemed in November for fireworks.

LES DUKES , FRED MORGAN , JOHN O'DONNELL , JACK HAYTER , *TONY O'DONNELL*, STAN WATERMAN, DON KEEPING, CHARLIE HIBBS, DICK WATERMAN, COLIN EDE, ALAN EDE, JOHN JOLLY   (RIGHT)

EMPLOYMENT

Three of the fathers of the boys above were postmen with the same number employed by the railways and in hotel work. The remaining three were a golf professional, a builder, and a gardener. Work was often found within the family network, with sons going into family businesses e.g. hairdressing, as *Sid Frowde* did, or - as *Cecil Hill* - being found employment where the father worked. Others got local jobs such as *Harold Cleveland*, who worked in Holtom's the butchers or *Alfred Shilleto* who worked for the New Forest Rural District Council at Lyndhurst. Many others were employed in service as gardeners, chauffeurs or general handy-men. The railway was the biggest employer, with hotels reportedly nearly in the same league. The Post Office provided a steady job for about twenty-five people and small building firms employed tradesmen, as there was little sub-contracting.

Some still joined the Services. *Leslie Myles* and **George Johnson** both joined the Army in 1933, whilst in 1936 *Ronald Read* joined the Royal Air Force as an apprentice. Indeed, apprenticeships continued to be an accepted way that a 14-year old - like *Tony O'Donnell* - was introduced to a trade. The indenture for *Jack Dunkinson*, on the next page, reflects the pay and conditions of the time.

148

This Indenture made the twenty first day of August,
one thousand nine hundred and thirty five.

Witnesseth That Jack Dunkinson,
of "Belmont", Waters Green, Brockenhurst
in the County of Hampshire
Son of John and Sarah Dunkinson

by and with consent and approbation of his the himself testified
by h is executing these Presents, doth put himself Apprentice to

R. PURKESS, LIMITED,
of Brookley Road, Brockenhurst.
in the County of Hampshire
to learn the Art, Trade or Business of

Baker, Pastrycook & Confectioner

and with him after the manner of an Apprentice to serve from the
first day of September, 1934 until
the full end and term of four years from thence next following, fully to be complete
and ended. During which term the said Apprentice his Master faithfully shall serve, his
secrets keep, and his lawful commands obey;—he shall do no damage to his said Master or his
Goods, nor suffer it to be done by others, but shall forthwith give notice to his said Master of
the same, when necessary;—he shall not waste the Goods of his said Master, nor lend them
unlawfully to any; nor shall he do any act whereby his said Master may sustain any loss, with
his own Goods or others' during the said term;—without Licence of his said Master, he shall
neither buy nor sell during his Apprenticeship; nor shall he absent himself from his said
Master's service day or night unlawfully; but in all things as a faithful Apprentice shall behave
himself towards his said Master and others, during the said term. And the said

R. Purkess, Limited shall instruct

Jack Dunkinson his said Apprentice in the Art, Trade, or
Business of Baker, Pastrycook & Confectioner
which he useth by the best means in his power shall teach and instruct or cause to be taught
and instructed;—the said R. Purkess Limited,
will pay the said Apprentice the Wages following—that is to say
The first year he shall receive 10/- per week.
The first six months of the second year he shall receive 12/6 per week.
The second six months of the second year he shall receive 15/- per week.
The first six months of the third year he shall receive 17/6 per week.
The second six months of the third year he shall receive £1. per week.
The first six months of the fourth year he shall receive £1.2.6 per week.
The second six months of the fourth year he shall receive £1.5. 0. per week.

These Presents shall be handed over to the said Apprentice
on the completion of the said term, with a Certificate of such service endorsed thereon.
AND for the true performance of all and every of the said Covenants and Agreements the
said Parties bind by themselves by these Presents. IN WITNESS whereof the said parties
have hereunto set their Hands and Seals the day and year first above written.

Signed, Sealed and Delivered in the presence
of *Reginald J. Purkess.*
Director.
Holm
Addison Road
Brockenhurst.

Sarah Dunkinson

Jack Dunkinson

FOR AND ON BEHALF OF
R. PURKESS LIMITED.
Stanley A. Purkess. SECRETARY

1935-1938: THE APPROACH OF WAR

Although war-clouds were not generally perceived in 1934 local emergency services maintained a high degree of efficiency that was to prove itself only five years later.

The British Red Cross Society. The village branch, under the command of Miss Gilham Smith, was inspected annually by the War Office. The inspecting officer on 2nd May 1934 was Major Rennie R.A.M.C., from Netley Military Hospital. Other inspectors included Lady Malmesbury, General Woodyatt, Colonel Deas and Mrs Moray-Williams. All expressed approval of what they had seen. The Red Cross Society and St. John's Ambulance Brigade were to underpin the effectiveness of the A. R. P. in the Blitz.

The Parish Council Fire Brigade. This photograph was taken on 23rd January 1934 when Fireman Fred Marden handed over duties of driver/mechanic to Fireman Cliff Gulliver.

THE CROSSLEY FIRE ENGINE AND THE NEW "PULSOMETER" TRAILER PUMP

At a Parish Council meeting on 17th April 1934 a cheque for £27.16.8 was sent to the County Treasurer as the first instalment of the repayment of the loan for the purchase of the Trailer Fire Pump. By a majority of one vote it was decided to insure the Tender and Pump under a Comprehensive Policy for £300.

The entry for **The Parish Council Fire Brigade** in the May 1934 edition of the Brockenhurst Bulletin reads

> **"Station Fibbards Road. Fire Bell, opposite Lloyds Bank. Captain, Mr. W. Hiett. Second Officer, Mr R. J. Stevens (Telephone 89) Hon Sec Mr. J. W. Martin Brookley Road (Telephone 16). Medical Officer Dr. D. K. Gaitskell."**

An article on its activities reports:

Brockenhurst Fire Brigade.

A strenuous time during the last month involving much hard work has been experienced by our Members but one and all have quite enjoyed the drills, though the consequent hose drying and clearing-up in the evenings after drills has not perhaps, been quite so pleasant but there we take the rough with the smooth and still the Brigade go merrily on with their work. As advertised in our last issue the Brigade gave their first public demonstration of the powers of their new Pyrene Pulso-meter Pump on Tuesday evening April 24th on Culverley Green, before a great number of ratepayers. Mr. W. Hiett, captain of the Brigade, was in charge, and the pump itself was in the capable hands of Fireman C. Gulliver.

Water was pumped from the stream, and the Brigade demonstrated with one, two, three and four jets at about 70lbs. pressure to the square inch, although the pump is capable of much more than this.

The demonstration was voted by one and all to be highly satisfactory, and the pump should be a great asset to Brockenhurst, especially to the outlying districts.

On Tuesday, May 1st. just a week later one of the outlying districts was visited viz: Whitley Ridge with a view to test the possibility of being able to cope with an outbreak, should one occur, at this country residence. The result proved very satisfactory and the Brigade were able to throw 3 strong jets over the house, this proved that the hose and equipment were quite adequate, though we had not much to spare after the long distance from the river to the house had been covered. Owing to the steep rise in the ground full pressure had to be used from the Pump, luckily our 3 new lengths of hose (just added by the Brigade themselves) were coupled directly on to the Pump, and consequently stood the 120 lbs. pressure admirably, but we shall certainly have to keep our hose in good condition in the future, and try to add 3 new lengths each year. The Brigade were most kindly entertained at the close of the drill by Mr. Fairhurst, who express great satisfaction and admiration at the way the Members carried out their duties, and the lads all voted that the good fare provided amply balanced the discomfort of handling wet hose and getting it all packed away dry and clean for the next fire, or drill.

At the same time political realism was apparently less positive.

New Forest and Christchurch Conservative and Unionist Association. (Brockenhurst Branch).

A short address on the European situation was delivered by Mr. G. R. B. Whitehead, vice-chairman of the New Forest Conservative and Unionist Association, at a meeting of the Brockenhurst branch, at the Railway Inn, on Tuesday, March 18th.

The speaker alluded to Germany's aspirations to regain her liberty and equality amongst other nations, and expressed the view that England had no cause for alarm over Germany's natural desire to regain her lost status and put right those things in the Peace Treaty which had proved to be unworkable.

Germany was faced by many problems, particularly on her eastern boundaries, and he hoped that her efforts to restore her self-respect would not be a disturbing element, but a contribution to the peace of Europe.

Mr. E. D. Townsend Rose presided, and a smoking concert, with an entertainment given by Mr. Reginald Fry and members of the Motley Follies, was much enjoyed.

The Railway Inn is now The Snake Catcher.

The death of King George V, who had inspected so many units before they went to France or another theatre of war, hit the country hard.

The Brockenhurst Bulletin.

A Monthly Magazine of News and Interesting Items. Printed and Published by John R. Stevens, Printer & Stationer. Brockenhurst. Joint Editors:—J. R. and E. L. Stevens. Copyright.

Vol. XII. No. 10. FEBRUARY 15th, 1936. Price, Threepence.

Editorial Notes.

The death of our beloved King George V. is still fresh enough in our minds to make this number of the Bulletin a memorial one.

Through the kindness of Mr. J. W. Martin who spent a whole Wednesday afternoon going through old negatives, we are enabled to present our readers with a picture which we believe is unique. We have seen one something like it but not one that shows Her Majesty Queen Mary whom you will observe just behind the King The tall gentleman at the side was the O.C. Col. Lloyd and we believe he is still living in the district. We have inserted this special memorium in the middle of the book so that if our readers would like, they may detach this quite easily. We have also obtained from a member of "the rank and file" his impressions of the Memorial Service held at the Parish Church on Tuesday, February 28th (the date of King George's funeral) which we are printing in this inset.

May we here record our great sorrow at the passing of a good King, our sincere sympathy with Her Majesty Queen Mary, and all the other members of our royal family and to express our loyalty to our new sovereign, His Majesty King Edward VIII. May his reign be a long, happy and prosperous one. He has already made for himself a warm corner in our hearts, and as the years go on may he endear himself to us all, as his wonderful father did.

While Kings and Courts are in our mind may we mention how honoured our Village is to have three of its residents occupying such high positions at the Court. Of course we refer to Lord Claude Hamilton, Col Mansel-Jones, v.c. and Col. Grace. Truly we are well represented.

When Tennis Time comes round again, a very familiar figure will be missing. We refer to Admiral Hill who passed away in December last. He was keenly interested in the New Forest Club. A very indefatigable worker, he will be greatly missed at the tournaments.

We should like to express our sympathy with the relatives of Mr. J. Young and Mrs. Welling, who have both passed over since our last issue.

As we go to press we hear of the sudden death of Mr. P. Sherard. May we extend our sympathy to his wife and family and pay a tribute to a man who was a good friend to us when we first came to Brockenhurst.

The "promise" of Edward VIII was not to be realised.

Home Defence. By 1937 the Air Raid Precautions organisation, which was to become so essential to Britain in the war, was being established by the Government. Interestingly the silver cap-badge, shown right, has a hallmark showing it was made in 1938/9.

Preparations for home defence in Brockenhurst were at a surprisingly aware stage, as the following report shows:

REPORT ON AIR RAID PRECAUTIONS.

<u>October 1937</u>

The response to the circular letter sent to all householder on the 2nd July was disappointing. While 18 ladies volunteered as nurses for the First Aid Post, only some 11 gentlemen offered their services as Air Raid Wardens, 2 as Stretcher Bearers and 1 for the Cycle Corps. There were no volunteers for either the Rescue & Demolition or Decontamination Squads. In consequence various employers of labour, including Capt Sutton and the Secretary of the Golf Club, were approached with a request to bring the matter to the notice of their employees. The Secretary of the R.A.O.Bs was also written to. There have been no additions to the above volunteers. Finally it was decided to solicit the assistance of the British Legion and at a Committee meeting held last night (14th Oct:) - after the members had been addressed by Capt Hay who is co-ordinating the training of all parish organizations in the N.F. - it was decided to call a public meeting at the Foresters Hall on 28th October. It is felt that until this meeting has been held and the result of it known nothing further can be done at present.

The following notes under each head will explain the position in more detail.

<u>AIR RAID WARDENS.</u> The village has been divided into 6 wards. It will be necessary to establish a post (with a telephone) as centrally as possible in each. A minimum of 3 Air Raid Wardens will be required for each ward - one to man the post, one to patrol and one in reserve. One Air Raid Warden for each of the 6 outposts is also required. An absolute minimum of 24 Air Raid Wardens is therefore necessary. But more than this number of volunteers is desirable to enable some selection to be made. All Air Raid Wardens will require anti-gas training. Capt Hay has undertaken to give this when the cadre is complete.

<u>RESCUE AND DEMOLITION SQUAD.</u> A squad of 8 - 12 men is required. Mr Thompson of Father's Field has undertaken to raise one. The men will require anti-gas training.

<u>DECONTAMINATION SQUAD.</u> A squad of 8 - 12 men is required. No volunteer. Anti-gas training will be necessary.

<u>STRETCHER BEARERS.</u> Major N.H.C.Russell has informed me that 3 stretcher and up to 12 men of the St John Ambulance will be available when required. The men will require anti-gas training.

FIRST AID POST. Capt Sutton has assented to this being established at the Morant Hall,i.e.,in the same building as the Casualty Clearing Station. Training is being undertaken by the British Red Cross Society,but all details of the organization have not yet been worked out. Nurses will require training in (i) First Aid and (ii) Anti-gas. Anti-gas lectures have already begun,but it is to be regretted that of the 18 ladies who volunteered only 5 have attended both the lecture already given. Seven have attended one lecture. It is thought that there cannot be too many volunteers as nurses as knowledge of First Aid and simple anti-gas treatment will be of value to everybody in an emergency and ladies with anti-gas training will be able to disseminate knowledge on such matters as how to make a room gas-proof,how to fit a respirator and simple anti-gas treatment to householders generally.

HEADQUARTERS. A room with a telephone (not in a private house) is required for an emergency and for use when testing the organization from time to time. I have considered all possibly suitable places, I think,and have come to the conclusion that a room in the Church Schools will be the most suitable. The sanction of the Council to have a telephone extension put in is solicited.

HOUSEHOLDERS GENERALLY. I consider that as soon as possible steps should be taken to ensure that every householder has the following knowledge :—

    (1)   How to make a room gas-proof.

    (ii)   How to fit a respirator.

    (iii)   Simple anti-gas treatment.

I should appreciate the advice of the Council as to how this problem can best be tackled. *Equipment. Gasmasks & suits of protective clothing have been indented for for instructional purposes.* The above report does not profess to be complete,but is submitted as a summary and basis for discussion.

Oct 28th Foresters Hall 7.30 p.m.

                         V.H.T.Fields-Clarke,

                         Hon: A.R.P.O.

                         15. 10. 37.

The Munich Crisis occurred in 1938 and a year later we were - once again - at war with Germany.

The Second
World War
1939 – 1945

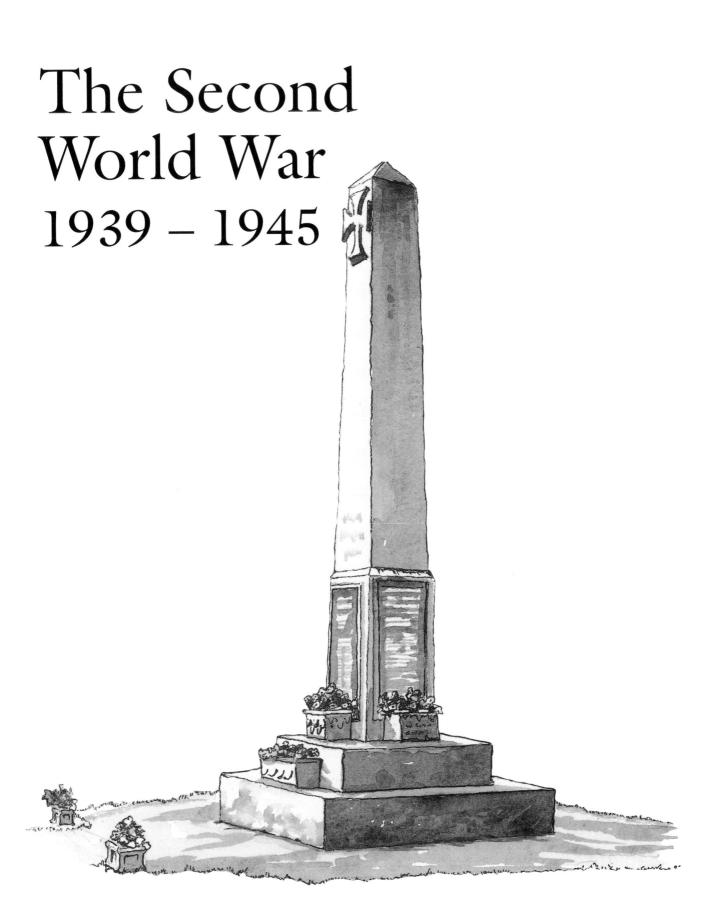

SOME THINGS YOU SHOULD KNOW IF WAR SHOULD COME

PUBLIC INFORMATION LEAFLET   NO. 1

Read   this   and keep   it   carefully. **You   may   need   it.**

Issued from the Lord Privy Seal's Office July, 1939

1939

THE HOME FRONT

War was declared on 3rd September 1939.

The Schools. On 1st September the Portsmouth South Secondary School for Boys arrived to be billeted in the village. This was done more according to the accommodation available than the capabilities or inclinations of some of the householders. Some elderly spinsters had to make adjustments for town lads billeted on them. This was resolved when Marlpool, on the Lymington Road, and The Briars Hotel, on the site of the flats at the bottom of Avenue Road, were taken over as hostels for the pupils. The County School had just vacated their old buildings in Highwood Road and these were taken over by the Portsmouth school after the first month - during which the Brockenhurst students were taught in the mornings in their new school, which was then used for the Portsmouth pupils in the afternoon.

Pupils returning to the Church of England School in September found a large number of new girls all dressed in uniform from the Hampshire Girls Orphanage, sharing their school. These children had been evacuated from Southampton to Marden House on the Rhinefield Road.

Evacuation. The government also had plans should the anticipated bombing of Britain require mass evacuation from the targeted cities:

FOOD SUPPLIES FOR EVACUATION

The Government evacuation scheme, of which you have already been told, will mean a considerable shift of population from the more vulnerable areas to safer areas. This will lead to additional demands on shops in the reception areas. Traders have been asked to have plans in readiness for increasing the supplies in shops in reception areas to meet the needs of the increased population. It would, however, take a day or two for these plans to be put into full operation.

The Government are, therefore, providing emergency supplies for children and others travelling under the official evacuation scheme. These supplies would be issued to them on their arrival in their new areas and would be sufficient for two days. Those who receive them will be asked not to make any purchases, other than small ones, in the local shops during those two days.

Those making their own arrangements to travel, should take food with them sufficient for two days, and should buy in advance, as part of their arrangements, the non-perishable food which they would require. As already said, anyone who, in time of emergency, buys more than normal quantities, would be doing harm, as such buying must draw on stocks which should be available for others.

Food. At the beginning of the war there was a large riding school attached to Captain Blackmoor's riding stables in Avenue House, Avenue Road. It extended over the area now occupied by Auckland Place and Gates new garage. This was taken over by Ranks Solent Flourmills who filled it with sacks of flour and grain. A room at the Church of England School was used for storing cases of canned goods and Purkess the grocers took over the Coach House at Black Knoll as a food store.

With wartime paper shortages labels on tins were reduced to a third size; sugar, dried fruits and many other lines had to be put in paper bags. Biscuits were sold loose and vinegar was dispensed from barrels into bottles.

The "Blackout". Restrictions on lighting at night, which would have aided enemy bomber navigation, caused a few problems in the village for those walking around without a torch. Forest ponies were one such hazard, as they could not be relied upon to always sense the approach of humans and take the necessary avoiding action. Road traffic, with shaded lights, inevitably hit a few.

John Jolly recalls the story of the South Weirs resident who, having fully enjoyed an evening's drinking, was escorted home and deposited in the darkness in the wrong house by an equally drunken mate.

THE WAR

THE ARMY

A number of villagers, like *Harold Cleveland, Leslie Dukes* and *Reg Meaden* were immediately mobilised and joined their Territorial units.

The British Expeditionary Force (BEF) proceeded as planned to Northern France and by 11th October had landed 160,000 men. The French armies occupied the Maginot Line and the BEF's task was to move into Belgium, when required, to stop the predicted German outflanking movement to the north.

There was little enemy activity at this time so the BEF trained and planned against the expected enemy invasion. At home it enabled the Services to be expanded and the economy and the civilian population to be organised onto a war footing.

THE AIR WAR

When war was declared the RAF was partway through an urgent programme of "catching up" with the air forces of the Axis powers in both quantity and quality of aircraft. For some 15 years after the First World War development had been slow. Germany was forbidden by treaty from establishing an air force and RAF duties in colonial policing as in Iraq, on the Northwest Frontier of India, did not call for much development. First World War aircraft, such as the Bristol Fighter, were still in service in the early 1930's.

The Air Ministry had a policy of not acquiring monoplanes, as these were considered unnecessarily hazardous. It took Germany's occupation of the Rhineland and other territories and - even more alarmingly - the performance of their aircraft in the Spanish Civil War in 1936 to expose the dangers of our obsolete equipment. In 1935 the RAF began to place large orders for new aircraft, at first for existing types and then for later developments as they became available. Even so, Hurricanes did not reach squadron service until 1937 and Spitfires a year later - the year Chamberlain met Hitler at Munich.

In a similar way our bomber force was transformed by the arrival of the Blenheim in 1937. It was the result of a private venture and had been ordered "off the drawing board". It proved to be faster than our fighters. The Wellington and Hampton followed into service in 1938.

At the outbreak of war the RAF Advanced Air Striking Force (AASF) was sent to France to support the BEF and Blenheims and Wellingtons (one piloted by *Ken Smith*) attacked German naval units in their bases on the North Sea coast.

RAF bomber operations over Germany were then confined to leaflet dropping, which at least provided valuable experience of night navigation over Europe. However the RAF was directed not to attack land targets, as the government was anxious not to provoke the bombing of our own cities. A similar restriction appears to have been placed on Luftwaffe operations. This "Phoney War" lasted until Germany attacked the Low Countries in May 1940.

THE WAR AT SEA

Unlike confrontation with the enemy on land or in the air, the Navy experienced no "phoney" phase of the war before battle was joined.

On the very day that war was declared, 3 September 1939, the liner ATHENIA was torpedoed and sunk with the loss of some 200 lives. By the end of the first month, U-boats had sunk 32 merchant ships as well as the aircraft carrier COURAGEOUS. The new German magnetic mine was also causing the loss of ships in coastal waters, both naval and merchant marine.

Before the end of the year, the Royal Navy suffered two further losses, the armed merchant cruiser RAWALPINDI - sunk by the German battle cruisers SCHARNHORST and GNEISENAU - and the battleship ROYAL OAK, torpedoed by a U-boat in Scapa Flow. The second of these two disasters sadly caused the first war casualty for the village. *Able Seaman Ronald Chalk* was among the 600 men lost.

However, in some measure to redress the balance, a number of U-boats were sunk and the year ended with the British success at the Battle of the River Plate.

RONALD GEORGE CHALK

Ordinary Seaman, Royal Navy

HMS ROYAL OAK

Who died on

Saturday 14th October 1939, Aged 18.

Ronald Chalk was the only son of Ralph and Violet who ran the friendly greengrocer's shop in Brookley Road.

The family had lived for many years in Brockenhurst. Ron's Uncle Frank ran the fishmonger's business which was later taken over by his own son Reg.

Ralph Chalk had also at one time been a mechanic at Cooper's Garage in New Milton.

Both Ronald's father and his uncle, Mr Frank Chalk served throughout the First World War. His father was in Mechanical Transport, whilst Frank initially served with the Hampshire Regiment and, later, in the Black Watch.

Ron went to the village school and joined the Navy as a boy seaman in 1937.

RONALD AND HIS COUSIN REG CHALK

After passing out from the training school ST VINCENT at Gosport he joined IRON DUKE, the old battleship that had been Admiral Jellicoe's flagship at Jutland, as a signalman.

HMS ROYAL OAK

He was transferred to the ROYAL OAK when she was re-commissioned in July 1938. This was one of the 5 Royal Sovereign class dreadnoughts and had been built in Devonport in 1914. She was completed in December 1915 and armed with 10 x 15 inch guns and had a displacement of 25,750 tons.

On 14th October 1939 U47 commanded by Lieutenant Commander Günther Prien attacked ROYAL OAK in the naval base at Scapa Flow. He fired three torpedoes, one of which hit ROYAL OAK in the bows. As the ship was moored behind anti-submarine defences it was initially thought to be an internal explosion. Six minutes later, however, Prien fired three more torpedoes, all of which hit his target. All lights went out and the ship rapidly listed to starboard and sank.

Of the 950 men in the ship's crew 833 were lost - one of whom was Ronald Chalk.

He was the first casualty of the war from Brockenhurst.

His name is commemorated on the **Portsmouth Naval Memorial**:

Column 3, Panel 34.

1940

1940 was dominated by the evacuation of our forces from Dunkirk.

At 3.0 a.m. on 10th May German land and air forces launched an attack on Holland, Belgium and Luxembourg, simultaneously carrying out extensive bombing raids on French airfields and towns. Only then did Belgium allow British and French forces to rapidly deploy forward to their planned positions on the river Dyle. After fierce fighting, however, the allies found themselves retreating in the face of the German Blitzkreig of coordinated tank and air attack. The "miracle" of Dunkirk was the saving of 337,000 men from the beaches. It was at the cost, however, of losing all their heavy equipment of tanks, guns, lorries etc. and of leaving mainland Europe in the hands of the Germans.

William Dickinson lost his life in the chaos of the retreat to Dunkirk.

The local paper reported that two of the soldiers taken off the beaches were Brockenhurst men:

> **Gunner Charlie Purse**, of the Royal Artillery, Brockenhurst.

> **Lance-Cpl Eric Charles Rhodes**, 1st Bn. Royal Welch Fusiliers, son of Mrs. Rhodes of St Andrews, Rhinefield Road, wounded.

At least one other villager was taken off the beaches.

Sergeant Dennis Sherard. Dennis Sherard joined the Royal Signals in 1933 and served in India and Palestine before the war.

He was evacuated from Dunkirk to Dover. En route to his depot the troop train passed through Brockenhurst. John Jolly remembers hearing that it paused there briefly - but long enough for Dennis to pass a note to a porter, which was then delivered to his mother at Addison Road, saying

"Safe and well."

After the war he worked in America, married a Canadian girl and in the mid 1950's emigrated to live in Canada.

THE HOME FRONT

In late May, David Jackson-Smith went to the County High School one morning only to find that it was filled with French Poilus who had been evacuated from Dunkirk. Whilst they left fairly quickly, the damage they did with their boots to the parquet flooring lasted long after their departure!

During the year an Air Training Corps was established at the School with Mr Gallimore, a French master, in command. Mr Halliday and Mr Cockrill commanded the Army Cadet Force.

Forces Canteen. The original premises of the village store, next to the Morant Hall, was furnished to be used as a Forces Canteen. It was run by local volunteers.

Bombed-out families from Southampton began to arrive by train and were accommodated in the Morant Hall and in the Methodist Church schoolroom.

Lumberjacks came from Newfoundland to work in the forest. They built themselves a log-cabin camp in an area near the Victorian Tilery off the Balmer Lawn Road. It is remembered that in the beginning they occasionally had the habit of felling trees 5 feet off the ground, making a forest look like a battleground!

All enclosures were leased to the Ministry of Supply for the extraction of timber. Trees were sawn into planks and pit props were made from the tail ends.

The nearest sawmills were at Park Hill - near the tile yard - Frane Heath, Wootton Bridge and Holmsley. These sawmills provided employment for local tractor drivers hauling timber. In 1941 a new sawmill was built at Denny Lodge with band saws to cut the larger trees.

"Lumberjills" ran small offices on all these sites. They also had to go into the woods to measure the length and girth of all felled timber. Each tree was numbered and the Home Grown Timber Production Department (HGTPD) records annotated with its cubic footage.

UNKNOWN CANADIAN LUMBERJACK

After the war the camp was taken over by the Hampshire Association of Youth Clubs for weekend and summer camps. The camp was later destroyed by fire.

The Church Bells ceased to ring, as the nationwide ringing of bells was to be the signal of a German invasion.

Registration for Military Service was also quickened and men aged from 25-29 reported between 6th April and 22nd June. This produced 1,250,000 potential recruits for the three services. National Service was also introduced for all British subjects between the ages of 19 and 36 years of age.

Enemy Bombing. The first bombs were dropped on the village at about 3.00 a.m. on Wednesday 13th August. At that time Gates Garage was only the old building and the new showrooms and workshops was a field. As the stick of bombs fell, one fell:

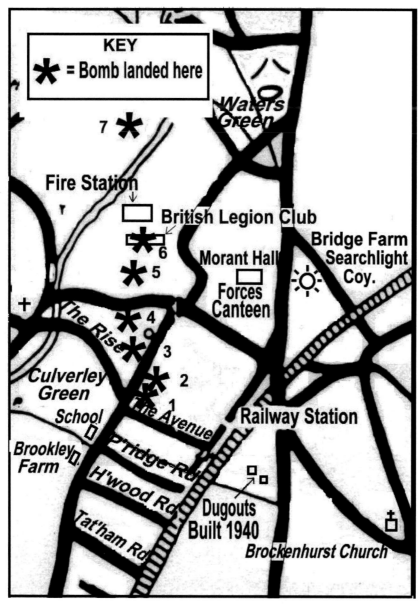

1. Next to their building and made a hole in the roof

2. On the other side of the field

3. Slid under the conservatory of Wide Lane Cottage (now Cottage hotel)

4. Took the front off Purkess bakery shop (where the Jack Hull memorial is)

5. At the bottom of Cairo Cottage garden (undertakers garage)

6. On the British Legion club.

7. In Careys Cottages.

WHERE THE BOMBS FELL

The Daily Express reported the bombing of Purkess's shop and the British Legion Club.

Next day it said that a South Coast baker had put up a sign saying

"DONT LET **HITLER**
SPOIL YOUR APPETITE
BREAD & CAKES
AS USUAL"

Necklace

THE steward at a British Legion club in the south-east of England was asleep when a bomb fell through the roof. He found himself sprawled on the wreckage of the bed. A pair of antlers hanging on the wall had fallen round his neck. Otherwise he was unhurt.

John Purkess remembers that the steward was sleeping on the premises as relatives who had been bombed out occupied his house.

His escape from the club had been so hasty that his steak pie and milk pudding were still to be seen on the side of the bar the following morning!

165

Brockenhurst Fire Brigade. In 1939 the village-manned fire station had been reclassified as an Auxiliary Fire Service (A.F.S.) station. This released full-time fireman for service at first line units e.g. Lyndhurst, which responded immediately to air raid and other emergencies.

VILLAGE CREW WITH THE BERESFORD-STARK "LIGHT" TRAILER PUMP ISSUED IN JANUARY 1940

Back Row Dick Jenvey, Rowland Hewitt, Stan Jenvey, David Baker, XXX
                              Ron Burnett.
Front Row Phil Waterman, Bill Dunkinson, Arthur Stevens, Ken Martin,
                      Reg Street, Jack Dunkinson (Senior), Walter Holland, Fred Field.

The reorganisation of the Brigade and the removal of some of its equipment were criticised at the April meeting of the Parish Council. It was also noted that the village would have to wait for Lyndhurst to respond to ordinary local fires. The local crew responded to the many incendiary attacks on the area with great effectiveness, however, and the fears of the Council do not appear to have been realised.

A.F.S. units were placed on alert at night and attended many calls.

The Brockenhurst tender and A.F.S. crew were usually sent on standby to Lyndhurst before being allocated to incidents. Thus on the 20th June they were sent to Dibden and fought fires whilst under bombing in what was the first serious raid of the war. This was repeated on the 30th November, when they went to Boldre and again on 1st December when they went to Hythe. On this latter callout they came back without the pump as a later bomb cratered the access road making it temporarily impassable.

The Fire Service was not the only organisation fighting fires as it really was "all hands to the pump" as the following letter shows:

The Rural District Council of New Forest.

W. A. TURNER, Grad. I.F.E., L.A.G.C.,
Principal Fire Officer,

Council Offices,
Lyndhurst, Hants.

WAT/DP/AFS   26th September, 1940.

Dear Sir,

    I should like to take this opportunity to place on record my gratitude and admiration for the way in which the members of the Stirrup Pump Parties in Brockenhurst tackled the Incendiary Bombs during the air raid last night.   Through their efforts, what may have been several serious fires were quickly extinguished with little or no damage.

    I should consider it a favour if you would kindly convey my appreciation to the personnel concerned.

Yours faithfully,

W. A. Turner

Principal Fire Officer.

R.E. Tiller, Esq.,
Clerk to the Brockenhurst Parish Council,
"Waynflete,"
Southampton Road,
LYMINGTON, Hants.

Emergency Powers.   The new government, under Churchill, provided itself with exceptional authority under the Emergency Powers Act which gave it control over all persons and property in the country.

Requisitioning.   In the village the following buildings were requisitioned:

Balmer Lawn Hotel   Carey's Manor   Whitley Ridge
Lawnside (in Meerut Road)
Orchard House (in Wilverley Road).
Nethermoor (in Rhinefield Road) - used as a Red Cross medical station.

Rationing was introduced with food ration books being issued to everybody in January 1940. Customers had to register with a preferred supplier in order to obtain regular supplies of the rationed goods. Shops received supplies based on the number of such registrations.

Coupons were exchanged for sugar, butter, margarine, cheese, bacon, preserves, tea and meat.

Some foods, like cheese were on such small rations that they were sold on alternate weeks so the portion was larger. Other foods were accumulated until there was sufficient stock for each registered family. This resulted in "Pickle and Sauce" or "Biscuit" weeks when such commodities could be bought.

It could be many weeks before such foods could be purchased again.

Romance. Bert Wallis met and married Olive Marsh when he came to Brockenhurst as a member of a searchlight team located at Bridge farm (see page 164). Their wedding cake was the last one produced by Purkess Bakery before the imposition of food rationing.

Anti-Invasion measures included not only removing sign posts, but also changing the colour of the Ten Shilling and One Pound notes to frustrate and detect enemy agents using old currency.

A post for the Royal Observer Corps was completed at Marlpit Oak. It was situated just off the track that runs from the Marlpit Oak - Wilverley Road down to the site of No. 10 Gates on the railway line.

THE WAR

THE WAR AT SEA

There were many naval encounters in the course of the ill-fated Norwegian campaign in the spring of 1940, including the two battles of Narvik.

May saw the Royal Navy conducting the evacuation from Dunkirk. In doing so it lost nine destroyers sunk and numerous small craft manned by volunteers and RNVR officers. In the Mediterranean there were the first skirmishes with the Italian Fleet, which in turn suffered attack from the Fleet Air Arm at Taranto. In the broad Atlantic, our convoys came under increasing attack by both U-boats and surface raiders and sustained heavy losses.

THE AIR WAR

Following the German invasion of Holland and Belgium, the main tasks of the RAF Advanced Air Striking Force was to delay the German advance and cover the withdrawal of the allied armies. As in Norway, a month earlier, much of our equipment was shown to be obsolete. Most of the RAF bomber squadrons were equipped with Fairey Battles. When, on 12th May, five of these attacked and hit a vital bridge over the Albert Canal, all five were lost. The leading crew were awarded posthumous VCs. Late on 14th May all remaining 71 Battles and Blenheims were used to attack enemy forces massing at Sedan; only 31 aircraft returned.

Four additional squadrons of Hurricanes were sent to France, but further reinforcements were refused in order to conserve UK reserves. By the end of May most operations over NE France were from bases in Kent.

For a month after the fall of France, German forces were reforming and preparing for the invasion of England. Then in early August Luftwaffe attacks started. This developed into the Battle of Britain with enemy attacks initially concentrating on shipping in the channel but quickly changing to attacks on airfields in SE England. Losses were heavy on both sides and there was considerable damage on the airfields. RAF reserves of aircraft were being seriously depleted. In September the Luftwaffe inexplicably switched to targets in London, thus relieving the pressure on airfields but increasing the losses on both sides. For the first half of the month the RAF was losing the equivalent of one squadron a day. By the end of October it became clear that the German plans for invasion had been postponed, if not abandoned. The Luftwaffe's attacks changed to the night bombing of cities. The Blitz had started.

THE ARMY

After Dunkirk the army prepared to resist the expected invasion. The troops saved from Dunkirk were quickly reorganised but were poorly equipped - and remained so for some time. Coastal fortifications were rapidly created and the second line of defence, mainly pillboxes and dugouts, was manned by the newly created **Local Defence Volunteers**.

BROCKENHURST HOME GUARD.

The Local Defence Volunteers (LDV) were formed in May 1940.

The evacuation of the British Expeditionary Force from Dunkirk and the subsequent fall of France made the threat of a German invasion of England very real. In the First World War seven well-equipped Regular Divisions had been retained in Britain to meet a similar danger. In 1940 the threat was not only very imminent but the Germans possessed an airborne option which increased the scope and depth of any invasion.

The LDV was therefore tasked to work with both the military and the emergency services to counter enemy activity in the immediate locality. Though poorly armed their initial recruitment was largely of First War veterans who had experienced war, had discipline, knew the local area and were well motivated to defend their homes and villages. A local pony patrol was even suggested as being appropriate for area defence.

CAPTAIN BLACKMORE AND HIS SUCCESSFUL HOME GUARD SHOOTING TEAM

Back row (Centre)	**SGT EEDE**
Middle Row (Centre)	**H. ANSTY**
Front Row (Second from left)	**TED BLATCHFORD** (See *William Janes* Page 39)

Two months later the LDV became **The Home Guard**. Brockenhurst provided two platoons, one being commanded by Lieutenant-Colonel Hotham, the father of **John Hotham** (see page 204). The other made up of railway employees under the command of the Station Master, Reg Prosser. The local Quartermaster was CQMS Frank Perkins, who had lost a leg in World War 1. His well-pressed uniform trouser leg was neatly pinned-up except for special parades, when it properly enclosed his artificial leg.

Initially they were tasked with watching the coastline at Lymington and guarding vulnerable points, railways, bridges, etc. in the village. As an anti-invasion measure, two dugouts were built in Blackbridge field, overlooking the Lymington Road. The outline of one can still be seen by the path. The remains of a concrete gun platform has also been sighted in the area.

JEFFREY CREMER (see page 218)

Whilst intended to attract men up to 51, many "old soldiers" enlisted by being economical about their age. The improvisation of the first few months began to disappear as better weapons and equipment became available and effective training given by instructors from the Army and the Royal Marines.

In October 1942 the local sector was organised into three battalions - the 28th (Bay), commanded by Lieutenant Colonel Sir Morgan Crofton, Bt. DSO, who lived in the village, 9th (New Forest) and 8th (Avon Valley).

The training of the Home Guard became more integrated with Allied forces and its role began to embrace the preparation of 17-year-olds for military service. *Jeffrey Cremer,* (pictured), *Ronald Mutter* and many other village lads joined and learnt their drill, weapons training, and how to get on with other people, as well as a positive attitude and a military sense of humour from service in the local Home Guard units.

By the time the Home Guard stood down in December 1944, the 28th Battalion was not only fully manned but it had also discharged 220 men, posted 350 either to other units or for service in the mines, and 245 had joined the Regular Services.

Issued by the Ministry of Information *in co-operation with the War Office and the Ministry of Home Security.*

If the
INVADER
comes

WHAT TO DO — AND HOW TO DO IT

THE Germans threaten to invade Great Britain. If they do so they will be driven out by our Navy, our Army and our Air Force. Yet the ordinary men and women of the civilian population will also have their part to play. Hitler's invasions of Poland, Holland and Belgium were greatly helped by the fact that the civilian population was taken by surprise. They did not know what to do when the moment came. *You must not be taken by surprise.* This leaflet tells you what general line you should take. More detailed instructions will be given you when the danger comes nearer. Meanwhile, read these instructions carefully and be prepared to carry them out.

I

When Holland and Belgium were invaded, the civilian population fled from their homes. They crowded on the roads, in cars, in carts, on bicycles and on foot, and so helped the enemy by preventing their own armies from advancing against the invaders. You must not allow that to happen here. Your first rule, therefore, is :—

(1) IF THE GERMANS COME, BY PARACHUTE, AEROPLANE OR SHIP, YOU MUST REMAIN WHERE YOU ARE. THE ORDER IS " STAY PUT ".

If the Commander in Chief decides that the place where you live must be evacuated, he will tell you when and how to leave. Until you receive such orders you must remain where you are. If you run away, you will be exposed to far greater danger because you will be machine-gunned from the air as were civilians in Holland and Belgium, and you will also block the roads by which our own armies will advance to turn the Germans out.

II

There is another method which the Germans adopt in their invasion. They make use of the civilian population in order to create confusion and panic. They spread false rumours and issue false instructions. In order to prevent this, you should obey the second rule, which is as follows :—

(2) DO NOT BELIEVE RUMOURS AND DO NOT SPREAD THEM. WHEN YOU RECEIVE AN ORDER, MAKE QUITE SURE THAT IT IS A TRUE ORDER AND NOT A FAKED ORDER. MOST OF YOU KNOW YOUR POLICEMEN AND YOUR A.R.P. WARDENS BY SIGHT, YOU CAN TRUST THEM. IF YOU KEEP YOUR HEADS, YOU CAN ALSO TELL WHETHER A MILITARY OFFICER IS REALLY BRITISH OR ONLY PRETENDING TO BE SO. IF IN DOUBT ASK THE POLICEMAN OR THE A.R.P. WARDEN. USE YOUR COMMON SENSE.

III

The Army, the Air Force and the Local Defence Volunteers cannot be everywhere at once. The ordinary man and woman must be on the watch. If you see anything suspicious, do not rush round telling your neighbours all about it. Go at once to the nearest policeman, police-station, or military officer and tell them exactly what you saw. Train yourself to notice the exact time and place where you saw anything suspicious, and try to give exact information. Try to check your facts. The sort of report which a military or police officer wants from you is something like this :—

> " At 5.30 p.m. to-night I saw twenty cyclists come into Little Squashborough from the direction of Great Mudtown. They carried some sort of automatic rifle or gun. I did not see anything like artillery. They were in grey uniforms."

Be calm, quick and exact. The third rule, therefore, is as follows :—

(3) KEEP WATCH. IF YOU SEE ANYTHING SUSPICIOUS, NOTE IT CAREFULLY AND GO AT ONCE TO THE NEAREST POLICE OFFICER OR STATION, OR TO THE NEAREST MILITARY OFFICER. DO NOT RUSH ABOUT SPREADING VAGUE RUMOURS. GO QUICKLY TO THE NEAREST AUTHORITY AND GIVE HIM THE FACTS.

IV

Remember that if parachutists come down near your home, they will not be feeling at all brave. They will not know where they are, they will have no food, they will not know where their companions are. They will want you to give them food, means of transport and maps. They will want you to tell them where they have landed, where their comrades are, and where our own soldiers are. The fourth rule, therefore, is as follows :—

(4) DO NOT GIVE ANY GERMAN ANYTHING. DO NOT TELL HIM ANYTHING. HIDE YOUR FOOD AND YOUR BICYCLES. HIDE YOUR MAPS. SEE THAT THE ENEMY GETS NO PETROL. IF YOU HAVE A CAR OR MOTOR BICYCLE, PUT IT OUT OF ACTION WHEN NOT IN USE. IT IS NOT ENOUGH TO REMOVE THE IGNITION KEY; YOU MUST MAKE IT USELESS TO ANYONE EXCEPT YOURSELF.

IF YOU ARE A GARAGE PROPRIETOR, YOU MUST WORK OUT A PLAN TO PROTECT YOUR STOCK OF PETROL AND YOUR CUSTOMERS' CARS. REMEMBER THAT TRANSPORT AND PETROL WILL BE THE INVADER'S MAIN DIFFICULTIES. MAKE SURE THAT NO INVADER WILL BE ABLE TO GET HOLD OF YOUR CARS, PETROL, MAPS OR BICYCLES.

V

You may be asked by Army and Air Force officers to help in many ways. For instance, the time may come when you will receive orders to block roads or streets in order to prevent the enemy from advancing. Never block a road unless you are told which one you must block. Then you can help by felling trees, wiring them together or blocking the roads with cars. Here, therefore, is the fifth rule :—

(5) BE READY TO HELP THE MILITARY IN ANY WAY. BUT DO NOT BLOCK ROADS UNTIL ORDERED TO DO SO BY THE MILITARY OR L.D.V. AUTHORITIES.

VI

If you are in charge of a factory, store or other works, organise its defence at once. If you are a worker, make sure that you understand the system of defence that has been organised and know what part you have to play in it. Remember always that parachutists and fifth column men are powerless against any organised resistance. They can only succeed if they can create disorganisation. Make certain that no suspicious strangers enter your premises.

You must know in advance who is to take command, who is to be second in command, and how orders are to be transmitted. This chain of command must be built up and you will probably find that ex-officers or N.C.O.'s, who have been in emergencies before, are the best people to undertake such command. The sixth rule is therefore as follows :—

(6) IN FACTORIES AND SHOPS, ALL MANAGERS AND WORKMEN SHOULD ORGANISE SOME SYSTEM NOW BY WHICH A SUDDEN ATTACK CAN BE RESISTED.

VII

The six rules which you have now read give you a general idea of what to do in the event of invasion. More detailed instructions may, when the time comes, be given you by the Military and Police Authorities and by the Local Defence Volunteers ; they will NOT be given over the wireless as that might convey information to the enemy. These instructions must be obeyed at once.

Remember always that the best defence of Great Britain is the courage of her men and women. Here is your seventh rule :—

(7) THINK BEFORE YOU ACT. BUT THINK ALWAYS OF YOUR COUNTRY BEFORE YOU THINK OF YOURSELF.

(52194) Wt. / 14,300,000 6/40 Hw.

WILLIAM ARTHUR KIRWAN DICKINSON

Major, 39319

Royal Tank Regiment, Royal Armoured Corps,
Attached
2 Ordnance Field Park, Royal Army Ordnance Corps.

Who died on

Wednesday 29th May 1940, Aged 31.

William was born on 23rd May 1908, one of the three sons of Arthur and Eileen Dickinson who lived in Orchard Cottage, Brockenhurst. Dot Street recalls that Pat, (Patric Thomas) the youngest son, wrote poetry which she remembers him reading on the radio. He later became a well-known poet, playwright and freelance broadcaster.

The Dickinsons were a Service family. His grandfather was Commander Thomas Dickinson, Royal Navy. His father, Major Arthur Dickinson was commissioned into the 51st Sikhs (Frontier Force) of the Indian Army and was killed in Mesopotamia on 22nd November 1915. His name is recorded on the Basra Memorial in Iraq.

It was natural, therefore, for William to become a regular soldier. Dr Peter Thwaites, a Sandhurst lecturer, has researched this early phase of William's career. He joined No 1 Company at the Royal Military College Sandhurst as an Officer Cadet on 3rd September 1926 and passed out 52nd out of 157 cadets on 20th December 1927.

He was then gazetted as a Second Lieutenant in the Royal Tank Regiment on 3rd February 1928.

At some stage William married. His wife, Margaret, later lived at Liss in Hampshire.

He was with the BEF in France. In the confusion of the retreat to Dunkirk William was killed and his body was never found.

His name is therefore recorded on the **Dunkirk Memorial**, Nord, France, on:

Column 4.

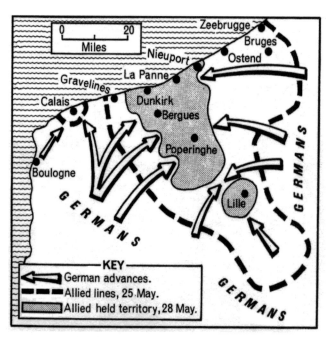

THE DUNKIRK BRIDGEHEAD

174

1941

THE HOME FRONT

The building of Holmsley, Beaulieu and Stoney Cross airfields brought a lot of activity to the village. Setley pond was dug by Wimpy to extract the gravel that was used to help make the runways at Stoney Cross airfield.

The Prisoner-of-War camp at Setley was initially built to house Italians captured in Africa. They were employed in the forest and each morning and evening were seen in lorries going to and from work with just one soldier with a rifle sitting amongst them. There were no attempted escapes.

Later in the war the camp housed German prisoners, some of whom - like Max Mueller who became the manager of Holtoms the butchers - later married local girls and settled in the area.

The Battle for Fuel was taken very seriously.

Fuel Communique No 8 makes curious reading now, but at the time was very positively received by the populace.

Saving for Victory was a continual occupation.

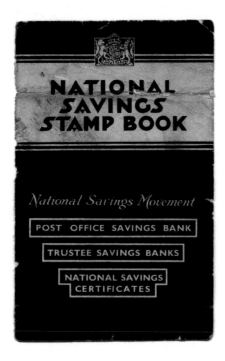 

Weekly National Savings were a Monday morning ritual in schools, but it took a lot of 6d stamps to get a 15/- certificate!

There were special weeks for "war weapons" "warships" and the like, which always led to an increase in in the social activity of the village.

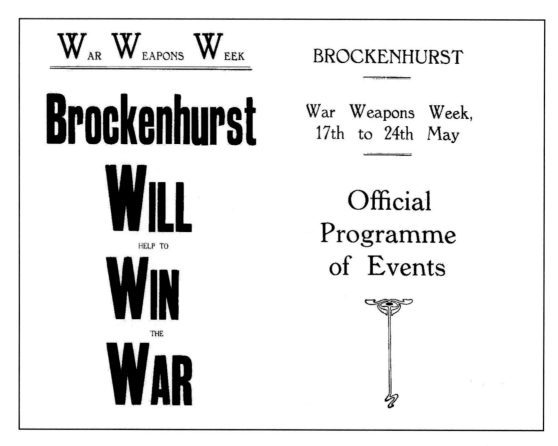

This normally started with a parade on Saturday, a service on Sunday, Films in the Morant Hall on Monday and dances and a variety show during the week. The Armed Forces usually had a display of some sort as can be seen in this programme from May 1941.

WAR WEAPONS WEEK.   BROCKENHURST.
MAY 17TH—24TH, 1941.

OFFICIAL PROGRAMME OF EVENTS.

17th, Saturday.	11 a.m.	**Opening Ceremony** at **Morant Hall.** Speakers—Colonel J. D. Mills, M.P., Colonel V. W. Roche. Followed by a **Military Display** in the Car Park and a **PROCESSION** through the village.
	2.30 p.m.	**Cricket Match**—Brockenhurst v. Army.
	7.30 p.m.	**Grand Dance, Morant Hall**—Moderniques Band. Prizes 4 War Saving Certificates. Entrance 2/6.
18th, Sunday.	11 a.m.	**United Service at the Parish Church.**
19th, Monday.	8 p.m.	**Special Boxing Exhibition** at **Morant Hall.** Tickets 3/-, 2/-, 1/-. (*by permission of A.B.A.*)
20th, Tuesday	6 to 9 p.m.	**Table Tennis** (Knock-out) **Competition** at the **New Forest Club.** Entries 6d. to be made before 6 p.m. at the Estate Offices or at the Club.
21st, Wednesday.	2.30 p.m.	**Whist Drive** at **New Forest Club.** Entrance 1/-
	8.0 p.m.	**GRAND CONCERT & CABARET.** at **Morant Hall.** Stage Band, Community Singing, Songs, Tap Dancing, Pipers, Comic Sketch, etc. Entrance 3/-, 2/- 1/-. *The War Weapons Week Draw will be made during the evening.*
22nd, Thursday.		All day **Golf Competition** (Open) at **Brokenhurst Manor Golf Club—PUTTING IN GAS MASKS.** Entrance 6d. Prizes—War Savings Stamps, etc.
	7.30 p.m.	**Whist Drive** at **Morant Hall.** Entrance-1/3d. Prizes
23rd, Friday.	6.15 & 8.15 p.m.	**Cinema** at **Morant Hall**—"Oh Mr. Porter" (Will Hay), Mickey Mouse, etc. 6.15 p.m.—Entrance 1/-, children 6d. 8.15 p.m.—Entrance 2/-, 1/-, 6d.
24th, Saturday.	2-5 p.m.	**Children's Sports** at **County High School.** An array of Sideshows. Entrance—Adults 3d., Pupils 1d.
	8 p.m.	**Special Dance** at **Morant Hall**—Moderniques Band. Entrance 2/6. Prizes—4 War Savings Certificates.

During the whole week there will be an Open Golf Competition at Brokenhurst Manor Golf Club. Entrance 1/- a Card.

All profits on Entertainments during the Week will be invested in Government Securities for the Brockenhurst Nursing   Association.

Salvage. The collection of paper and metal for salvage was also encouraged to help the war effort. The iron rails around the War Memorial may well have contributed to the manufacture of tanks or ships.

THE WAR

Eight villagers died in the three Services during 1941.

THE WAR AT SEA

1941 saw the deaths of no less than five Brockenhurst men serving with the Royal Navy.

Two of these, **Commander Walter Marshall-A'Deane** and **Able Seaman Jack Dunkinson,** were lost in the Battle for Crete that followed the evacuation of our forces from Greece in April of that year. Although the German intention to attack the island was known through our ability to read their coded messages, we were unable to prevent an airborne landing and the enemy enjoyed complete air superiority throughout the area.

German seaborne landings, however, were largely frustrated by the Royal Navy, although in so doing, many ships were lost including, on 22 May, the destroyer GREYHOUND and the cruiser GLOUCESTER in which these two villagers, respectively, were serving. Five days later, the Government ordered the evacuation of Crete.

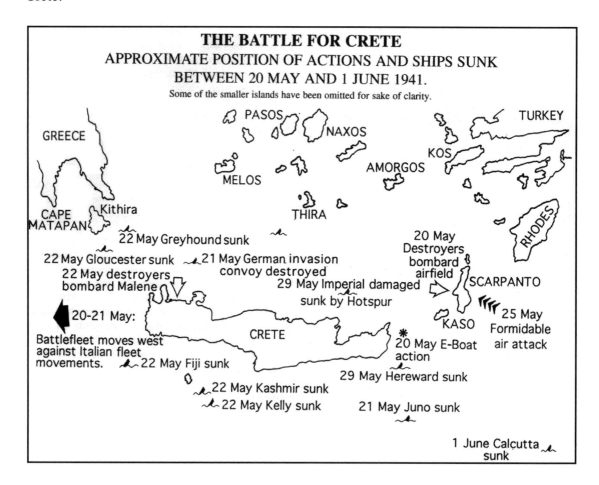

The first of our two submariners was lost in July, when **Lieutenant Peter Banister** failed to survive the sinking of the newly commissioned submarine UMPIRE, of which he was the First Lieutenant. UMPIRE was unhappily sunk on her maiden voyage in collision with an escort vessel when in convoy off the East Coast of England.

Two further village casualties occurred in December, in widely separated areas. First there was the loss of **Lieutenant George Ferguson** in the battleship PRINCE OF WALES, off the coast of Malaya. PRINCE OF WALES, in company with REPULSE, had been sent to the Far East to help counter the Japanese threat of invasion, but, operating without air cover, both ships were sunk by four squadrons of Japanese torpedo-carrying aircraft. The loss of these two ships was one of the heaviest blows of the war.

Then, only twelve days later, came the loss of **Lieutenant Anthony Moore**, who was drowned when the merchant aircraft carrier AUDACITY was sunk in the Atlantic whilst escorting a homeward bound convoy from Gibraltar. The defence of this convoy proved to be one of the epic battles of the anti-U boat war, confirming beyond doubt the value of integral air cover in support of well-trained escort groups.

But the long drawn out Battle of the Atlantic continued to be waged with desperate determination on both sides. It was not until the spring of 1943 that, with the increasing effectiveness of air cover, the introduction of improved weaponry and developments in radar, the Navy started to gain the upper hand.

THE AIR WAR

A new generation of RAF heavy four-engined bombers began to reach squadrons in late 1940, starting with Stirlings and followed by Halifaxes and Lancasters. They had far greater range and load capacity than preceding types and were equipped with power-operated gun turrets for defence.

Early targets in 1941 were on the North coast of France concentrating on naval installations and airfields. An attack on the latter cost the life of **Frederick Holden**, who was the first RAF casualty for the village. Gradually, however, the force was directed onto industrial targets in Germany. In April the raids were extended to Berlin.

Associated with these developments was the need for a huge expansion of the training programme. Although the RAF had built many new airfields in the 1930's, increasing their number from 52 to 138, their use to meet the training needs reduced operational capacity as well as rendering them vulnerable to air attack. The Empire Air Training Scheme was therefore set up, providing many flying schools in Canada and South Africa for all categories of aircrew.

John Short died in South Africa whilst undergoing pilot training.

THE ARMY

Whilst most of the army was retained in England to repel the expected German invasion a number of divisions were in the Mediterranean operating against the Italians. 1941 began with General O'Connor's continued success in North Africa with Indian, British and Australian forces against Graziani's Libyan and Italian troops. The capture of Bardia and Tobruk by the British in February led to German troops arriving in North Africa later that month.

The Italian attack on Greece in October 1940 had led to some RAF squadrons being sent there. This was sufficient until the German invasion of Greece on 6th April 1941. Despite Australians and New Zealander reinforcements from North Africa, Greece could not be held and the allied forces withdrew to Crete. Crete was of strategic importance for bomber attack against the Rumanian oilfields. On 25th April the Germans therefore invaded the island. The key to its defence was the destruction of seaborne reinforcements for the initial parachute attack. Whilst this was largely achieved German ad hoc air reinforcement led to the capture of Crete on 2nd June.

Back in North Africa the advent of Rommel and the loss of the divisions sent to Greece led to the allied withdrawal back towards Egypt and the German siege of Tobruk.

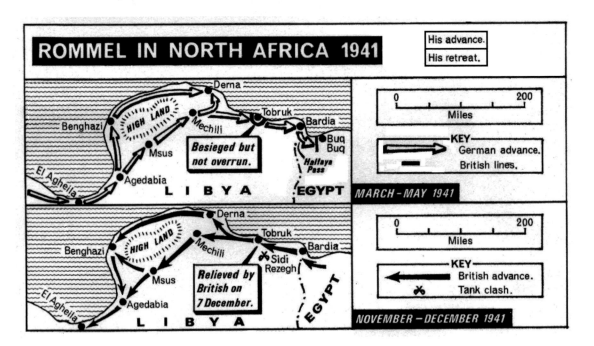

Auchinleck's attack on 18th November was initially frustrated by Rommel. After 12 days of changing hands the capture of Sidi Rezegh forced Rommel to retreat. It was in this phase of the fighting that *Pat Painter* was killed. The British then advanced into Libya, with Benghazi being taken on Christmas Eve.

The Far East. Reinforcements intended for Auchinleck's offensive were, however, diverted to Malaya in the face of the threat from Japan.

FREDERICK WILLIAM HOLDEN

Pilot Officer, 45096

Royal Air Force

Who died on

Friday 18th April 1941, Aged 28.

Fred Holden was a son of Mr & Mrs William Holden of Brockenhurst. He married Lottie and lived with her in Seaford, Sussex. This may account to some extent for the regrettably complete absence of any other information about him.

By 1941 he was flying with 61 Squadron in Hampden bombers as an observer.   It is recorded that on 18th April 1941 he took off from RAF HEMSWELL at 1520 hours to attack the large German airfield at Malpertus near Cherbourg.

The crew of the Hampden Mark 1 AD732 QR comprised:

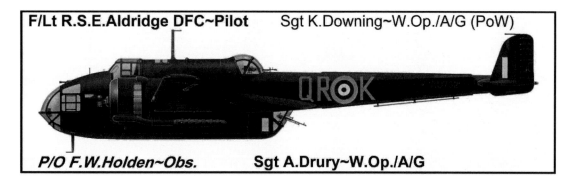

The aircraft was shot down by flak in the target area.

Sgt K Downing became a prisoner of war, but the remainder of the crew - including Fred Holden - are buried in **Cherbourg Old Communal Cemetery** in:

Grave 2 Plot 6, Row B,

JACK DUNKINSON

Able Seaman, Royal Navy

HMS GLOUCESTER

Who died on

Thursday 22nd May 1941, Aged 21.

Jack Dunkinson was born in Brockenhurst on 4th February 1920 and was the eldest son of John and Sarah.

He attended the local school and worked initially for Purkess bakery before joining his father in the family coal merchant business. He was over 6 feet in height, neither smoked nor drank, was a keen cyclist, played football for the village team and won all ten of his bouts when a member of the Lawrence Boxing Club in Lymington.

His father had served in the Royal Navy in the Great War and so in 1938 it was natural for Jack, who was also encouraged by Dr Marshall, to join the RNVR.

In 1939 he was called up with Archie Cleveland and Arthur Purkiss, all of them going to Skegness for their basic training. Jack and Arthur then went on to Plymouth for advanced training.

After qualifying, he was sent to Trincomalee to join GLOUCESTER, a City Class cruiser completed in 1937.

She later joined the Mediterranean Fleet and on 28th March 1941 took part in the victory against the Italian Fleet at the Battle of Matapan.

JACK DUNKINSON

182

In late April the GLOUCESTER began to evacuate the Garrison from Crete. When the Germans assaulted the island on 20th May, however, British naval units were ordered to attack at night and withdraw beyond enemy aircraft range in the daytime.

The Royal Navy dominated the waters at night and sank many small caiques and other troop-carrying craft.

On 22nd May, however, enemy air attacks sank the GLOUCESTER, along with the cruiser FIJI and the destroyer GREYHOUND.

Of the GLOUCESTER's crew of 801 only 81 were saved.

Jack was not amongst their number.

His name is commemorated, with those of his shipmates, on the **Plymouth Naval Memorial:**

Column 1 Panel 474.

His name is also inscribed on the family headstone in **St. Nicholas Churchyard,** Brockenhurst.

WALTER ROGER MARSHALL A'DEANE DSO DSC AM

Commander, Royal Navy

HMS GREYHOUND

Who died on

Thursday 22nd May 1941. Aged 38.

Bill Dunkinson recalls that Walter A'Deane lived in Foster's Cottage at Water's Green with his wife and three daughters.

In 1931 Walter was a Lieutenant (with seniority of 15th August 1924) serving in VEGA, a "V" Class destroyer. In 1932 he was promoted Lieutenant Commander and 4 years later served in ESCORT, an "E" Class Destroyer built in 1934.

Promoted to Commander on 30th June 1939 he became Commanding Officer of GREYHOUND, a modern "G" Class destroyer of 1335 tons built by Vickers Armstrong. Armed with 4 x 4.7-inch guns and capable of 36 knots, she had been commissioned in 1936.

GREYHOUND had an incredible war:

8th April 1940	Involved in combined operations in Norway.
26th May 1940	Operation Dynamo – involved in the evacuation of the British Expeditionary Force from Dunkirk.
23rd September 1940	Operation Menace – involved in abortive attack on Dakar.
11th November 1940	Involved in Fleet Air Arm attack on Italian battleships at Tarranto.
27th November 1940	Involved in action off Cape Spartivento, Sardinia, against Italian Fleet.
19th January 1941	Sank the Italian submarine NEGHELLI.
28th March 1941	Involved in the Battle of Matapan, where GREYHOUND's searchlights illuminated the Italian cruisers POLA, ZARA and FIUME, which were promptly sunk by the guns of WARSPITE.

HMS GREYHOUND

In July 1940 Walter was awarded the Distinguished Service Cross

"For good service in the Royal Navy since the outbreak of the War"

and in August he was Mentioned in Despatches

"For good service in the withdrawal of the Allied Armies from Dunkirk."

He was subsequently, in July 1941, appointed a Companion of the Distinguished Service Order for his

"Courage and skill in a successful attack on an Italian submarine".

At the battle for Crete in May 1941 the GREYHOUND was bombed and sunk in the same action that saw the loss of the GLOUCESTER.

Alec Dennis from the sister ship GRIFFIN reports that in the course of this action GREYHOUND was detached to sink a caique. On the way to rejoin (still alone) she was set upon and sunk in the early afternoon by eight JU87s.

> *"About one hundred men got away in rafts and a whaler. While in the water they were machine-gunned.*
>
> *Poor old GREYHOUND – the last of the flotilla apart from ourselves."*

This action is described in the official citation for the Albert Medal, posthumously awarded to Commander A'Deane.

> *"When his ship HMS GREYHOUND was bombed and sunk Commander Marshall-A'Deane was among the survivors picked up by HMS KANDAHAR later in the day.*
>
> *HMS FIJI was sunk and HMS KANDAHAR again went to the rescue. Commander Marshall-A'Deane, despite the ordeal he had already been through that day, dived overboard in the gathering darkness to rescue the men in the water. He was not seen again.*
>
> *This was the last proof of his great gallantry. Commander A'Deane had already in this war been appointed Companion of the Distinguished Service Order, won the Distinguished Service Cross and was twice Mentioned in Despatches."*

By Warrant of December 1971 surviving recipients of the Albert Medal were invited to exchange their awards for the George Cross, the highest gallantry award for civilians as well as service personnel in actions for which purely military honours would not normally be granted.

Bill Dunkinson recalls that a New Milton sailor, Brian Thatcher, from the GREYHOUND, always referred to Walter A'Deane as

"What a good skipper".

The news of his death arrived in Brockenhurst on the same day as that of the death of Jack Dunkinson. Mrs A'Deane visited the Dunkinsons that very day to offer sympathy.

His name is recorded on the **Portsmouth Naval Memorial** on:

Column 1, Panel 45.

186

PETER CHARLES M^CCONNEL BANISTER DSC

Lieutenant, Royal Navy

HM Submarine UMPIRE

Who died on

Sunday 20th July 1941, Aged 23

Peter Banister was the eldest son of Charles and Phyllis Banister. He was born on 3rd September 1917. He attended West Downs Preparatory School in

PETER BANISTER

Winchester and in 1931 joined the Britannia Royal Naval College at Dartmouth as a 13-year-old Cadet. The family moved to the village in 1932, initially into Armstrong Farm House, and later in 1956 built and moved into Armstrong Farm Cottage.

His younger brother Robert remembers him at this earlier time as a dashing handsome man; good company, an excellent all round sportsman who was clearly an extremely competent and highly regarded young Naval officer and submariner.

He came to Brockenhurst when he was 15 years old and was quickly a central part of the lively pre-war active social scene whenever he was not away at sea. This included tennis and dancing at "the (Morant) Club".

In 1934 and joined the battleship BARHAM in the Mediterranean as a Midshipman. Five years later, having passed his submariner's course, he was appointed to SALMON, which later became the first submarine to sink a U-boat.

In December 1939 he became engaged to a Brockenhurst girl, Rosemary Whittow, whom he married in March 1940 in St Nicholas Church.

In April 1940 he went as Liaison Officer to the French submarine ORPHEE, which also sank a U-boat whilst he was aboard. For this he was awarded the Croix de Guerre. He then went, briefly, as Third Hand to CLYDE. This submarine hit the German pocket battleship SCHARNHORST with torpedoes.

Peter then served in CACHALOT as Third Hand from July to November, during which time she sank two U-Boats. For this he was Mentioned in Despatches.

In November he joined H 32 as First Lieutenant and then attended the First Lieutenants course at Rothesay. On completion he was appointed in January 1941 as First Lieutenant of the new submarine UMPIRE then building at Chatham. As soon as she was completed in July UMPIRE sailed for trials and training to the Clyde. Four days before the submarine set sail, Peter received the Distinguished Service Cross

"For good services in HM submarines in recent successful patrols and operations against the enemy"

from the hand of King George VI at Buckingham Palace.

HMS UMPIRE AT CHATHAM DOCKYARD

UMPIRE joined a northbound convoy on the 19th July 1941.

That night the submarine was accidentally rammed and sunk by a Dutch escort of a southbound convoy.

As the senior officer remaining in the sunken submarine, his Captain having been washed off the conning tower, Peter took charge of the escape drill enabling nearly all who had survived thus far, including Peter himself, to reach the surface. Sadly he was not among those rescued. His story is told in *"One of our Submarines"* by Edward Young.

After Peter's death Rosemary gave birth to their daughter, Carol, who now lives in Washington DC with three grown children of her own. Rosemary herself subsequently joined the Air Transport Auxiliary as a pilot towards the end of 1943 and ferried about 300 aircraft, nearly half of which were Spitfires and Seafires, from factories to squadrons across the UK.

Lieutenant Peter Banister is recorded on the Memorial to All Lost from the College, at the RN College, Dartmouth as well as in their Book of Remembrance. His name also appears on the **Portsmouth Naval Memorial** on:

Panel 5, Column 1

He is also commemorated on his brother's gravestone in **St. Nicholas Churchyard,** Brockenhurst:

"IF I TAKE THE WINGS OF THE MORNING AND REMAIN IN THE UTTERMOST PARTS OF THE SEA THERE ALSO SHALL THY HAND LEAD ME AND THY RIGHT HAND SHALL HOLD ME."

PSALM 139

JOHN LAWRENCE SHORT

Corporal, 546794

Royal Air Force

Who died on

Wednesday, 13th August 1941.

Jack Short was born in Brockenhurst, one of several sons and daughters of George Short, a village coal merchant. A brother, Joe, served in the army during the war.

JACK SHORT

He enlisted into the RAF at the beginning of the war and then married a local girl. They lived at Rosita Cottage opposite Lloyds Bank, Sway Road, Brockenhurst.

He was selected for pilot training and was posted to No. 61 Air School at George Aerodrome in the Western Cape area of South Africa. This air school, part of the Empire Training Scheme, trained pilots and aircrew on Ansons and Aeroncas aircraft.

He is reported to have died in an accident during pilot training.

Jack is buried in the **Church of England Allotment** of

George Cemetery, Western Cape, South Africa.

190

PATRICK CHARLES PAINTER

Lance Corporal, 7908968

44th Royal Tank Regiment, Royal Armoured Corps

Who died on

Saturday 22nd November 1941, Aged 21.

Patrick was the only son of Frederick and Alice Painter who lived in Westmoor, Meerut Road, Brockenhurst. His father Frederick, who was an ex-navy man, worked for the GPO as an engineer. He is also remembered as teaching knots to the local scout troop of which Pat was a keen member.

Patrick enlisted into the Royal Armoured Corps and served with the 44th Royal Tank Regiment.

In November 1941 this was part of the 4th Armoured Brigade operating against Rommel in Cyrenaica. On 18/19th of the month Operation CRUSADER was begun with the aim of relieving Tobruk. The operation succeeded in getting to within 10 miles of the perimeter but a successful German response frustrated the relief.

Two days of very confused fighting followed in which 4 Armoured Brigade played little part, being in reserve. On the night of 22nd November, however, the 15th Panzer Division surprised 4-Armoured Brigade and shattered it as a fighting entity. Patrick Painter was one of the many casualties in this German attack.

PATRICK PAINTER

He is buried in **Halfaya Sollum War Cemetery**, Egypt in:

Collective Grave 5 G 1-10.

GEORGE CUTHBERT IRWIN FERGUSON

Lieutenant-Commander, Royal Naval Volunteer Reserve

HMS PRINCE OF WALES,

Who died on

Wednesday 10th December 1941, Aged 38.

George, Robby, Helen and Ursula were the children of Major Spencer and Agnes Ferguson. The family hailed from Carlisle but between the wars moved to Homewood, The Rise, Brockenhurst. They later rented this house to Lord Northcliffe. It is now the Watersplash Hotel.

George Ferguson was a career naval officer who joined the Royal Naval College, Dartmouth, as a cadet at the age of 13. He later retired from the Royal Navy and, amongst other things, was secretary to the New Forest Point-to-Point. He married a Brockenhurst girl and had two sons and two daughters. The family lived at Copythorne and were very regular in attending the Church of St Mary, George being a member of the Church Council. His wife was noted for her church flower arrangements. His sister reports that he had a keen sense of humour and was an excellent sailor.

HMS PRINCE OF WALES ARRIVING AT SINGAPORE. 2nd DECEMBER 1941

He rejoined the navy at the outbreak of war and first served in CARDIFF, one of the new 6 inch gun Town Class cruisers, before being appointed to the PRINCE OF WALES. This newly commissioned battleship of the King George V Class carried 10 x 14-inch guns in three turrets. The need for a heavy anti-aircraft defence that could double as anti-destroyer armament led to the adoption of a dual-purpose secondary armament of 16 x 5.25-inch guns. These high angle/low angle guns were grouped amidships. George Ferguson was put in charge of one of these batteries.

PRINCE OF WALES saw action against the BISMARCK and service in the Mediterranean, where she had supported Force H on escort duty for Malta convoys. She was then sent with REPULSE to Singapore to discourage Japanese aggression.

HMS PRINCE OF WALES SINKING

The Japanese started their assault on Malaya on 7/8th December 1941. Force Z, consisting of the PRINCE OF WALES and REPULSE with destroyer escort, but no air cover, set sail from Singapore on 8th December to intercept the Japanese landing force at Kota Bharu. The following day this order was changed to attack an enemy landing at Kuantan. This, however, was a false alarm and early on the 10th December the force headed back to Singapore. Japanese aircraft located the force and attacked with torpedoes, two of which hit the PRINCE OF WALES aft. This jammed her rudder, causing the ship to list to port and cutting power to half the anti-aircraft batteries. After further air attacks the crew were taken off by destroyers and the ship sank at 1318 hours. George Ferguson was not amongst the survivors.

His name is commemorated on both the Copythorne and Brockenhurst War Memorials. It is also recorded on the **Plymouth Naval Memorial:**

Panel 61 Column 2.

ANTHONY DAVID WALTER MOORE

Lieutenant, Royal Navy

HMS AUDACITY

Who died on

Monday 22nd December 1941, Aged 27.

There is, unfortunately, no detailed memory of Anthony Moore in the village today. This may be because after marriage he lived with his wife Ebba in Wotton-under-Edge in Gloucestershire.

Mary Richardson recalls, however, that his father, John Walter Barnwell Moore CBE, lived in Weirs End whilst serving as a Royal Naval padre. He later lived at "Sundowners" in Meerut Road. A plaque in his memory is to be found on the right-hand front wooden kneeler in St Saviour's Church. He died in 1969 aged 84 and was buried at sea.

Archie Cleveland, an ex-Navy man and village undertaker at the time, remembers John Moore as

"A hell of a nice man."

Anthony joined the Navy as a Midshipman in 1932 and served before the war in the cruiser AJAX and in the aircraft carrier COURAGEOUS. By late 1940 he was a Lieutenant aboard HAVELOCK a modern "H" Class destroyer which had taken part in both battles of Narvik earlier that year. In September 1941 he joined AUDACITY as a watch-keeping officer.

The story of the loss of AUDACITY, after an operational life of only seven days, is a brave one.

Early on in the war the need for convoy air cover was recognised and in January 1941 the ex-German cargo ship HANOVER began conversion to a Merchant Aircraft Carrier (MAC-ship). Her superstructure was razed and the upper deck rebuilt and topped with a wooden flight deck. She was fitted with the barest minimum of equipment necessary for flying – two arrester wires and a crash barrier. There was no hanger, as the Martlet aircraft were parked and serviced on the open deck.

H.M.S. AUDACITY

Initially named the EMPIRE AUDACITY she sailed on 13th September with her first convoy for Gibraltar. Although six ships were lost, the EMPIRE AUDACITY provided the convoy with continuous air cover during daylight hours and actually shot down two enemy FW 200 reconnaissance aircraft.

Renamed AUDACITY she sailed from Gibraltar on 14th December 1941 with convoy HG76. The story is told on Page 10 of a book called **"Fighting Captain"**. The convoy consisted of 32 ships, and was escorted by Commander Johnnie Walker's well-trained 36th Escort Group of two sloops and seven Flower Class corvettes. The convoy was under continuous air and U-boat attack until 23rd December. On 17th December AUDACITY lost one of its Martlets, which was shot down by U131. This submarine was later forced to scuttle itself and another, U434, was also sunk. The AUDACITY's aircraft also shot down two enemy planes on 18th December. This tally was repeated the following day.

In a night action on 21/22nd December the carrier moved away from the convoy and was sunk by U571. Nine officers, including her Captain with Anthony Moore and 63 men lost their lives. After seven days of continuous action the enemy had sunk AUDACITY, a destroyer and two merchant ships at the cost of four U-boats and four aircraft.

Lieutenant Anthony Moore is commemorated on the **Plymouth Naval Memorial:**

Column 3 Panel 44

1942

Eight people from the village were killed during 1942.

THE HOME FRONT

Two very large bombs were dropped one night in the field between the Lymington Road and the railway end of Church Lane. The following day John Jolly and some friends went from Avenue Road to the blackened craters in search of shrapnel. These craters can still be seen.

At the time of the raid Mr Lodge, the Foreman-Shunter, and his gang dived under the nearest wagons for shelter - until they realised that the train was loaded with explosives.

As John Purkess graphically describes it:

"**A large chunk of Brockenhurst would have gone missing if the bombs had only been 200 yards closer to their target.**"

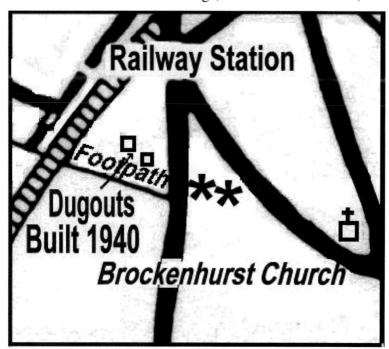

WHERE THE BOMBS DROPPED IN 1942

In June **Colonel Conwyn Mansel-Jones** V.C., C.M.G., D.S.O., Legion d'Honneur, late West Yorkshire Regiment, (14 June 1871-29 May 1942) was buried in St Nicholas churchyard. He lived at Weirs End and won his Victoria Cross. in February 1900 in the Boer War.

On 18th October Bill Street, who was serving in the Royal Marines, lost his wife Phyllis and his two daughters Molly and Beryl, along with their aunt Lily Reay and her two daughters Ruth and Marion when an aircraft of a Czechoslovak squadron of the R.A.F. crashed on a park in Ruislip. *Phillis, Molly* and *Beryl Street* are buried alongside *Lily, Ruth* and *Marion* in St Nicholas Churchyard.

THE AIR WAR

The RAF continued to re-equip and expand to meet the needs of the campaigns in the Middle and Far East as well as the war at sea. The bombing of Germany was intensified in 1942 and extended to include the Skoda works in Czechoslovakia and the armaments factories of Turin in Italy.

In January **Sergeant Donald Cockburn** did not return from a raid on Hamburg.

THE ARMY

By 1942 the threat of German invasion was receding in the light of the German advance into Russia. Britain was therefore becoming one vast training area and forces built up for the projected invasion of Europe. The ill-fated Dieppe raid was part of this scenario.

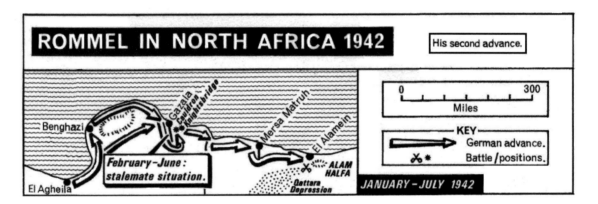

The British successes in the desert of late 1941 came to a frustrating halt as reinforcements were diverted to the Far East. Rommel resumed the offensive, but by mid June German supply problems and stiffening British resistance under Montgomery led to stalemate.

The containment of German activities before the battle of El Alamein was achieved only at the expense of many lives - one of whom was **John Hotham**. By mid 1942 the war in North Africa was beginning to turn away from continued German success and the subsequent Battle of Alamein turned the tide in the Allies favour.

The Far East. The Japanese invasion of Malaya and Burma, however, was beginning to require more forces.

THE WAR AT SEA

The last village Royal Navy casualty came at the end of 1942, when *Lieutenant Commander Drummond St. Clair-Ford* was lost in the submarine TRAVELLER. Like all too many of our submarines at that time, TRAVELLER failed to return from patrol and was presumed to have been mined off Taranto.

That year had seen some of the toughest battles of the sea war, with convoys being fought through to North Russia as well as across the Atlantic. Equally hard-fought had been the landings in North Africa, the convoys to Malta and the relentless interdiction campaign waged by our submarines in the central Mediterranean against the enemy's supply line to North Africa, which made such significant contribution to ultimate victory.

The Merchant Navy. The ships within convoys were manned by the Merchant Navy of all the allied nations. In the early years of the war their casualties were severe with one in four merchant Navy men being lost at sea. In 1942 two such were *William Judd* and *Eddie Jackson Smith*.

Neither of these war casualties is commemorated on the War Memorial.

Happily, there were no further recorded naval casualties in action among Brockenhurst seamen for the remainder of the war.

DONALD WILFRED COCKBURN

Sergeant, 1168673

Royal Air Force Volunteer Reserve

Who died on

Wednesday 14th January 1942, Aged 31.

Donald was the son of George and Florence Cockburn who owned the Island shop. George was reportedly a great character who ran his shop with great aplomb. Regrettably, nothing more has been remembered about Donald other than that he joined the RAF at the beginning of the war and that he trained as an air-gunner.

By 1942 he was serving with 50 Squadron at RAF SKELLINGTHORPE in Yorkshire. At this stage of the war the Admiralty had requested RAF help against The U-boat menace. The German North Sea ports therefore began to be targeted and Hamburg, with the Blohm and Voss U-boat yards, was frequently bombed. Accurate bombing was more possible with port targets as the recognisable coastline and highly visible port profile aided target identification.

In fact it was to bomb these yards in Hamburg that Sergeant Baddeley's Hampden crew took off at 1635 Hours on 14th January 1942.

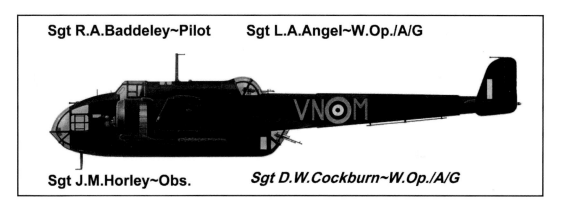

Sgt R.A.Baddeley~Pilot   Sgt L.A.Angel~W.Op./A/G

VN○M

Sgt J.M.Horley~Obs.   Sgt D.W.Cockburn~W.Op./A/G

50 Squadron's Record Book quite simply records

> *"Nothing heard from this aircraft after takeoff."*

All crew members are therefore recorded on the **Runnymede Memorial** on:

Panel 80

EDWARD JACKSON SMITH

Cadet, Merchant Navy

S.S. TRAVELLER

Who died on

26th January 1942, Aged 17.

Eddie was born in Southampton on 14th January 1925, ten minutes ahead of his identical twin brother David. Before the war their father ran a fruit-importing business, but on the outbreak of war the family moved to Keith Lodge, Forest Park, Brockenhurst.

EDWARD JACKSON SMITH

Both boys continued to attend Taunton's School, which had been evacuated to Bournemouth. The twins had been brought up to be strong swimmers and between them held every swimming record in the school. Although only 15 years old Eddie also won the men's quarter-mile swimming championship. He also gained his colours at the same age by playing Centre-half for the School football team. David remembers his brother, at this time, as being

"A very determined character."

German bombers at this stage of the war were guided onto their targets in Britain by navigational beams, one of which lay over the Isle of Wight and Brockenhurst. The boys therefore became accustomed to listening to the de-synchronised engines of enemy aircraft.

When the Germans bombed Coventry one of their bombers was shot down by "Cats-eyes" Cunningham, flying a Night fighter out of Middle Wallop. It crashed north of the Ornamental Drive and the following day the twins and a friend set out to find the wreck. David, not yet 16, was driving his father's car when they found a wounded German airman crawling across a forest road. They took him to the old police station at Lyndhurst where they were relieved of their prisoner. The next day their mother made them return to the police station to hand in the German Mae-West inflatable life jacket they had liberated from the airman! A reporter for a Sunday paper describing the incident covered for David being under age for driving by describing him as being 17 years old. His father, reading the story in Scotland, was, however, not amused!

At the end of the Fifth Form neither boy had a chance in wartime to go to college so David was placed as an apprentice marine engineer with Thorneycroft in Southampton, while Eddie decided to join the Merchant Navy.

In this he was undoubtedly influenced by his grandfather, Thomas Hughes, who also lived with the family in Keith Lodge. Thomas had been born in North Wales and in 1869 had gone to sea at the age of nine. Initially he had sailed in a two-masted Barque carrying slate to wherever it could be sold. He soon advanced to larger ships and became a "Cape-Horner." In 1912 he was the Quartermaster on board the White Star vessel *"Carpathia"* which rescued many survivors from the *"Titanic"*.

The owner of the "Cat and Fiddle" at the time suggested that Eddie could join the Harrison line of Mersey Chambers, Liverpool. This was effected and in September 1941 Eddie was kitted out with his uniforms by Miller, Rayner and Haysom, naval and civil outfitters of Southampton, for a cost of £32.12.0. This was paid for by his uncle, Mr F. C. Wootten. David's last memory of his brother in Brockenhurst was of sitting one evening with Eddie, who was dressed in his cadet's uniform and bridge coat, on the bench by the War Memorial talking to Millie Perkins, who lived in Partridge Road.

David and a cousin then travelled with Eddie up to Liverpool to see him on board his ship. They stayed overnight in a Royal Naval hostel, full of mateloes, and then saw him onto the S. S. *"Traveller"*.

Keith P. Lewis

The "Traveller", 3,963 grt, built in 1922.

This was a steamship of 3963 tons, which had been built on the Clyde in 1922 at a cost of £190,555. At this time it was under the command of Captain Fitz-Simmons.

At the end of September *"Traveller"* joined an outward convoy bound for the East Coast of the United States. It soon ran into bad weather but, as Eddie wrote from New Orleans in a letter posted 10th January 1942:

> *" The old Traveller is a dirty ship, but an excellent sea-boat and although she did everything except stand on her head, we reached our destination.*
>
> *The work on board is hard, but I feel it is doing me good and by my brown face and body know I am not having such a bad time. I have, since we left Liverpool, been on the 8-12 watch night and day and do also day work such as painting and sweeping the decks. The day before yesterday I went down into the notorious bilges, except for a smell like bad walnuts they were not so bad as Fred told me.*
>
> *I have chummed up with the 4th engineer and 2nd and 3rd sparks and I have had many good times ashore with them, going to the pictures and having a good meal. My Spanish has come in jolly useful, especially in buying presents. I was very excited to get ashore, especially as it was my first foreign port and I had not put my feet on terra firma for over a month. I went ashore with the 3rd sparks, a true Irishman who stands in his stocking feet 3 foot nothing. It was good to see shops and people again although they were not the same as in England.*
>
> *Although I have enjoyed myself ashore, seen some wonderful scenery, take it from me there is nothing better than the English countryside and I shall be glad to see good old Brockenhurst again and the trees of the forest."*

"Traveller" then called at Norfolk, Virginia, to coal. America had just entered the war but had not yet appreciated the need for the convoy system to be introduced, or even for the need for coastal blackout. As a result German U-Boats were diverted to the Eastern American Seaboard to great effect. *"Traveller"* was, by this stage, on charter or requisitioned by the Admiralty as she was loaded with 600 tons of ammunition.

On 26th January, twelve days after his 17th birthday, *"Traveller"* was steaming unescorted at 8-10 knots, bound for Halifax, to join a Liverpool-bound convoy. At 2.30 a.m. She was attacked by U-106, commanded by Oberleutnant-zur-see Herman Rasch, in position 39 34 n, 64 05 W, 306 miles south of Halifax. Rasch fired two torpedoes, both of which hit, and the ship sank within 6 minutes with the loss of all fifty-one hands.

On 2nd August 1943, whilst under the command of Oberleutnant-zur-see Damerow, U-106 was attacked in the Bay of Biscay by a Hampden of Coastal Command and seriously damaged. Later that day she was sunk by two Sunderlands of the Australian Air Force. Her captain and 36 other members of her crew were saved. Herman Rasch also survived the war.

Eddie's mother received £8.13.6d in wages due and a weekly pension of 10 shillings.

Edward Jackson Smith is commemorated on **The Tower Hill Memorial** to the Merchant Navy on:

Panel 109

His name is also recorded on his mother's grave in **St. Nicholas Churchyard**.

JOHN ALTHAM HOTHAM

Major, 65327

1st Royal Tank Regiment, Royal Armoured Corps

Who died on

Monday 27th July 1942, Aged 29.

John Hotham was born on 5th June 1913 to Lieutenant Colonel John Clarence Hotham (1882-1959) and Margaret Wilmer. He was a kinsman of Baron Hotham and very much part of a Service family. His great-grandfather was an Admiral, who had blockaded the French Mediterranean ports with Nelson in 1795. His maternal grandfather was a naval Commander and his father, John Snr., transferred to the Indian Army after service with the Suffolk Regiment in World War I and in the Afgan War in 1919. Colonel Hotham was Remount Purchasing Officer, Calcutta (1924-7) and Director of Remounts, Simla, (1931-32). He settled in Brockenhurst in 1932, about the time John left Stowe School.

JOHN HOTHAM

Not surprisingly young John and his two sisters were accomplished riders. Aileen, his elder sister, won numerous trophies in India, before, sadly being killed there in a riding accident in 1932.

Diana, his other sister who was born in 1918, served as a war-time Voluntary Aid Detachment (VAD) nurse, firstly in the UK and then in Italy. She ended her war service in Rome and later married John Whatley-Smith, living at Hordle House Milford.

John was educated at Stowe. He played 1st XI cricket and had a knack of getting on well with people. On leaving school he joined the RAF and trained as a pilot, but retired due to eyesight problems. He later joined the Army and was commissioned into the 1st Royal Tank Regiment (1 RTR).

In May 1939 he married Osra Aubrey Porteous. Osra died on 16th February 1944.

By 1942 he was a Major and was attached to 6 RTR in North Africa. as the Squadron Commander of "C" Squadron. An extract from the War Diary (15th July 1942) of that Unit shows that his squadron had been newly-equipped with 12 Grant Tanks.

His crew comprised:

Comd	Maj. Hotham
Driver	Cpl. Williamson
Driver/op.	Sgt. Bennett
37 mm	Tpr. Nottage
75 mm	Tpr. Day
Loader	Tpr. Neal

A GRANT TANK OF 6 RTR IN JUNE 1942

On 27th July 1942 6 RTR were supporting the Durham Light Infantry. After the initial engagement "C" Squadron went forward to deal with enemy anti tank guns that were stopping the advance. The squadron destroyed a 50-mm and a 75-mm gun but in this action lost 2 Grant tanks.

Major Hotham was initially reported missing but the following day it was confirmed that he

"was killed in yesterday's action".

From the Battle Casualty Return his crew appear to have survived.

He is commemorated on the **Alamein Memorial** in Egypt on:

Column 19

His name is also on the **Stowe School Memorial** as well as on his wife's grave in **St Nicholas Churchyard.**

205

Mrs. Phyllis Street, Aged 37

Molly Street, Aged 12
and
Beryl Street, Aged 4

Who died on

Sunday 18th October 1942.

Bill Street was one of the eight children of Fred and Laura Street who lived in Railway Terrace in Avenue Road. Fred had fought in the First World War, serving in a Pioneer battalion in France. At one stage he had been involved in running a Prisoner of war camp for German soldiers. He returned to the village in 1919, worked as a gardener and served as an Air Raid Warden in the Second World War.

The Street family can be said to have "done their bit" during the war. Of the five sons Fred worked on the railways (a reserved occupation) but was a member of the Home Guard. Frank and Ted joined the Army. Bill and Reg enlisted into the Royal Marines; the latter becoming a commando who - as a frogman - helped clear the Normandy beaches before the D-Day landings. The end of the war found him serving in the Far East.

FRED STREET (Snr.)

Of the three daughters Mary joined the Fire Service and Dorothy and Rose both worked at the Masonic hall (the ex-Kiora Club of the First World War) in Brookley Road making aero-engine parts for Wellworthys.

Fred's son John now lives at Calshot and has provided all the information on Phyllis and her family.

PHYLLIS AND MRS REAY

BERYL AND MOLLY

Bill Street had married Phyllis Le Fevre before the war and had worked as a van-driver for Messrs. Purkess Bakers and Grocers. The Street family lived in Ringwood Terrace, Brockenhurst.

Bill joined the Royal Marines in 1941. In the summer of 1942 he had been home on leave and then returned to his unit in South Wales. Phyllis had wanted to go and stay with him in Wales but Bill had been unable to get rooms. She then decided to go to visit her sister, Mrs. Reay, who, with her own children - Ruth and Marion - had stayed with the family in Brockenhurst in the summer. Phyllis and the girls therefore left home on Friday afternoon to spend a fortnight's holiday with the Reay family at Ruislip.

Mrs Vera Waterman, who worked in the Post Office and had lived with the Streets for twelve years, reported to **THE ECHO** at the time that

"Mrs Street and the children went away on Friday a happy party. They had been looking forward to the holiday, but it was curious that at the last moment, with everything packed, Mrs Street was reluctant to leave. Now I am wondering whether she had an intuition."

On Sunday the Street and Reay families set out to visit friends.

THE ECHO, for Monday October 1942, reported:

BIG DEATHROLL IN PLANE CRASH

Children Killed at Play

CHILDREN at play in open ground, and number of women were among civilians killed when an R.A.F. 'plane crashed and burst into flames in the Home Counties yesterday afternoon.

The crew were also killed, and other casualties included Servicemen who had left trains at a station nearby.

The deaths number 20.

When the 'plane was preparing to land at an aerodrome it is thought that it suddenly developed trouble and that the pilot decided to land on the open space to avoid crashing into a group of houses.

-The ground is used as a playground by children from the surrounding houses, and the adjoining road is a popular Sunday walk for local people.

NO TIME TO ESCAPE

"It was not realised until a moment before the crash that the 'plane would not reach the aerodrome." an eye-witness said. "Men and women scattered hurriedly, but they had no time to escape.

"The 'plane apparently undershot the landing ground, crashed on its nose and burst into flames."

Several of the casualties were due to burns, and a woman and her 18-months-old baby, who were taken to hospital with extensive burns, died shortly after admission.

207

A letter from the MOD (RAF), dated 26th November 1999, confirms that on 18th October 1942 a Wellington Mark 1c T2564 of 311 (Czechoslovak) Squadron spun into the ground and caught fire off a steep turn near the ground half a mile east of Northolt. All fifteen personnel on board were killed. It is understood that the 13 Czechoslovaks, a Belgian and the Yugoslav aboard were to have attended a medal ceremony at Headquarters Coastal Command.

Bill had heard the dreadful news in South Wales and travelled straight to London. Mrs Reay's husband was, at the time, serving abroad. Father Fred met Bill in London for the sad task of identifying the two families.

The funeral of the two mothers and four children of the Street and Reay families was conducted by the Vicar, the Reverend Haslam, on 24th October. They are all are buried in **St Nicholas Churchyard**.

Bill returned to duty to serve in Italy, where he was later wounded.

Family postscript. Of Fred Street's original war-time family Dorothy married a Sergeant from the 4th Hampshires in 1945. She now lives in Fawley. Rose, the family's youngest daughter, married a Canadian soldier whom she met whilst he was stationed in Careys Manor, Brockenhurst. She is now a widow living in Ontario. Her seven children are all married with families. Reg now lives in Lymington.

WILLIAM GEORGE JUDD

Greaser, Merchant Navy

M.S. WARWICK CASTLE

Who died on

Saturday 14th November 1942, Aged 45.

William George Judd was born on the 11th August 1897 to William and Rebecca of 5 Cambridge Terrace, Chapel Street Bitterne, Southampton.

During 1943 the local paper reported that:

> *"Mr **William George Judd**, of "Lindum", Avenue Road Brockenhurst, a greaser and cleaner in the Merchant Navy, is officially reported to have lost his life through enemy action."*

The Mail Ship *"Warwick Castle"* was the third ship of that name to enter service with the Castle Line. The 20,000-ton motor vessel entered service in 1931 and was completely refitted in 1938. In 1942 it was in the Far East, leaving Java just before the invasion of the Japanese.

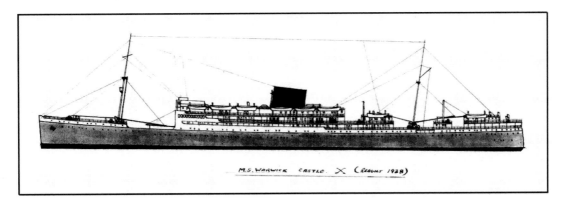

M S WARWICK CASTLE

In October 1942 she was in a convoy that carried part of the American army to North Africa and landed the troops at Oran on 8th November. With this satisfactorily achieved she made a dash to Gibraltar where a U.K.-bound convoy was to be formed.

This convoy left Gibraltar at 4.30 p.m. on Thursday 12th November with the *"Warwick Castle"* as the last ship in the column. Mid-morning two days later she was torpedoed by a U-Boat and quickly sank. One hundred survivors were rescued but William Judd was not amongst their number.

The First Officer of the *"Warwick Castle"* did, however, survive and on the 20th November wrote a letter to the Union-Castle offices in Glasgow

---

Dear Sir,

I enclose the sum of sixty-nine pounds, ten shillings, this being the proceeds of an entirely voluntary subscription among the one hundred surviving members of the crew of the Warwick Castle rescued and subsequently landed from HMS ACHATES. It is intended as a small token of gratitude to the Captain, Officers and Ratings of the destroyer for their great help and kindness during the time of danger and privation. I will appreciate it if you will be good enough to arrange to have this sum of money placed at the disposal of the ACHATES.

I feel that we are especially indebted to the Captain of the ACHATES, Lt-Cdr Johns and to the First Lieutenant, Lieut Paton Jones,(sic) for their outstanding ability and courage........

During the whole of the rescue operation Lieut Paton Jones placed himself in a Precarious position in order to give greater assistance to the survivors, as they were brought on board, and on one occasion he dived into the rough sea, in order to save the life of a man who was exhausted and sinking..........

Commander Loftus Edward Peyton Jones CVO, DSO, DSC, MBE, RN. died in Brockenhurst earlier this year.

William Judd is amongst the 209 Union-Castle seamen who remain missing from the Second World War. His name is therefore recorded on the **Tower Hill Memorial** on:

Panel 117

DRUMMOND ST. CLAIR-FORD

Lieutenant Commander, Royal Navy

Commanding Officer, HMS TRAVELLER

Who died on

12th December 1942.

Drummond St. Clair-Ford came from a well-known Service family. Captain and Mrs Anson St. Clair-Ford had moved to Bentley, in Sway Road, Brockenhurst, in1928. Prior to this they had lived in The Crossways, Pennington, and later at Hordle. Captain Anson St. Clair-Ford, late Gloucester Yeomanry, served both in the South African and in the 1914-18 war.

In 1940 all three sons were serving in the Royal Navy. Drummond's elder brother, Captain Sir Aubrey St. Clair-Ford DSO RN Bart., served with distinction in the destroyer KIPLING in operations off Crete in May 1941, when her sister ships KELLY and KASHMIR were sunk. He rescued his Flotilla Captain, Lord Louis Mountbatten, who had been in command of the KELLY. For this action he was awarded his first DSO, gaining a bar later in the war.

A younger brother, Sub-Lieutenant Vernon John St. Clair-Ford was awarded the MBE in 1940

> *"For seamanship, devotion to duty and saving many lives at sea on the occasion of the bombing by the enemy of S. S. Domala on November 3rd 1939.*

A brother-in-law, Captain G W Preston, R.E., also served during the war in the Army.

Drummond, ("Sam,") who was married and lived at Bentley Grange in Sway Road, had been a well-known rugby player before the war, representing the Navy over several seasons. He had joined the submarine service in 1929 and was therefore an experienced submariner. John Purkess relates that whilst home on leave during the war Drummond was woken by the smell of burning. Believing it to be caused by a burning night-light, which he extinguished, he went back to sleep - only to find out later that, at the time, the front room had actually been on fire.

In November 1942 Sam was actually the Commanding Officer of PARTHIAN and had only taken over command of TRAVELLER as a temporary replacement for its Captain, Lieutenant Michael St. John, who had been taken ill.

TRAVELLER, one of the new T Class submarines, was built at Greenock and commissioned on 1st March 1942. Armed with 11 x 21-inch torpedo tubes and a 4-inch gun she had a surface speed of 15 knots. She carried a complement of six officers and 59 ratings.

HMS TRAVELLER

Her motto was:

> *" Fidenter Perge Viator"*

(Push Forward in Faith, Traveller)

As part of the preparations for an attack against the Italian capital ships in Tarranto TRAVELLER sailed from Malta on 28th November 1942 on a reconnaissance patrol of the harbour approaches. This was known to be heavily protected by mines. TRAVELLER failed to answer signals and never returned to harbour. The most likely cause of her loss was mining around 4th December 1942.

His name is commemorated on the **Portsmouth Naval Memorial** on:

Panel 61, Column 3.

and also on the family grave in **St. Nicholas churchyard**.

The date of death on this grave is distinguished by his records and Death Certificate both of which show "12th December 1942".

1943

1943 saw the preparation for the planned invasion of Europe taking tangible form.

It was also the worst year for the village with ten war deaths.

THE HOME FRONT

The construction of new railway sidings was started. The Lymington road was widened from the railway crossing through to Setley and at the railway bridge along the Balmer Lawn Road the road was lowered to enable transporters to take aircraft parts to and from Beaulieu.

At Wood Fidley on the north side of the railway line there is a short stretch of road in the shape of a dumbbell. At the Brockenhurst end is an excavation, now a pond, material from which was used to make this short road. Local belief was that it was an experimental activity with sections of the road made to different formulas - possibly to enable roads and airstrips to be built quickly from local materials. What is known is that train passengers always noticed some poor chap who was continuously driving round this road. As it was a military truck being driven it could also have been connected with M.E.X.E., who were experimenting with roads and bridges at Christchurch?

Rationing. With the war at sea focussing on convoys and the transportation of supplies around the world rationing of most commodities became tighter for the civilian population.

Clothes rationing, in particular, was something that taxed the ingenuity of families, especially of those with teenage daughters.

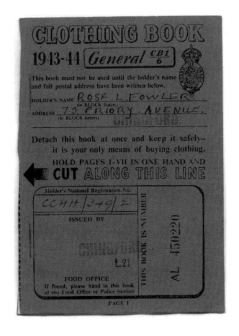

War food production under the Hampshire War Agricultural Executive Committee (HWAEC) became an increasingly important part of the local economy. It had a depot in Holland's Wood where huts were built for truck maintenance and the accommodation of workers. Their task was to produce food in the open forest so they cleared gorse and small trees from large areas of forestland, ploughed it and grew potatoes and other crops. Cleared areas closest to the village included the area behind Holland's Wood, all around the allotments and on the other side of the path to Queens Bower. At Whitemoor the cultivated acreage was both sides of the Rhinefield Road. At Wilverley it stretched the length of the enclosure. The other area was at Longslade Bottom. These latter locations have been retained as large cleared lawns. When Holland's Wood was vacated at the end of the war it became, some years later, a natural location for a caravan site.

Recycling. In the village re-cycling was in full swing with all bottles and jam jars being returned by rail to their manufacturers.

Children. The village school ran competitions - one of which was to collect books for the forces. Collectors were rewarded with small badges according to the number collected from "Private" for twenty up to "Field Marshall" for hundreds. There was keen competition to get to senior rank! Rosehips were also gathered by children for the manufacture of syrup and the Forestry Commission rewarded the collection of acorns, chestnuts and other tree seeds.

The Canadians. The Canadians came to the New Forest in 1943. A headquarters contingent occupied Careys Manor and the Balmer Lawn hotel. Troops were also accommodated in hutted camps towards Stoney Cross and Hollands Wood.

HOW MANY VILLAGERS CAN FIND THEMSELVES IN THIS PHOTOGRAPH?

They were soon assimilated into wartime Brockenhurst and are still remembered today for the Christmas party they gave on 23rd December at the County High School for all the village children. For many children it was the first taste they had had of ice cream or peanut butter. Each Canadian was given the responsibility of looking after two children - which they did in style! John and Roy Purkess were looked after by a French Canadian, who was then, as many soldiers were, invited home to share Christmas lunch.

The Canadians were then moved to Bournemouth where, unfortunately, some of them were killed when a bomb hit a hotel at the Lansdown one Sunday lunchtime.

THE WAR

THE AIR WAR

Plans were being made for the invasion of Europe. As a precursor to this the RAF was seeking to extend its air superiority into France. During this phase *Jeffery Cramer* lost his life over the Channel.

The bombing offensive continued with increased intensity. *Ron Read* was killed over Germany in January, as was *Ken Smith* in April and *Francis Hodder* in September. In June *Anthony O'Donnell* was killed in a bomb dump explosion at RAF SNAITH.

THE ARMY

The British success at Alamein in November 1942 had opened up the North African campaign. Rommel's losses in trained manpower, armour and supplies caused him to retreat westwards. The Anglo-American landings in Morocco and Algeria caught him in a pincer movement and the allied plan to occupy Tunis was almost successful. Rommel, however, occupied Tunisia and was resupplied through the ports of Tunis and Bizerta. Subsequent German counter-attacks were contained and on 20th March Montgomery breached the German defences of the Marenth Line. On 7th April he linked up with the Americans advancing from the west.

By 5th May the British First Army occupied Tunis and the Americans were entering Bizerta. The Axis Forces surrendered on 13th May. Sadly, both *Bill Close* and *Reg Meaden* were killed before the surrender.

The North African campaign, which had broken the spirit and power of Italy, provided a base for the invasion of Sicily and the subsequent invasion of mainland Italy. This occurred on 3rd September - the same day Italy withdrew from the war. Later that month *Roger Ash* was to be killed in a road accident in Palestine.

In the Far East the Japanese advance in 1942 had driven British forces back to the frontiers of India. In early 1943 the allies responded with Wingate's First Chindit expedition. This proved the concept of aggressive jungle patrolling. The line gradually stabilised and air resupply enabled units cut-off by the Japanese to survive and continue fighting. The monsoon period compounded the confused fighting during which *Cecil Hill* was killed.

Walter Clark died in November as a prisoner of the Japanese.

RONALD WILLIAM READ

Sergeant, 542180

Royal Air Force

Who died on

Sunday 17th January 1943, Aged 23.

Ronald Read lived with his parents in the Thatched Cottage (Cherry Tree Cottage) opposite the Forester's Arms. His father, Bill, was a postman who is still remembered for his skill at cricket and football. He was the eldest son in a family with two brothers Roy, Stan and a sister Nora. He was a prominent member of the Brockenhurst football team (his brothers were also in the team) and reportedly a leading player in the New Forest Junior League.

When he left the village school he joined the pre-war RAF in 1936 as an apprentice. After training he was posted to Iraq for three years where he captained his squadron football team and was vice-captain of the Flying Training Squadron Sports Team. As a hurdler he won seven cups and was only once beaten when competing for the RAF. He also represented the RAF in the high jump and the long jump and won numerous prizes.

In February 1942 he was posted to 83 Squadron at RAF WYTON. During the year the airforce received new aircraft, equipment, navigational aids, and more effective bombs. Tactics were also changing. The sum of these improvements was to make bombing raids against the enemy more effective.

In January 1943 a new Air Ministry Directive called for a renewed offensive against U-Boat bases in France. Air Vice Marshal Harris, who wished to continue attacks on German cities and industries, did not welcome this diversion of his forces. However the Directive did permit the continued attack of important objectives in Germany and Italy.

The first attack on U-Boat bases at Lorient on 14/15th January 1943 was not a success. The next raid on Berlin two days later by 201 aircraft saw the use, for the first time, of red Target Indicators by Pathfinders. Despite cloud cover a distinct red glow gave the main force an aiming point, and only one aircraft was lost.

On 17th January 1943 Ronald Read took-off at 1707 hours from RAF WYTON as flight engineer on a Lancaster 1, Serial number R5630 OL-T. 83 Squadron was one of the Pathfinder units for this operation, again against Berlin. The Germans, however, anticipating the RAF. tactic of targeting the same city on successive nights deployed their night-fighters around Berlin.

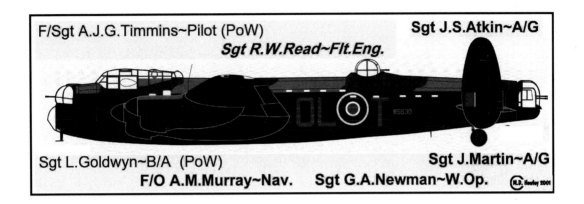

As a result 22 of our bombers were shot down.

What happened to Lancaster R5630 OL-T is not reported. Whilst F/Sgt Timmins and Sgt Goldwyn became prisoners of war the rest of the crew, including Ronald, were killed.

He is buried in **Kiel War Cemetery** in:

Collective Grave 2, G. 19.

JEFFREY MARTIN CREMER

Flying Officer, 127940

Royal Air Force Volunteer Reserve

Who died on

Sunday 14th March 1943, Aged 19

Jeffrey was born in Freshfield, Lancashire on 24th June 1923. He was the eldest son of Arthur and Gwyneth Cremer, who at the time were on UK leave from Tanganyika. Arthur was a colonial auditor whose next appointment was to Mauritius, where Jeffrey grew up and Gwyneth also gave birth to Ursula and Donald

In 1932 the family settled in Ingoldesthorpe, Armstrong Road, Brockenhurst. Arthur then took up his final posting to the Gold Coast – an area considered not suitable for young children in those days.

JEFFREY CREMER

Jeffrey initially attended Furzey Close Preparatory School in New Milton before going, in 1934, to the Junior King's School, Canterbury. There he proved to be a good sportsman – representing the school at Rugby, Hockey and Cricket.

In 1937, being also an able scholar, he won a scholarship to the senior school. He left King's in 1941 with a Higher School Certificate in Classics (Latin and Greek) and English Literature.

The headmaster wrote later:

> *"I thought the world of Jeffrey – so good and kind, such a loving disposition. I did hope he would be ordained and, at times, he thought he would be."*

In April 1941, however, he joined the RAF (VR) and went to Gonville and Caius College, Cambridge on the first RAF University course, where he converted from Classics to Science. In October he did his basic training and in December sailed to Canada and onward to California where he trained as a pilot at the Polaris Flight Academy. On 12th August 1942 he was awarded his Wings, commissioned as Pilot Officer and returned to the UK for operational training.

Between October 1942 and February 1943 he flew Spitfires on advanced operational training from RAF stations in Cheshire and Glamorgan. In February he joined 610 Squadron at RAF WESTHAMPNETT, near Chichester. This squadron was led by Johnny Johnson, a well-decorated and experienced pilot with a score of 33 enemy aircraft. It had Norwegian, Dutch, Polish, Australian and Canadian as well as British pilots and was tasked with defeating enemy raiders as well as conducting aggressive sweeps over France and Belgium.

On 14th March 1943 Jeffrey was reported "missing on air operations". He was on patrol flying low over the channel in his Spitfire looking for German raiders trying to get in under our radar cover. His plane crashed into the sea, cause unknown. Other planes circled overhead but nothing further was seen and the Spitfire was never recovered.

As his obituary in the school magazine records:

> *"So passes yet another King's scholar, young, able, of strong and winning personality; one who would have done much for the cause of humanity had he lived – and who has done everything for it in giving his young and promising life."*

His name is recorded on the **Runnymede Memorial** on:

Panel 124

It is also recorded on the Memorial at **The King's School, Canterbury**.

WILLIAM HAROLD TWEED CLOSE

Private, 5503656

2nd Battalion, Hampshire Regiment

Who died on

Tuesday 16th March 1943, Aged 26.

Bill Close was baptised on 23rd February 1917. He lived in 5 Tattenham Road, Brockenhurst, with his parents Ernest and Annie and brothers Percy and Sid. Ernest worked on the railway. A classmate at the local school remembers Bill as being very good-natured. On leaving school he worked for Frank Chalk as an errand-boy.

He joined the 2nd Battalion, the Hampshire Regiment (2 HAMPS) at the beginning of the war. On 11th November 1942 the battalion sailed from Liverpool to North Africa to take part in the campaign against Rommel. It arrived in Algiers on 21st November, only a week after the initial allied landings had taken place. 2 HAMPS were placed under the command of 78th Division in the British First Army.

BILL CLOSE

The advance went well until it was within 20 miles of Tunis. On the 29th November the unit was allocated to 11th Brigade and ordered to defend Tebourba against determined German counter-attacks. These were supported by strong armoured forces operating under total air supremacy. The battle lasted four days and turned into a vital rear-guard action that covered a general withdrawal. Without it the Allies could have been driven out of Tunisia. The Battalion went into action 689 strong but was reduced to an effective strength of 194 all ranks.

After the battle 2 HAMPS had 3 weeks to reorganise and re-equip. Nine Officers and 260 other ranks reinforced the unit sufficiently to enable it to move to Munchar where it dug new positions. The Germans continued to try to drive the Allies back, and for months there was heavy fighting before the link-up of the British 1st and 8th Armies was to be achieved.

On 5th March 2 HAMPS were supporting the Hampshire Brigade which had taken the brunt of the German attack on Hunts Gap. For the next three weeks they remained in defensive positions patrolling at night and being subject to constant enemy shell and mortar fire.

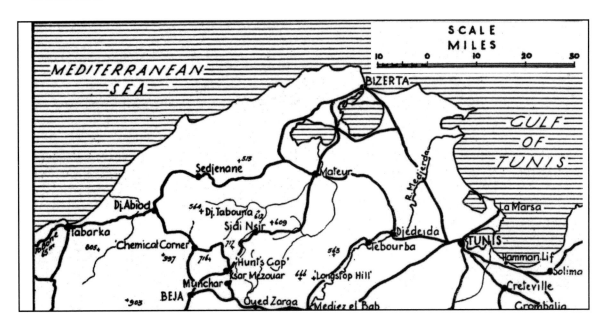

On 16th March 1943 Bill was reported as *"wounded and missing."* His parents appealed through **The Lymington Times** for any further news of their son from any soldier who may have returned or served about that time. However Captain W E Jukes, his Company Commander, had written on 20th March:

> *"I am indeed sorry to inform you that Private Close is missing. He was out with his platoon recently and was wounded, and we believe that he is a prisoner of war. I sincerely hope that he will return safely in due course.*
>
> *His mates and I are particularly sorry to lose him, as he was an excellent soldier, very popular and efficient. He was extremely gallant in the action in which he was wounded and undoubtedly did his job very well. He is a great loss to the Company."*

Bill was, however, not captured but killed in action. He is buried in **Beja War Cemetery**, Tunisia in:

Joint Grave 2 E11-12

There is also a memorial to the 2nd Battalion on **Tebourba Way**, Southampton.

KENNETH BROOKE FARLEY SMITH DSO

Wing Commander, 36042

Royal Air Force

Who died on

Sunday, 11th April 1943, Aged 30.

Kenneth was the third son of Mr and Mrs Thomas E Smith of Lyndhurst.

KEN SMITH by WILLIAM ROTHENSTEIN

His father was Clerk to both to the New Forest Magistrates and to the New Forest Rural District Council and Guardians.

He was educated at Charterhouse and Corpus Christi College, Oxford. Commissioned into the RAF in 1935, he was promoted to Flight Lieutenant in March 1939. He married Esme, elder daughter of Captain Cecil Sutton MBE and in 1940 they had a son, named Bruce.

On 3rd September 1939 his bomber was amongst those which attacked units of the German Grand Fleet in Wilhemshaven in the first raid of the war. He was promoted Squadron Leader in 1940 and acting Wing Commander in November of that year.

He was rated as being one of the RAF's most experienced pilots being twice "Mentioned in Despatches" and was awarded the Distinguished Service Order in May 1941 whilst commanding 58 Squadron at RAF LINTON-ON-OUSE.

In announcing the award the citation stated that he had been engaged in active operations against the enemy over a long period. After recalling his participation in the first raid of the war added that:

"Since then he has taken part in many bombing missions over Germany in addition to many convoy escorts.

Throughout the whole period he has displayed exceptional powers of leadership, courage and determination and has undoubtedly contributed in a large measure to the operational efficiency of the squadron."

He assumed command of 9 Squadron on 15th March 1943. Ten days earlier, what Harris called the Battle of the Ruhr, had started with an attack on the Krupps works at Essen. Such raids now had the benefit of support from high-flying Mosquito aircraft equipped with the blind bombing device called "Oboe". This beam-device placed pathfinder aircraft over the target and signalled when to release Target Markers, thus significantly increased bombing accuracy.

In order to keep the defences spread across Germany, other more far-ranging raids were also made. On 11 April 1943 Kenneth took-off from RAF WADDINGTON on one such an operation to Frankfurt. He was piloting a Lancaster III bomber serial number ED501 WS-R. He took most of F/Lt. Cowan's crew for this, his fourth sortie since taking command.

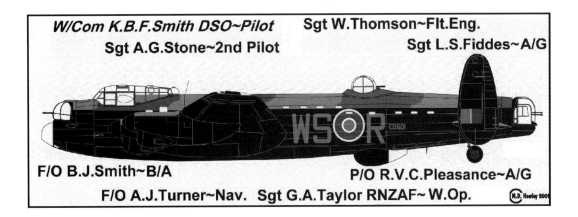

The aircraft crashed near Mainz.

Sgt Taylor has no known grave. Kenneth Smith is buried with the other members of his crew in **Rheinberg War Cemetery**, Germany in

Plot 8, A 6.

REGINALD MEADEN

Warrant Officer Class II, 5500234

5th Battalion, Hampshire Regiment

Who died on

Thursday 22nd April 1943, Aged 22.

Reg's father, George Meaden, hailed from near Winchester. He was a gardener by profession, specialising in the restoration and development of gardens in all parts of southern England. The return for this skill was 30 shillings a week and a house. It was therefore in the nature of things that the family was very mobile and that his sons

REG MEADEN

Reg and Ron both had an unsettled education. In the 1930's George worked at Hincheslea, where he was cowman, gardener and bailiff. He then moved on to work as head gardener for the Morants, living in Reynolds Cottage in Mill Lane. After the war he moved to Ford Cottage to look after the Morant's 9-acre smallholding.

According to Reg Meaden, who lives in Lyndhurst and shares the same name as his cousin, Uncle George was always talking of his experiences as a Sergeant in the First World War. It was therefore no surprise when, before the war, Cousin Reg joined a Territorial battalion of his father's old regiment - the Hampshires.

In 1939 the 1/4th, 2/4th and 5th Hampshire Territorial battalions formed the 128th Brigade of the 43rd (Wessex) Division. In 1940 this brigade became part of GHQ Mobile Reserve before moving to East Kent for coastal defence duties.

In August 1942 it became part of 46th division and on 6th January 1943 it embarked on the LEOPOLDVILLE at Gourock for North Africa.

The brigade arrived at Bone on 17th January and by the end of the month occupied a defensive position astride Hunts Gap (see Bill Close page 219). 5 HAMPS were posted, with 155 Battery RA, 12 miles ahead at Sidi Nsir to blunt the expected attack on the main position.

Von Arnim attacked Sidi Nsir on 26th February using three battalions of parachute troops and heavy tanks. By evening, the battalion and the 9 survivors of its supporting 25 Pounder battery withdrew, having stopped an enemy who were desperately determined to break through to Hunts Gap. The 200 survivors of the battalion then occupied a portion of the defences at Hunts Gap and awaited their next battle. By 2nd March the German attack at Hunts Gap was finally defeated, although the brigade remained in contact with the enemy there until early April.

On 5th April 128 Brigade moved 100 miles south to take part in an attack on the Fondouk gap. The capture of the Gap would enable 6th Armoured Division to pass through and intercept the Africa Corps retreating in the face of Montgomery's advance from Egypt. This was successfully achieved with 5 HAMPS capturing the northern part of the Gap. On 11th April 128 Brigade was withdrawn for a ten-day rest prior to taking part in its next battle at Bou Arada.

The brigade attacked the rocky ridge of Bou Arada at 3.30 a. m. on the 22nd April 1943. The Herman Goering Division, who were expecting the attack, held this feature. The objective of 5 HAMPS was a hill they called "Brer Rabbit" This they initially believed they had captured, but as the mist cleared, Ber Rabel was seen to be still ahead. It proved too strong to take and, for the rest of the day, the unit was heavily shelled and mortared.

Reg Meaden was one of the many Hampshire men who died that day.

The following day the Germans withdrew. On the 7th May Tunis was captured and the North African campaign was over.

Reg is buried in the **Medjez-el-Bab War Cemetery**, Tunisia, in

Grave 11.A.9.

ANTHONY CHARLES O'DONNELL

Aircraftman 2nd Class, 1600881

Royal Air Force Volunteer Reserve

Who died on

Saturday, 19th June 1943, Aged 21.

Tony was the youngest son of Mr & Mrs George O'Donnell of Broceste, Meerut Road, Brockenhurst. This house has now been absorbed into the complex of the Cloud Hotel. He was born on 14th February 1922 and was admitted aged 5 to the Catholic School at Lymington on 10th January 1928, when the school records noted

TONY O'DONNELL

that the school opened with an attendance of 45 out of 47 scholars. Six weeks later, on 23rd February, the same records note that his sister Betty, aged 10, was killed in a motor accident.

The family was a large one comprising older siblings David, Roderick, Leonard, Kathleen, Elizabeth and John all of whom travelled daily to and from school by train. They all left school when they reached 14 years of age.

At the age of 15 years Tony was apprenticed to Gamble & Son, the builders at Lyndhurst where he mainly did carpentry. He was a popular lad who enjoyed sports and played for the village football team. He also had a reputation as a long distance runner.

He also joined the local unit of the St. John's Ambulance Brigade. When war was declared he automatically became a member of the First Aid Party of the local Civil Defence. Later, he joined the Brockenhurst Air Training Corps.

He enlisted into the RAF in 1941 and was posted to 51 Squadron, part of 4 Group at RAF SNAITH, an airfield near Selby in Yorkshire. Family memory recalls that Tony trained as an air gunner and completed several missions over enemy territory.

On Saturday 19th June 1943 the Station armourers were at work preparing the high explosive bombs, some of which were delayed-action fused, for that night's attack against the Le Creusot armaments factories.

At 1320 hours a serious explosion in the bomb dump shook the airfield. Fire broke out amongst some incendiary bombs and further explosions continued to occur well into the night. A reconnaissance of the dump the following morning showed 22 live 1000-lb bombs, some of which were fused with a delay time of up to a week. The dump was therefore cordoned off and the nearby LNER main line to the North closed. An aerial reconnaissance reported a number of bodies.

The following Saturday work began on defusing ammunition in the wrecked dump. Anthony O'Donnell was one of the ten bodies that were recovered. One body, however, remained unidentified. This started a rumour that the explosion was not an accident, but sabotage.

The funeral for all the dead was held at Selby Abbey on 30th June and was attended by relatives. Anthony was buried with full military honours in **Selby Cemetery** in:

Grave 5278.

**NOT MY WILL BUT THINE
BE DONE, O LORD.
MOTHER OF SORROWS
PRAY FOR HIM. R.I.P.**

FRANCIS SAMUEL HODDER

Group Captain

Royal Air Force

Who died on

Monday 6th September 1943, Aged 37.

Frank was born on 11th February 1906 in Johannesburg, the elder son of Colonel Samuel and Maud Hodder. He was brought up in County Cork and joined the RAF on a Short Service Commission in 1925. Five years later he was granted a Regular Commission as a Flying Officer in the General Duties Branch of the RAF.

"TWINKLE" AND FRANK ON THEIR WEDDING DAY

During the following 7 years he was engaged on flying operations in cooperation with the Army in Iraq and Aden. He also had a spell at RAF CALSHOT in 210 (Flying Boat) Squadron as well as experiencing other operational and engineering duties. He was assigned to various courses with the Army in Armament and Gunnery and Chemical warfare. During these years he flew a wide range of aircraft ranging from fighters and bombers to seaplanes.

Frank was an outstanding athlete, representing both the RAF and the Combined Services at rugby and cricket. He also played rugby for the London Irish, and for Kent, and gained an Irish international trial.

In 1937 he attended the Staff College at Andover, after which he was assigned to Intelligence duties in HQ No.1 (Bomber) Group at Abingdon. From here he flew around the country identifying locations for new airfields required for the forthcoming conflict.

For the first five months of the war he was in France and was Mentioned in Despatches for brilliant work with the Advanced Air Striking Force headquarters staff.

In January 1940 he married Evelyn "Twinkle" Bowden Smith, whose family was formerly of Careys Manor Brockenhurst.

He was promoted Wing Commander in March 1940 and was appointed Liaison Officer on engineering duties firstly with Messrs. Rootes at Speke in Liverpool and then with the Handley-Page Aircraft Company in North London. In March 1942 he was promoted Group Captain. and was attached to HQ Bomber Command before being appointed, in July 1943, Station Commander at RAF SYERSTON in Nottinghamshire.

This RAF Station was home to 61 and 106 Squadrons, part of 5 Group, Bomber Command. August 1942 had been an awful month for 61 Squadron with 13 of its 16 operational crews reported missing - more than the combined total of its losses for the rest of the year. Station Commanders were not required to fly but, clearly, this was widely ignored as, in 1943, six were either killed or became prisoners of war.

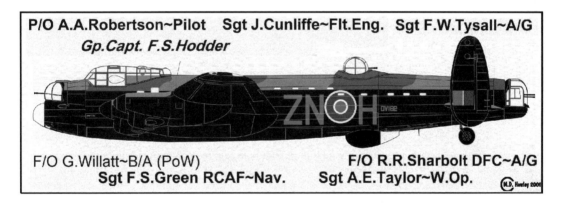

P/O A.A.Robertson~Pilot   Sgt J.Cunliffe~Flt.Eng.   Sgt F.W.Tysall~A/G
Gp.Capt. F.S.Hodder

F/O G.Willatt~B/A (PoW)   F/O R.R.Sharbolt DFC~A/G
Sgt F.S.Green RCAF~Nav.   Sgt A.E.Taylor~W.Op.

Frank Hodder took off at 1950 on the 6th September 1943 from SYERSTON in Lancaster Mk. 111 DV 182-ZN to bomb Mannheim. The aircraft was attacked by a night fighter whose opening burst of fire killed the pilot and mortally wounded the flight engineer. Fire engulfed the aircraft after which there was no further communication. Seven of the crew including Frank Hodder and Sgt. Taylor – an American from Boise Idaho - were killed. Only one member of the crew, F/O G Willatt, survived as a prisoner of war.

Frank left a widow and two sons who lived at Ash Cottage. They all moved to Springers Cottage in 1944, where "Twinkle" lived until 1998. She still lives in Brockenhurst.

Group Captain Hodder is buried in **Rheinberg War Cemetery**, Germany in:

Collective Grave 16, A 3-7.

ROGER ASH

Captain

31 Field Regiment Royal Artillery

Who died on

23 September 1943, Aged 32.

Roger's father was a dentist who is remembered as having his practice, before the war, in Fern Cottage - opposite Lloyds Bank in Sway Road. At some stage during the war he gave up the practice to Mr Cork, who had been bombed out of his premises in Southampton.

Roger was born in Stanmore or Bushey, the eldest of three brothers - the others being Mark and Michael

He joined the Gunners and was posted to 31st Field Regiment Royal Artillery which, in 1943, was operational in North Africa under the command of Lt. Col. S. L. A. S. Rudd- Clarke. The War Diary provides an interesting insight into the activity of a gunner unit in Egypt at that time.

__Sept 1.__ Six of our 6 year or more men left for home as a result of the new procedure whereby 1/5th of all such men leave monthly. Universally felt to be a step in the right direction, which should have been taken months ago. Yet letter from GHQ accused all units of not making adequate efforts to get their men home.

__Sept 2.__ Div Arty W/T exercise. Lecture for all officers in 7 Bde NAAFI tent. __Capt. R. B. Ash and Capt R. B. W. G. Wake rejoined unit from ME School of Arty.__

__Sept 3.__ Memorial service. C.O. left for Cairo to see Col. Cavanagh about officers.

__Sept 4.__ Orders for move. C.O. returned.

__Sept 5.__ Advance Party under Capt. T. B. Wood left for Palestine. Major J. F. Gilbertson rejoined from hospital.

__Sept 6.__ Road party left under command of Major T. A. Temple. C.O. left independently for Palestine. Lecture for all officers by Major T. Kitcat MC RA on "Submarines".

Sept 7/8. *Cleaning up of camp area and returning of tentage to stores.*

Sept 9/10. *Baggage sent off by train. Lieut E. S. A. Antrobus rejoined from Camouflage Course. Lieut A. H. Chambers proceeds on Messing Officers Course.*

Sept 11. *Train Party left for Palestine.*

Sept 12. *Train party arrived Rehovoth 1730 hrs. Met with transport at station. Area had been changed from Qastine to near Jerusalem. Arrived there about 2000 hrs. Lieuts. G. F. Thompson and O. N. Roberts rejoin unit from courses at M.E. School of Arty.*

Sept 13/14. *Organising of new camp areas. Lieut D. Radcliffe proceeds to No. 1 MEOSB for interview in respect of application for Permanent Regular Army Commission.*

Sept 15. *Lt (QM) arrived with Rear Party.*

Sept 16. *Training now in full swing. Btys each having one Bn. and one Bty day per week.*

Sept 17. *Weekly medical class started, to be held every Friday. One officer and two NCO's arrived on attachment from 10 Ind Div. Visit of CRA and BMRA. Lieut J. A. Evens rejoined unit from Offrs MT Course. Lieut A. E. Burrows posted to unit from BDRA.*

Sept 19. *2 Officers and 4 NCO's arrived on attachment from 10 Ind Div. Lieut A. H. Chambers rejoined unit from Messing Officers Course.*

Sept 20. *C.O. and Adj left for visit to Mtn W. T. C. RQMS T. C. Light left the Regiment. Five Lieuts posted to this unit from BDRA.*

Sept 21. *FFI and foot inspections.*

Sept 22. **C.O. and Adj returned from Mtn W.T.C. to learn the sad news that Capt R. B. Ash and L/Bdr Smith V. had been killed in an accident in which their carrier had overturned.**

Sept 23. **Funeral of Capt R. B. Ash and L/Bdr Smith V. at Ramleh. Large attendance from Regiment.**

The grave of Captain Roger Ash is to be found at **Ramleh War Cemetery**, Israel, in

Plot 3. G. 19.

231

THOMAS ERIC KIRWAN DONALDSON

Commander, Royal Navy

HMS KONGONI

Who died on

Tuesday 26th October 1943, Aged 44.

Eric Donaldson was born on 28th May 1899 to Walter and Claribel Donaldson. Walter was, at the time, the postmaster at Brooklands, Surrey.

The Electoral Roll for Brockenhurst for 1924-1926 shows him living in The Weirs Cottage. On 31st July 1926 he married Muriel Jean MacBaimy at the Church of St. Michael and All Angels at Lyndhurst. After the Second World War Muriel moved to Litchfield, Staffordshire.

Eric joined the Royal Navy in May 1912 as a Cadet. On the outbreak of war, aged 15, he was appointed Midshipman aboard HOGUE, an obsolete 12,000-ton cruiser of the CRESSY class, completed in 1902.

Seven weeks later this ship, as part of the Seventh Cruiser Squadron, was patrolling the Dogger Bank and Broad Fourteens area looking for German warships. On 21st September bad weather forced escorting destroyers to return to Harwich. In an effort to conserve coal and thus stay longer at sea the HOUGE and its sister ships ABOUKIR and CRESSY reduced speed to 10 knots and steered a steady course. In calmer conditions the following day the German submarine U-9, commanded by Lieutenant Commander Otto von Weddigen, sighted the squadron and torpedoed ABOUKIR. The other two cruisers stopped to lower boats and rescue survivors - and within the hour were promptly torpedoed in their turn. Weddigen, Germany's most successful U-Boat commander at this stage of the war, was promoted to command the much superior U-29. On 18th March 1915, this new submarine was rammed and sunk, with the loss of all hands, by the battleship DREADNOUGHT.

Eric survived this sinking and after three weeks leave "to recover from the shock" was appointed to ORION, a 22,500 ton Super-Dreadnought completed in 1912 and the first ship to be armed with 13.5 inch guns. He served on this modern battleship for most of the war. Twelve days before the Battle of Jutland, when the ship was on its way to Cromarty, he was wounded by a bullet in the left leg and hospitalised. Captain Buckhouse, however, noted his conduct as

"Promising in development"

and Eric was promoted to Senior Midshipman in April 1917.

In September 1917 he was appointed to MARIGOLD, a "Flower Class" Fleet Minesweeper of 1200 tons. Completed in May 1915 it was manned by 77 Officers and Ratings. Despite not impressing Captain Holland he passed his exams and was promoted to Sub-Lieutenant in March 1918. He finished the war serving in BELLEROPHON; an obsolescent Battleship completed in 1909. In the course of this commission Captain Chetwold noted that

"He will make a good officer."

After the war he continued his Naval career being promoted Acting Lieutenant on 15th December 1919. After courses and brief service on the destroyer PARKER he applied for service on submarines. Promoted Lieutenant in 1920 he did his submariners course at the end of the year and was appointed Third Hand to L 18 in October 1921, moving later to L 52. It was noted, at this time, that he was

"Conscientious, keen and anxious to get on."

Indeed in 1924 he was awarded both the Ryder Memorial Prize and £10 with a Certificate of Merit in the annual examination in French. The following year he was appointed to TITANIA as a reserve First Lieutenant for its Flotilla submarines. At the same time, however, he began to be hospitalised with a series of abdominal complaints. Despite being selected in 1926 to command the new fast submarine R10 a further deterioration in his health led, on 16th December 1927, to his being invalided out of the service. His disability was noted as being aggravated by service and his pension of £169 a year was consequently exempt from income tax.

In 1938 he was reassessed as

"Fit for service in an emergency"

and the following year saw him back in Naval uniform as a Commander attending a six months course in Naval ordnance. In 1941 he was on the staff of the Inspectorate of Naval Ordnance at Plymouth. Despite a reoccurrence of his ulcers and gastritis he was appointed to the Naval Ordnance Depot at HMS KONGONI, the Naval shore base at Durban, South Africa.

He died in Durban on 26th October 1943.

He is buried in **Durban (Stellawood) Cemetery**, Kwazulu Natal, South Africa, in

Block F Grave 41

WALTER CHARLES CLARK

Driver, T/275479

Royal Army Service Corps
Attached
35 Light Anti-Aircraft Regiment, Royal Artillery

Who died on

Saturday 13th November 1943, Aged 40.

Walter was the son of Henry and Susan Clark who lived in Martin's Road, Brockenhurst. He was born and brought up in the village attending the local school. He married Emily Jackson and had a son Owen and a daughter Edna Dorothy.

WALTER CLARK

Walter worked as a gardener for the Trotters in North Weirs. Being active he was a keen sportsman playing for both the cricket and football teams of the village. A knee problem, however, resulting in a cartilage operation, somewhat curtailed these pursuits. He was a member of the British Legion and frequently went to the clubhouse, informing the family that he was

"Going down to the Legion."

He was an early member of the Home Guard before being called up for army service.

He left home on 9th October 1941, aged 38 and joined the Royal Army Service Corps as a driver, being attached to the 35th Light Anti-Aircraft Regiment in 18 (Eastern) Division.

This Division left the UK to reinforce Malaya Command against the anticipated Japanese invasion. Churchill's attempt to divert the Division to the Middle East was frustrated by the Australian Prime Minister who warned that such an act would be "an inexcusable betrayal." It therefore sailed into Singapore in February 1942, in the last days before the Japanese captured the city.- virtually straight into captivity. Walter was initially presumed missing, but on 9th November 1943 his wife received notification that he was a Prisoner of War. He was one of the many sent to work on the Thai/Burma railway.

On 23rd January 1946 the family was notified that he had died of beriberi at Kanchanaburi Hospital on 13th November 1943.

Walter is buried at **Kanchanaburi War Cemetery** in Thailand in:

Plot 2.B. 34

Owen and his wife Glenda have twice visited Walter's grave.

On the first occasion in 1976 they asked a gardener for directions only to realise that he was actually, at that moment, cleaning Walter's grave.

'Father died in land of friends'

SIR: As a son of former prisoner of war I have just achieved a 30-year ambition to visit my father's grave in Kanchanaburi. He died during construction of the infamous "Death Railway."

Until now I have always felt as though he was buried in a far off land, having seen him go away a happy man, never to return, when I was twelve years old. I had already lost my mother at the age of four.

My wife and I have had the opportunity at last, to come with a group of ex-POW's and my feelings have changed completely. I find him not buried, as in the poem, "in some forgotten corner of a foreign land" but in a beautiful country with wonderful people.

It was difficult over the years to change those first thoughts as a young boy when I knew he had died so far away from home. At the service which was held in Kanchanaburi Cemetary, those thirty years seemed as a void and my wife and I felt as though we were attending his funeral.

The peace of mind I have now, though emotional, has made this journey so worthwhile it is difficult to express in words. My thoughts as a boy have now changed to knowing my father was not buried among strangers. The Thai people risked their own lives to help the prisoners and although my father did not return, I shall never forget them. They are people who are kind-hearted and with a deep sincerity.

I feel the warmth for them that they have shown to us, and I shall never again think of the place my father is buried as far away, but in a land of friends.

Yours Faithfully,
Owen W. Clark

In 1982, in Singapore, they accidentally met a Major John Marsh - who had been Walter's Commanding Officer. He was there to lay a wreath at Krangi Cemetery on behalf of the RASC, but insisted that it should be laid by Owen and Glenda.

CECIL ROBERT HILL

Private, 5505794

1st Battalion, The Queen's Royal Regiment (West Surrey)

Who died on

Thursday 2nd December 1943, Aged 28

Cecil was the only son of Alfred and Alice Hill who lived in Alva, Park Close, Brockenhurst. Cecil was born on 10th July 1915, the youngest of four children. He had three sisters; Alfreda, born in 1910, Mona, born in 1912 and Ellen, born in 1913. Ellen now lives in Birchy Hill, Sway; Mona lives in Park Close and Alfreda in Bentley Grange, Brockenhurst.

Cecil was educated at the Church of England School in Sway Road, Brockenhurst. He suffered alopecia and was bald at an early age. He was employed at Plumbley's Stores, Water's Green, Brockenhurst, which was managed by his father, who was also the preacher at the Methodist church in the village.

CECIL HILL

A gentle, quiet chap he loved the peace and solitude of the New Forest and was an accomplished artist with a sketchbook and pencil, which he used to capture local scenes. He also painted portraits and caricatures.

He had a developed skill in woodwork, which started as a pastime, producing fretwork items encouraged by the "Hobbies" magazine of that time. He went on to make model ships and a banjo. He could also play both the violin and mandolin.

He enlisted in the Queen's Royal Regiment and after training was sent to Burma by way of India.

Whilst in India he was browsing through a street market stall and found a book on the New Forest. With his great interest in the forest he purchased the book and sent it back to his parents in Brockenhurst. The book is still with a family member today.

He was killed in action in Burma on Thursday 2nd December 1943.

A letter from his Company Commander to the family dated 27th August 1944 reports:

"Your son was killed whilst returning from a company patrol.

It was through his giving the alarm and his unfortunate death that the warning was given to one of my posts that a Japanese patrol was trying to enter our defences.

The Jap patrol leader killed your son with his sword as a result of a typical Jap ruse of low cunning. The Jap announced himself as a Gurkha and naturally your son got up to investigate.

As a result of your son's action three Japs were killed, including the patrol leader, and more were wounded."

He lies in **Taukyan War Cemetery**, Myanmar (formerly Burma) which is administered by the Commonwealth War Graves Commission.

Grave 4.F. 20.

After the war the Pioneer Platoon of his Regiment built a **Memorial at Rangoon** to those of its members who had died in Burma. One of the inscriptions reads:

In Memory of
Private Cecil Robert Hill
1st Bn The Queens Royal
Regiment (West Surrey)
Thursday 2nd December 1943.
Aged 28.

RANGOON CATHEDRAL MEMORIAL DEDICATION

He is also remembered by his family with an inscription on his mother's grave in **St Nicholas Churchyard** at Brockenhurst.

His name is also commemorated on the **Methodist Church Memorial** (see page 119).

1944

Military activity was now becoming very focused towards the invasion of Europe.

THE HOME FRONT

In January 257, 263 and 486 (New Zealand) Squadrons of 2nd Tactical Air Force came to Beaulieu.

They stayed for three months and were tasked with attacking V1 launch sites in Northern France as these "Doodlebugs" were beginning to fall on southern England. They also attacked supply and communications targets as part of the pre-invasion disruption of enemy forces. To avoid radar they crossed the Channel at very low level!

From April the 365th Fighter Group of the 9th US Air Force, flying Thunderbolt fighters, occupied Beaulieu airfield making daily raids over France.

365 FIGHTER GROUP THUNDERBOLTS READY FOR TAKE-OFF FROM BEAULIEU IN 1944

At the end of June they moved to captured airfields in Normandy. They, in turn, were replaced by B26 Marauder light bombers.

With so many aircraft Beaulieu couldn't accommodate everyone so up to a hundred personnel - mainly officers - were billeted in Brockenhurst.

Robert Banister remembers that his mother had two such (one a Thunderbolt pilot, Harry Clark, who was subsequently killed in autumn 1944) who were collected by a Jeep around 7 o'clock and returned to sleep in the evening. Virtually all homes with spare rooms had airmen billeted on them.

Robert recalls

> *"They were a nice set and were welcomed and made as comfortable as possible - especially recognising the danger the operational ones faced every day. Certainly my mother became very fond of Harry Clark, who flew back from France one day, shortly before he was killed, to bring her some "Normandy" butter - a great treat at that time."*

Everyone was very conscious of their operations since with so many aircraft it took the bombers and fighters up to 15-20 minutes orbiting above Brockenhurst to form up for a raid. Approximately 2 hours later they would be back, but sometimes, sadly, as smaller formations. At the peak they were making two sorties a day. They were a very tangible evidence of the preparations for D-Day, whilst the soldiers waited and prepared for the landings.

In the village the area alongside Sway Road from Brookley Farm to Woodpeckers and from Robin Cottage to Collyers Road was covered in concrete blocks to provide hard standing for trucks. Up the right hand side of all the roads from Avenue Road to Woodlands Road numbered markers were put, spaced to accommodate medium-sized vehicles. Parking bays were marked out along Sway Road and also up the Lymington Road from Tile Barn Farm to Salmons (Q8) garage. A Nissen-hutted camp was built in Royden Wood and Brockenhurst Park was prepared for becoming a huge tented camp.

On the railway, trainloads of equipment were arriving. seven new sidings had been built at Brockenhurst to relieve pressure at Eastleigh. Tanks were being driven down the length of the trains - up and down the well wagons in order to unload. None were reported as falling off! The tanks, bren-gun carriers and trucks were driven to the coast to be prepared for shipment. The only casualties were when a Bern gun carrier shot across the Lymington road into the fence at the corner of Mill Lane and when a tank took the side off the Island Shop.

Early April saw the arrival of one of the first units - a Signals formation with some Engineers. It was an odd lot comprising a 10 ton wireless truck, a similar support truck, two Humber wireless cars and two half -tracks. They were parked in East Bank Road and stayed there until just before D-Day. Nearer to D-Day all the parking bays became filled and the Military Police set up their tents at all the road junctions - The Rise, Latchmoor, etc. The whole village became a one-way system. No traffic was allowed to enter Sway Road at Latchmoor. Nothing was allowed through the watersplashes. The only traffic allowed to travel along this road towards the village originated from its side roads which then had to turn down The Rise and go along Meerut Road, Waters Green and Grigg Lane before it could enter Brookley Road.

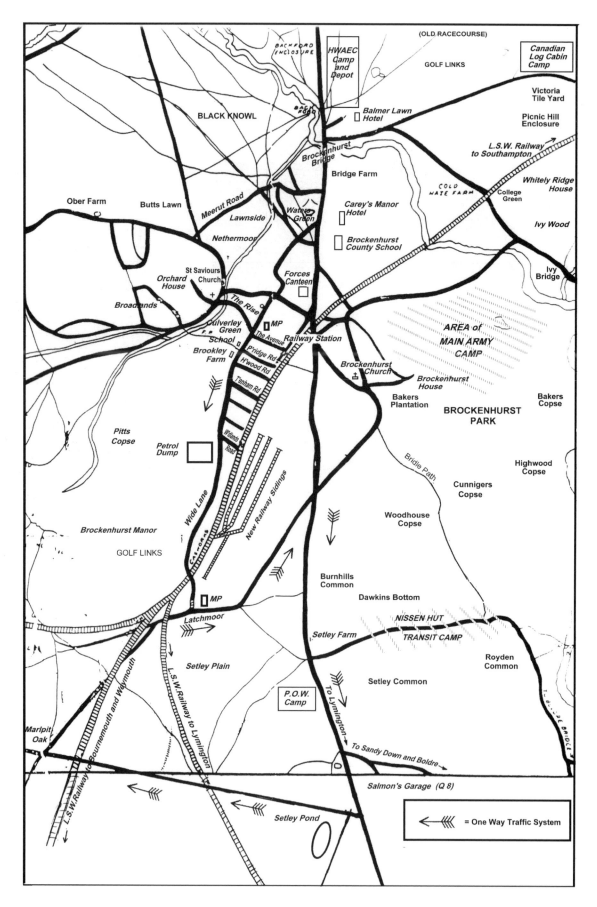

BROCKENHURST IN 1944

The Americans. During the year the Americans arrived in Brockenhurst, replacing the Canadians. They occupied the all the hotels and were billeted with some of the village families.

Their arrival signalled the opportunity for local children to be introduced to chewing gum. It is reliably reported that the opportunity was enhanced if an American at the Morant Hall dances befriended your older sister!

Stan Read, in this photograph, and John Larcombe were Telegraph Boys at the Post Office in May 1944 and so had daily contact with the U.S. Army Post Office located in the Cricket Pavilion at Balmer Lawn. One day they were told to position themselves at a particular spot of a closed road along which came a cavalcade carrying Churchill and Eisenhower to inspect the troops.

Harold Wheeler's memory of the occasion is that he was unable to go home for dinner because of the road's closure!

Terry Wingate gives a glimpse of this time:

> *"One spring day in 1944 my finely tuned 10-year-old ears picked up an approaching distinctive throb. Pausing, I waited to see if, whatever it was would turn off the main road into Meerut Road. It did. Looking across the green a bevy of white helmeted motor cyclists riding Harley Davidsons hove into view, followed by a Jeep, followed by more Harley Davidsons. They slowly meandered along giving me time to jump on my bike and pursue them.*
>
> *At the end of Meerut Road I saw a large number of troops formed up in a huge square. The Jeep turned onto the bridle path, travelled about 100 yards and stopped. "God", in the form of General Montgomery, stood up in the Jeep and gave a pep talk to the assembled men.*
>
> *My abiding memory is of some men in the rear rank talking amongst themselves. I remember feeling astonished, then angry, doing that - whilst the man who was controlling their fate was speaking!"*

In mid May the village suffered a bombing raid during which *Jean Gentle, William and Geoffrey Cumley* were killed.

As May progressed security dictated the imposition of a ban on troops fraternising with the locals. Relations between soldiers and the villagers were, however, good and a number of soldiers were making regular visits to homes for the luxury of a hot bath. With the aid of "lookouts" to give early warning of approaching "Red Caps" (Military Police), sergeants and all others in authority, such visits were able to continue. Bruce Smith, son of Ken Smith, remembers his grandmother - Beryl Sutton - advising him when he was four

> *"Not to approach the "Red Caps" as they were a dangerous breed."*

Bruce also remembers her in the garden of Heathfield House giving him a lesson as to the differences in sounds between German and British planes flying overhead.

> *"As far as I remember, the German ones sounded deeper, throatier, and nastier."*

As one convoy moved to a coastal assembly area so another took its place. At the beginning of June the village emptied and a total security blanket descended over the area. Bruce again recalls

> *"I remember going out one day and seeing nothing but tents and soldiers. One called Jim called me "Nipper" and gave me a football - bladder only. I suppose the poor devils knew that they wouldn't be using it again, or if they survived they would be too happy to worry. And of course they must have been British because of the nickname and the shape of the ball.*
>
> *I remember the tanks thundering down the road towards Lyndhurst on their way out. Then, suddenly, Waters Green was empty of soldiers. I went out to Waters Green with the football for days afterwards, hoping Jim would come back, kicking my precious football backwards and forwards till lunchtime."*

After D-Day, on the 6th June, reinforcement convoys continued to stage in Brockenhurst. After a while congestion eased and troops moved directly to the embarkation ports.

Robert Banister recalls the Flying Bomb, launched from near Cherbourg, that landed in the shooting range at Wilverley at the time of the invasion and notes that it was only the invasion itself that saved Brockenhurst and the whole surrounding South Coast area from heavy bombardment.

THE AIR WAR

The invasion on D-Day was supported by a greatly expanded and more flexible RAF, ranging from close-support aircraft and glider towing to short range bombers all covered by fighter escorts.

By this time, too, greater resources were being deployed to the long neglected Far East theatre and by mid 1944 we had started the advance to re-take Burma; a campaign in which air-borne and air-maintained army units played a significant part.

The unprecedented amount of flying inevitably led to an increase in flying accidents. In this context *James Banister* was shot down in April whilst completing pilot training and *Alfred Shilleto* died in September in a Wellington bomber training accident.

THE ARMY

The effect on the village of the "D" Day landings is described in the Home Front section. Happily no villager was killed in the landings or the subsequent breakout. *Ron Myles*, however, was killed in November in the subsequent advance through Holland.

Italy. By January 1944 the hard slog up the Italian peninsula had benefited from the Salerno landings and allied Forces had reached the Sangro and Garigliano rivers. The Anzio landings, however, 50 miles behind the German front, were not exploited and got bogged down. This stalemate was broken on 11th May when a concentrated advance up the Liri valley linked-up with the Anzio bridgehead. Rome was entered two days before the Normandy invasion. The Italian campaign, however, cost the lives of *Leslie Dukes* and *Sid Frowde*.

North Africa. Back in North Africa *Harold Cleveland* died from polio in September.

The Far East. The Burma Campaign continued in February and March with the Japanese attacks in the Arakan and at Imphal. This latter attack lasted for three months and cost the life of *Tony Eastwell* before being defeated. The successful defence of Imphal, however, broke the Japanese offensive.

By the end of the year the 14th army had crossed the Chindwin and Rangoon was taken in May 1945.

JAMES FRANCIS BANISTER

Flying Officer, 49769

Royal Air Force

Who died on

Friday 21st April 1944, Aged 24.

James - or "Jimmy", as he was always known in the family - was born on 24th January 1920. He was the second son born to Charles and Phyllis Banister, with Peter (see Page 187) being his eldest brother. The third and youngest son of the family - Robert Banister - presently lives in Kent and has been kind enough to provide information on his two brothers.

JAMES BANISTER

Jimmy followed Peter firstly to West Downs Preparatory School and then followed his father to Winchester College.

He started writing and drawing at an early age. All of his writing was complemented by sketches, which provided the material for later watercolours. He was a great countryman who loved the New Forest in all its facets. He walked and rode all over it recording dogs, horses, trees and views both for future use and to perfect his art.

He went up to Cambridge in 1938 and developed into a polymath expressing himself as a writer, poet and painter - particularly of the forest scenes. As well as being intellectually able he was a keen games player, possessed a great sense of humour and had a wide circle of friends. He lived his life by rigorous standards and his approach was that if there was a job to be done,

"Let's get on and get it done".

In wartime Britain this attitude had imbued the entire Banister family. His mother was the head of the W.V.S in Brockenhurst from 1942-45 and his elder brother Peter was already a career naval officer - a career that younger brother Robert was to follow in 1943.

246

Jimmy, therefore, volunteered to join the Army in November 1939 and was called up as a recruit to Canterbury Depot on 15th February 1940. He was commissioned into the Cheshire Regiment and served as a Platoon Commander in 1941/2 during the Siege of Malta.

The following poem, written at a difficult time in the Malta Siege, evokes both humour and reality.

LINES BY A STAFF OFFICER

WHO SEES NO FUTURE IN IT

1. Oh to be in Malta,
Now that April's here
And the drowsy hum of Junkers
Falls gently on the ear
The Spring is in the air, boys
And a big plot coming in,
And we're running short of whisky,
And we're running short of gin.

2. I feel I've got a touch of "Dog",
They're getting too b- near:
I think I'll just lie down,
But forty plus is coming in,
And heading for the town:
So we'll have to go below again,
And we're running short of ack-ack,
And we're running short of beer.

3. In rare moments of elation,
When I think they've made for home,
And I dream of all the bomb loads
That will shortly fall on Rome,
There's always that awakening
That shakes me all to bits,
As we're running short of Hurries,
And we're running short of Spits.

4. So there's very little left to bomb,
So they'll surely go away:
But there's nothing like vanity
To keep the ball in play:
So they have a crack at Hospitals,
And bomb the Gozo boats:
And we're running short of women,
And we're running short of goats

5. And we're running short of everything -
They've even rationed bread:
Pray God will help all future chaps
Who are sent to "HQ Med":
We've worn out all the Bofors guns
And every three point seven -
And the most we get for an epitaph
Is: "**Posted to HQ Heaven.**"

J. F. Banister, April 1942, Valletta.

Copyright Robert Banister 2001

In October 1942, having volunteered for the RAFVR, he transferred as a Pilot Officer and was sent to Moosejaw in Canada for flying training.

March 1944 saw Jimmy starting the final stages of his flying training as a fighter pilot with No. 7 (P) Advanced Flying Unit, before conversion to either Hurricanes or Spitfires. At this stage of the war the Germans had tasked a night flying unit 11/KG51, equipped with Messerschmitt 410s, to chase returning bombers and shoot them down as they landed at their bases in East Anglia. On 21st April Jimmy took off from RAF WALTON, flying an unarmed Miles Master on a night navigation exercise. He was shot down by one of these intruders and killed instantly.

In his final weeks he was fulfilled by the joy of flying.

Three days before he died he wrote his final poem "If I should Go" in the village of Wansford, near Peterborough, where an Elizabethan bridge crosses the River Nene, during what was an exceptionally warm and beneficent April. It reflects not only his talent but also his love of nature and what England meant to him.

His younger brother Robert visited the village in November 1999 and reports it as little changed.

After a service in St Nicholas Church Jimmy Banister was buried with full military honours in **Brockenhurst Churchyard**.

The inscription for Jimmy, taken from Psalm 139, reads:

"IF I SHALL CLIMB UP INTO HEAVEN THOU ART THERE.
IF I SAY PERADVENTURE THE DARKNESS SHALL COVER
ME THEN SHALL MY NIGHT BE TURNED INTO DAY."

IF I SHOULD GO

You cool grass of England will you remember me?
You April sky bluely through greening elm tops seen –
Will you think again of me great cedar tree
Whose quiet strength all afternoon has been
A shield about me, towering as a Church, and strong
Of root and husk, the reverend guardian of the lawn,
Will you remember me when I am gone?
And you, questing rivulet through gentle reed beds, bare
Beside you all this afternoon I've lain, and still
Caressed by cool grass fingers lie, and love the lullaby
Of the waters' murmuration by the mill:
Half asleep, and lulled there beautifully by
Rooks love talk, now harshly urgent, then
Gentle and beautiful, eloquent of spring.
Next year their nests will ride the elms again
And they'll be here, but not remembering.

Oh England, England, England you are mine
Locked in my heart, loved dearly
And all this day till stars shine
I'll lie with you, naked on grass, so nearly
Part of you; quiet grey roofs stand guard
Oh larks, sing on and river - who will sing when I have gone;
Sun shine near us daffodilled and daisy-starred
Among the grass; rooks speak your murmurous benison.

Oh England, England in the spring, I love
Your quiet elms, your daffodils,
Your spreading valleys, gentle skies above,
Quiet villages, the way your laughter fills
With lark song, rook and water talk,
And chiming of bells, murmur of bees,
And oh! Lingering May after May to walk
Among snow-blossomed cherry trees
To see the sunlight playing on ripples there,
And little fish jumping from quiet brownness,
And ducks happy among the mud; oh eye and ear
And memory are filled loving your loveliness!
Oh England you are in my heart and body - be it so -
You reared me, taught me how to love and to be free.
Oh faithless, heartless England, should I be called to go –
England beloved, beautiful, will you remember me?

J. F. Banister, 18.4.44 - Wansford, Near Peterborough.

ANTONY OWEN EASTWELL

Private, 6106839

1st Battalion, Seaforth Highlanders

Who died on

Monday 24th April 1944, Aged 21.

Tony Eastwell and his brother Geoffrey were the children of Cecil and Agnes Eastwell. The family lived above - and ran - the boutique shop in the village. One side of the shop catered for ladies, the other side for men. They later retired and lived in Partridge Road, Brockenhurst. Both brothers went to the village school.

Between the time Tony left University and joined-up he worked at Purkess's with deliveries.

He enlisted in the Seaforth Highlanders who, in 1943, were fighting on the Chindwin River. In February the battalion were part of a deception operation to confuse the Japanese over the location and intentions of Wingate's second incursion into Burma.

The scenario changed with the Japanese invasion of India in 1944. The Seaforths were tasked with cutting off part of the enemy forces by getting behind them to the west of Imphal at Kasom.

The Regimental History describes this phase of the battle thus:

> *"On 12th April, the battalion was given orders to attack and occupy the village of Kasom, destroy the Headquarters of the Jap 15th Division, which was thought to be there, and capture the Divisional Commander.*
>
> *According to Intelligence reports, the latter had an elephant to carry his personal kit, and was accompanied by his favourite Geisha girls."*

The village was taken, but not the Divisional Commander.

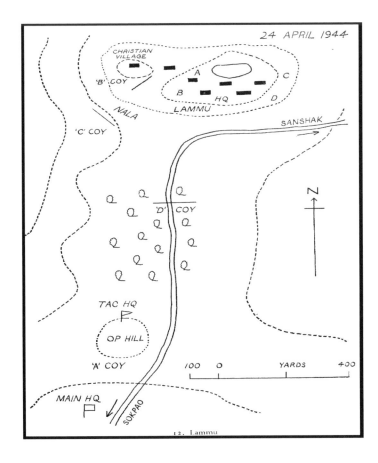

At 6.30 a.m. on 24th April the Battalion left Kasom with its objective being the next village of Lammu.

An hour later D Company came under heavy fire from Lammu, which was finally taken that evening by Battalion attack supported by artillery fire and air strikes.

Tony was killed in the attack, and his body not recovered.

His name is therefore recorded, along with 27,000 others, on the **Rangoon Memorial** in Burma on:

Face 17.

There is also a memorial to him on his grandparent's grave in **St. Nicholas churchyard.**

JEAN GENTLE, Aged 16,

WILLIAM CHARLES CUMLEY, Aged 43,
and
GEOFFREY CUMLEY, Aged 1,

Who all died on

15th May 1944,

Whilst all the pre D-Day activity was going a large air raid attacked Southampton in the early hours of 15th May and spilled over westwards. As a result Brockenhurst had its only air raid that resulted in fatalities.

The report on page 8 of the **DAILY ECHO** for Monday 15th May 1944 is graphic:

THREE DEATHS IN VILLAGE

When bombs fell on the outskirts of a South country village early today Mr Cumberley, a member of the Home Guard, was killed, and his year-old baby Geoffrey, and an evacuee child, Jean Gentle, also lost their lives. Mrs Cumberley is lying gravely injured in hospital. Their two other children, Charles and Jean, were only slightly hurt.

A bomb exploded at the rear of their bungalow, which was demolished.

Another bomb the front of a house occupied by Mrs Spencer and her five children. . .

"I heard it whistling," she said, "and it exploded outside my bedroom window. We all rushed into the passage. I grabbed the children and we took shelter in the kitchen, where we spent the rest of the night."

Mr Cumberley was on business in Belgium on the outbreak of war, and escaped from Brussels when the Germans invaded the country.

.

The rest of the Cumberley family were rescued by some American troops who were guarding a petrol dump on the other side of the road near the Golf Course. This dump contained stacks of 5-gallon square tins of fuel only protected by tarpaulins. As John Purkess has said - if the bomb had hit the dump it would have been an inferno.

Jean Gentle was buried on 20th May in **St Nicholas Churchyard** with the Reverend Haslam, Vicar of the parish, officiating. Her grave appears to be unmarked and has not been found.

Mary Pattison, the Clerk to the Parish Council, has confirmed that the Register of Deaths for the churchyard contains no mention of the burial of the two Cumberleys, or, indeed, anyone else at that, or near that, date.

Don Cording could not trace the appropriate Death Certificates for the two Cumberleys. His experience then led him to follow a phonetic approach, which resulted in successfully tracing death certificates for William Charles Cumley (43) and his one-year-old son Geoffrey, who both died in Brockenhurst

"Due to war operations"

on the 15th May 1944.

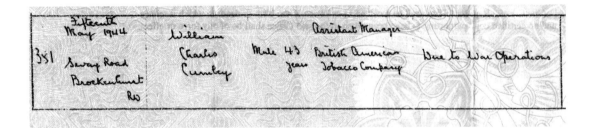

It is not known where William or Geoffrey are buried.

ALFRED CECIL SHILLETO

Flight Lieutenant, 122927

Royal Air Force Volunteer Reserve

Who died on

Thursday 13th July 1944, Aged 27.

Alfred was born in the village. When his mother died of TB he was brought up by his Grandmother Aida Dunkinson at Green View, Partridge Road, Brockenhurst. He went to the village school and was in the same class as Leslie Dukes and Harold Cleveland. All three of these classmates were to die over the coming twelve weeks. His photograph can be seen on page 142.

Ray Dunkinson, a cousin, knew him well and last met him in 1944 when both men were on leave. He tells Alfred's story.

From the local school he went to King Alfred's College, Winchester. He was a good dancer and a keen scout achieving King's Scout status. He was also interested in steam engines. He then went on to work for the New Forest Rural District Council at Lyndhurst.

In 1937/38, however, his Grandmother paid for some flying lessons. These changed his life. On gaining his private pilot's licence he joined the RAF Volunteer Reserve and thereby developed his flying skills.

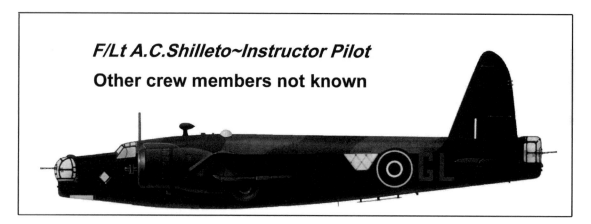

F/Lt A.C.Shilleto~Instructor Pilot
Other crew members not known

He was called up immediately war broke out and converted to Wellington bombers.

He flew on 39 operations and then was posted to train pilots at 14 Operational Training Unit at RAF MARKET HARBOROUGH.

Unfortunately on 13th July 1944, whilst taking a crew on a training flight, an accident occurred which resulted in two Wellingtons in a mid-air collision with the loss of all 16 crew, one of whom was Alfred.

He is buried in **St Nicholas's Churchyard**, Brockenhurst.

His name is also commemorated on the **Methodist Church Memorial** (see page 119).

HAROLD CLEVELAND

Gunner, 933652

144 (The Surrey and Sussex Yeomanry) Field Regiment, Royal Artillery

Who died on

Friday 1st September 1944, Aged 26.

Harold was born on 23rd June 1918 and was the son of Archibald and Ethel Cleveland of "Culverly View," Armstrong Road, Brockenhurst. The family also included his twin sister Bliss, two other sisters and a brother Archie. The Clevelands were a well-known family of Commoners owning cattle and horses in the forest.

His father served in the Royal Navy in the Great War and on discharge worked in a local garage. He was, for many years, a driver in the New Forest Ambulance, which was stationed at Brockenhurst. People still respect his excellent knowledge of First Aid acquired, apparently, during his naval service.

Harold was educated in the local school and is remembered as a good football player. He always wanted to be a butcher. He therefore started part-time work when he was 9 years old for Holtoms, the village butchers, and later, when he had left school, worked there full-time as a licensed slaughter man. His brother Archie, who still lives in the village, remembers that Harold enjoyed life and was

"A real lad."

He was particularly keen on motor cycles and at one time owned 11 of them in 11 months, either for use or for repair.

He was called-up at the very beginning of the war with two friends from the village - Fred Morgan and Bill Dorricott. They were all posted to the Royal Artillery and after training at Deepcut Harold was posted to 144 Field Regiment as a driver/mechanic.

HAROLD IN NORTH AFRICA IN JULY 1944

This regiment served throughout the North African Campaign. In August 1944, just before the regiment was due to return to England, he was given a weeks leave in Beirut. He wrote home during it saying that he was having

"A lovely time in the water, playing about with boats."

On 1st September 1944 the family received a telegram sent three days earlier, stating that Harold was ill in hospital. Another telegram received later that day reported his death. He died, aged 26, in a military hospital in Beirut from polio contracted locally.

He is buried in **Beirut War Cemetery** in

Plot 4 C11

LESLIE CYRIL DUKES

Private, 5500844

1/4th Battalion, Hampshire Regiment

Who died on

Monday 9th October 1944, Aged 27.

Leslie was the son of George and Emily Dukes who lived in Park Close, Brockenhurst. His father was a local builder whose name can still be seen on village manhole covers. Leslie appears to have gone to school in Sway but is well remembered, however, for playing football for Brockenhurst. After he had left school he went to work for Streets delivering, amongst other things, paraffin from their van. He later worked in his father's business. Les courted Kathleen, who worked in Brookley House, and after marriage they lived in Marchwood.

Les joined the Territorials just before the war, enlisting into 4th Battalion of the Hampshire Regiment.

There were so many volunteers that in August 1939 it became two battalions - the 1/4th and the 2/4th. With the addition of the 5th Battalion the Hampshire Regiment they became the 128th Brigade of 43rd Wessex Division.

This Brigade did not have an easy time in North Africa (see Reg Meaden page 222). 1/4th was particularly involved in the battle for Hunts Gap where they had taken the full brunt of the German attack.

On 7th September 128 Brigade sailed from Bizerta for Salerno. At 3.30 a.m. on 9th September 1/4th HAMPS landed on the left-hand beach as part of the initial wave of the assault. Despite heavy opposition the unit made good progress and moved into the foothills above Salerno.

LESLIE DUKES

The bridgehead held against strong German counter-attacks and on 20th the Germans began to withdraw northwards. Italy withdrew from the war on the 8th September and in the three weeks of fighting before Naples fell on 1st October 1/4th HAMPS lost 9 officers and 150 other ranks.

In the following six months 1/4 HAMPS fought their way northwards. On 12th October the unit was the assault battalion for crossing the Volturno and on the 19th January repeated the process for the crossing of the Garigliano. This was frustrated by the Germans who had opened sluices and caused the river to flood. They then attacked Monte Damiano, incurring casualties of 9 officers and 80 NCOs. and men. The 1/4th HAMPS gallantly defended Ornito on 19th February against three battalions of the Panzer Grenadier Regiment. The battle ended suddenly with the surrender of the Germans.

On 16th March 128 Brigade was withdrawn to Palestine for three months rest and retraining. It returned to Italy in August.

On 25th August 128 Brigade was the assault brigade tasked to

"BUST the Gothic Line."

In this phase 1/4th HAMPS captured and held Monte Gaudio. By the 31st August the battalion had penetrated the Gothic Line and a platoon commander, Lt. Norton, had been recommended for the Victoria Cross. This he was later awarded. In the last phase, four days later, 1/4th HAMPS captured Monte Gallera.

After resting the brigade was back in the line and on the 28th September tasked, once again, with leading the assault on a river crossing. Poor weather delayed the action on the River Fiumicino until the 7th October. 1/4 HAMPS crossed at midnight and occupied the Montigallo spur with the 2nd Battalion. This they held against fierce counter-attack for 36 hours cut off to their rear by the swollen river. The crossing of the Fiumicino is described in the Regimental History as

" A magnificent achievement."

Leslie Dukes, however, was killed in the heavy shelling and close-quarter fighting of this battle.

He is buried in **Assisi War Cemetery,** Italy in:

Plot II. H. 12.

His name is also commemorated on the **Methodist Church Memorial** (see page 119).

LESLIE RONALD MYLES

Corporal, 5495431

Royal Dragoons, Royal Armoured Corps

Who died on

Saturday 18th November 1944.

Leslie Myles lived in Sunnyholm, Partridge Road, Brockenhurst.

His mother was the local nurse who is still remembered kindly as "Nurse Myles." Part of the house was used for medical purposes and Molly Cleveland, amongst others, was born there. Nurse Myles also helped to lay out the dead, and often accompanied Archie Cleveland in the New Forest ambulance to accidents. In later years Leslie's father, Bernie sold Walls ice cream from a tricycle.

LESLIE MYLES

Leslie went to the village school and joined the 17/21st Royal Lancers in 1933. He served in this unit with fellow villager George Johnson in India for 6 years - without UK leave. They were both time-expired in summer 1939, but when war broke out both men were promptly called up into the Royal Dragoon Guards. Leslie was later posted to "A" Squadron 1st Royal Dragoons. This was an Armoured Car Regiment operating in a recce role in XII Corps under Lieut. Gen. N. M. Ritchie.

After the invasion of Europe in June this Corps had been involved in the advance through Belgium into Holland. On 3rd November the Royal Dragoons were ordered to relieve the Inns of Court Regiment on the Maas, just south of Grave. Here the 2nd Household Cavalry Regiment held a stretch of the river with Gunners and some Dutch Infantry. Ten days later the Household Cavalry were withdrawn and the Royal Dragoons took charge of the sector.

The enemy frequently put down shell and mortar fire and sometimes sent patrols across the river. The Royal Dragoons countered with aggressive patrolling. Leslie Myles was part of an eight-man patrol that went out on the night of the 18th November to lay mines. The Regimental History goes on to say that the patrol

"was caught, by complete coincidence, by a mortar bomb and entirely annihilated. Five men were killed and the remaining three injured."

In December 1944, Mr & Mrs Myles were officially informed that their second son, Leslie had been "killed in action" as a result of a mortar bomb exploding in a tree.

His Troop Commander wrote:

"As a corporal in charge of 6 men he was both competent and, at the same time, beloved by all who served under him – the greatest qualities a soldier can possibly possess. In his loyalty and honesty to me he was a man in whom I could place my utmost confidence to succeed in any job that he was called upon to carry out.

In the short time that I had the honour to be his commander he had carried out many deeds of the utmost bravery and devotion to duty, and I say that with complete sincerity.

Above all I admired and liked him as a man and it is in this respect that his loss will be so hard to replace, but it is to you that all my sympathies go, for to you his loss is irreplaceable."

At the time of his death Leslie had been recommended for "Mention in Dispatches". This was subsequently awarded posthumously.

He is buried in **Mook War Cemetery**, Holland in:

Plot II. E.8

SIDNEY HOWARD FROWDE

Corporal, 5501017

5th Battalion, Hampshire Regiment

Who died on

Monday 4th December 1944, Aged 25

Sidney was the son of James and Lisette Frowde who moved from Farnborough to "Fairfield," Avenue Road, Brockenhurst in 1938.

His father had been a barber in Selfridges in London and, when he came to the village, he bought the barber's shop next to the Foresters Arms. It was therefore a logical step for Sidney to become apprentice to his father in the trade. His sister still remembers that when his father was not present and the business was quiet it was not unknown for Sid to give free perms and hair styling to young ladies of the village. He had a good sense of humour, and was very enthusiastic about swimming and ballroom dancing.

SIDNEY FROWDE

Before the war he enlisted, with his brother, into the local Territorial unit of the 5th Battalion of the Hampshire Regiment. This battalion had fought in North Africa as part of 128 Brigade (see Reg Meaden on page 224) and had been in Italy since September 1943.

By the 15th September 1944 this brigade was once again part of a new fighting advance in which 5 HAMPS had an early success at Montescudo in surprising a platoon from an Austrian Mountain Regiment. On 7th October it took part in the assault crossing of the Fiumicino (see Leslie Dukes on page 259). On 7th November

HIS ORIGINAL GRAVE

5 HAMPS played a leading part in the successful battle of San Martino-in-Strada and by the 25th they had reached the Lamone river.

Sid was, at this stage, attached to the battalion's medics and had been trained as a unit chiropodist. Promoted to Corporal it is reported that he was very popular with the men of the battalion.

On the night of the 3rd December the brigade crossed the river and 5 HAMPS moved forward to capture Pideura. By the time they had fought their way close to this objective it was light and further advance was impossible. They therefore dug in and the village was finally captured three days later. This was the last battle the Hampshire Brigade was to fight in Italy.

Sidney Frowde was killed by a mortar bomb on 4th December 1944. He was one of the fifty-seven men of the battalion who had been killed in action since August.

At the time of his death he was engaged to a girl from London. Sid's sister Elsie still has the engagement ring, which was given to her by his fiancee.

Sidney is buried in **Forli war cemetery**, Italy, in:

Grave 1. C. 7.

1945

By February 1945 the Russians were occupying a front from the Baltic down to Hungary. The British were poised to cross the Rhine and the French and American Armies were driving the Germans out of Alsace. The Canadians were attacking into the Reichswald and the American Ninth Army under Patton had reached the Rhine at Coblentz.

On the 22nd March the Russians attacked strongly in Silesia, followed by advances against Hungary and Austria. By the 5th April they were in Vienna and by the 16th they started the final drive on Berlin. In Italy the allied 15th Army Group - including a Brazilian division - launched another offensive which this time led to the surrender of the German Armies in Italy on 2nd May. In Northwest Europe the western allied armies began, on 23rd March, the task of crossing the Rhine. This was successfully achieved but despite the end being near German resistance increased as the allied armies penetrated into Germany. It was in this late phase that **Ronnie Mutter** was to lose his life.

The Germans surrendered on this front on 4th May.

The Thanksgiving Service for the Second (British) Army records its part.

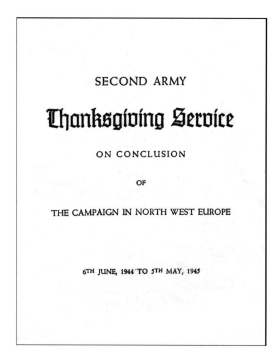

SECOND ARMY

Thanksgiving Service

ON CONCLUSION

OF

THE CAMPAIGN IN NORTH WEST EUROPE

6TH JUNE, 1944 TO 5TH MAY, 1945

THE PATH OF THE ARMY

1944

JUNE	6th	. . .	The Assault - NORMANDY
	27th	. . .	The ODON
JULY	9th	. . .	CAEN
	29th	. . .	CAUMONT
AUGUST	7th	. . .	MONT PINCON
	20th	. . .	FALAISE
	25th	. . .	The SEINE
SEPTEMBER	2nd	. . .	The SOMME
	3rd	. . .	BRUSSELS
	4th	. . .	ANTWERP
	3rd - 11th	.	The Canals - ALBERT and ESCAUT
	17th	. . .	ARNHEM
	17th - 29th	.	The Rivers - MAAS and WAAL
OCTOBER	22nd - 27th	.	'S HERTOGENBOSCH - TILBURG
NOV. 14th - DEC. 13th	.	The Rivers - MAAS and ROER
DECEMBER	21st	. . .	The ARDENNES

1945

JANUARY	13th	. . .	SITTARD
MARCH	24th	. . .	The RHINE
APRIL	5th	. . .	The WESER
	26th	. . .	BREMEN
	29th	. . .	The ELBE
MAY	2nd	. . .	The BALTIC

The Far East. In Burma an advance in the Arakan opened up new airfields and the defeat of the Japanese at sea enabled supplies to be landed on the Arakan coast. On 3rd May Rangoon was retaken. A planned invasion of Malaya proved unnecessary in the light of the Japanese surrender.

THE HOME FRONT

With the threat of invasion finally removed the six Church bells were serviced and rung again.

With night bombing also a thing of the past streetlights were fitted with shades and turned on up to 10.00 p.m. in the winter. They were maintained by Jack Place.

Cars that had been jacked-up on bricks for the duration were seen on the roads again as a small petrol ration became available to non-essential users.

Victory in Europe (VE) Day was celebrated in fine style by the village. Assuming that the announcement of peace would be made during the day the headmaster of the Grammar School had arranged that at a ceremony he would declare a two-day holiday. In the event the announcement was made on the Monday evening and the pupils just took two days off!

That evening there were bonfires in various parts of the village. John Larcombe recalls a large one on Waters Green, which was made larger through the involuntary addition of Captain Sutton's gates. Frank Rashleigh, the butler at Morant Hall, played his accordion for the communal singing.

Thanksgiving services and parades took place, with the Grammar School Cadet Forces parading at New Milton and Christchurch. These parades were popular with the cadets as the appearance of a Church Army tea wagon afterwards gave them the chance to buy a Mars bar without having to surrender coupons!

Victory over Japan (VJ) Day was celebrated in the village on 20th August, again with bonfires on Culverley Green and Waters Green. "Skip" Tiller, the headmaster of the Church of England School, had managed to get hold of some fireworks, which marked the celebration appropriately. The church bells were again rung.

The Peace. As time went on the troops were gradually demobilised and returned to the village and their civilian jobs. Rationing, however, remained and the war still seemed close with the Prisoner of War camp still full and local airfields still operational.

American and other troops departed, with some wartime romances blossoming into GI and Canadian Bride status.

Thankfully, so many did return.

The Cost. The war, however, had cost Brockenhurst - a village of just over 2000 people - at least forty dead.

RONALD GRAHAM MUTTER

Lieutenant, 314050

2nd Battalion Scots Guards

Who Died on

27th April 1945, Aged 19.

Ronnie was born on 16th July 1925 to William and Enid Mutter of Latchmoor House, Brockenhurst. A younger son Alan was born in 1931 and it is to him that the following information is mainly due.

RONNIE MUTTER

Ronnie spent his first 12 years in Scotland being educated initially at Ardvreck in Crieff, Perthshire and later at Harrow.

He returned to Brockenhurst in 1942 and joined the Home Guard. He loved dancing and would bicycle over to the Minstead hut, which seemed to be a favourite place during the war. He also had a horse, which was used to pull a trap. By 1944 however, after he was called up, his mother found that driving it to Brockenhurst had become perilous as all the armour and lorries awaiting D-Day upset the horse.

Ronnie also loved architecture and gardening, either of which could have been his future career.

He enlisted into the Scots Guards on 30th July 1943 and was commissioned into the 2nd Battalion on 24th March 1944.

After a last leave at Latchmoor, he joined his Battalion in France in March 1945 and took part in the advance towards Germany as a member of the Guards Armoured Division. Ronnie was in the Left Flank Company, which, on the 22nd April attacked Rotenburg capturing 600 prisoners. After two days rest and reorganisation the unit resumed its advance with the aim of cutting off 15 Panzer Grenadiers. There were also several Prisoner of War camps in the area to be liberated. At five in the morning the unit moved off and almost at once ran into strong opposition. They reached Ostertimke by evening at a cost of an officer and 4 guardsmen killed and 37 wounded. The next objective was to relieve the POW camp at Westertimke, which held nearly 8000 merchant seamen. The Regimental History records for the 27th April:

> *"There remained one more obstacle before Westertimke, and at 9 in the morning the Group moved forward to clear Kircktimke.*
>
> *Left Flank was on the right and F Company on the left, and the attack was made through the fields on either side of the road. Strong supporting fire was given by the 4.2 inch mortars and artillery, but the German shelling and mortaring was exceptionally heavy and Lieutenant R G Mutter, Left Flank, who had brought back valuable information about enemy positions after a patrol the previous night, was killed by a shell in the village."*

The report of his death arrived at his home on V.E. Day.

THE WAR MEMORIAL BENCHES ARE IN MEMORY OF RONALD MUTTER

He is buried at **Becklingen War Cemetery** Germany. The Grave Reference is:

1.C.8

THE AFTERMATH

Service personnel came back to a Britain were most of the wartime controls were still firmly in place. Travel abroad, apart from emigration was difficult due to severe currency controls. Finding employment was not necessarily easy as the full employment experienced during the war ceased as industries reorganised to peacetime trading conditions. Enemy prisoners of war continued to work in agriculture and forestry and call-up into the armed services happened to all 18-year-old men.

Identity Cards had still to be carried at all times and shown when required. John Jolly was issued this card on demobilisation in order to register to use a ration card in shops.

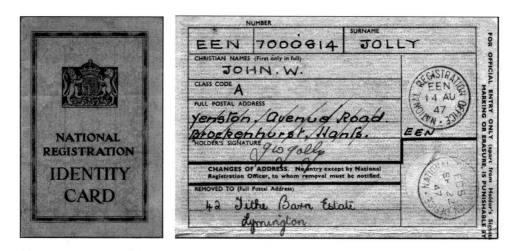

Rationing. This continued to ensure that a healthy diet was achieved by all. After the war some rations were even cut below wartime levels and bread was rationed for the first time in July 1946. Some examples include;

Item	Rationed	De-rationed
Tea	1940	1952
Clothes	1941	1949
Sweets	1942	1953
Petrol	1940	1950

and rationing of meat, butter and cheese continued until 1954.

The housing shortage was acute in the village as men returned and those amongst them who were married did not want to go back to living with in-laws. The District Council took over and refurbished some Nissen huts at RAF Ladywell for temporary accommodation. When the POW Camp at Setley finally closed this was also taken over for housing, as the accommodation was better! Edna Walker and Hilda Otter were amongst those locals housed on these sites. The site was developed and even had its own shop run by Harry Munden.

Returning Prisoners of War reportedly adapted well to these conditions. These included

> **Captain Robert Spencer Ferguson. He** served with the Royal Northumberland Fusiliers and was one of 500 officers who escaped from an Italian prisoner-of-war camp when Italy capitulated. He was recaptured and spent the rest of the war in Germany.

> Three other Brockenhurst officers escaped from Italian prison camps at about the same time. **Captain Fairhurst** and **Lieutenant Playford** were recaptured by the Germans. **Major Porter** reached Switzerland and was interned.

> **Lieutenant Playford** returned to his home at Forest Edge, Balmer Lawn, in 1945 aged 25. He had been captured in Tunis in 1942 when members of his unit dropped behind enemy lines and some of them were unable to link up. He escaped twice from the Germans in Italy. The third time he was captured he was put on a train and sent to Germany. He was in the same prison camp in Italy as **Captain Fairhurst**, whom he met again at Brunswick.

German and Italian Prisoners of War returned to Europe in 1946/7. Some stayed locally, however amongst whom was **Max Mueller**.

Ludwig Wilhelm Mueller was born in Aschafenburg on the River Main on 28th January 1913. He trained as a butcher before joining the German army and was captured in France in 1944. He was initially thought to be Max Schmelling, the

MAX MUELLER

famous German boxer, and retained the name of "Max" from this encounter. After travelling to England in a Landing Craft he was interned at Devizes. Whilst waiting for the Italians, and their cats(!), to leave Setley Camp he was tasked to be the leader of five local POW camps.

He was finally released just before Christmas 1947 and worked in agriculture, initially at Hatchett Mill and later in Pennington and then at Howletts Farm in Lymington. In April 1950 he married Molly Stupple and raised a family, with Michael Peter born in 1952 and Karin two years later. In October 1950 he was given an I. D. card which released him from the obligation to report weekly to the police. In May 1955 he returned to butchering firstly in Hordle and then as manager of Holtom's in Brookley Road. He is well-remembered for helping people. He collected villagers for Mass, drove people to Bingo in Sway and helped to run Bingo at the Football Club. He died on 3rd October 1988.

Victory Celebrations. The Government decided to hold the official celebration of both "Victory in Europe" (VE -Day) and "Victory in Japan" (VJ-Day) as "Victory Day" in 1946. Against a background of continuing Government control the following letter comes as no surprise.

Circular 44/46.

County Councils.
County Borough Councils.
Metropolitan Borough Councils.
County District Councils.
Parish Councils.

Ministry of Health,
Whitehall,
London, S.W.1.

27th February, 1946.

Sir,

Victory Celebrations

Local authorities will have received Home Office Circular No. 40/1946 regarding Victory Celebrations. The Minister of Health, acting in pursuance of his powers under the proviso to section 228(1) of the Local Government Act, 1933, hereby sanctions any reasonable expenses which may be incurred by County Councils, County Borough Councils, Metropolitan Borough Councils, County District Councils and Parish Councils, in connection with any public local Victory Celebrations, in so far as those expenses are charged in accounts subject to audit by a District Auditor.

This sanction is supplementary to that issued in Circular 80/45 in connection with the termination of organised hostilities in Europe, and the considerations set out in the second, third and fourth paragraphs of that Circular are also applicable to this sanction.

An additional copy of this Circular is forwarded for the information of the Chief Financial Officer.

I am, Sir,
Your obedient Servant,

F. L. Edwards.

Assistant Secretary.

The Clerk of the Council,
or
The Town Clerk.

Nevertheless Brockenhurst celebrated in its own particular manner, with a party for the school children - for which there were some official concessions such as an extra 4 ozs of margarine, some fresh fruit and a little extra sugar. Such gestures made an amazing difference psychologically, as well as gastronomically, to the celebrations.

Coda. The War Memorial. In 1947 a Works Order was placed with the Lettering Centre in Borough Road, London, for a tablet recording those who had lost their lives in the Second World War.

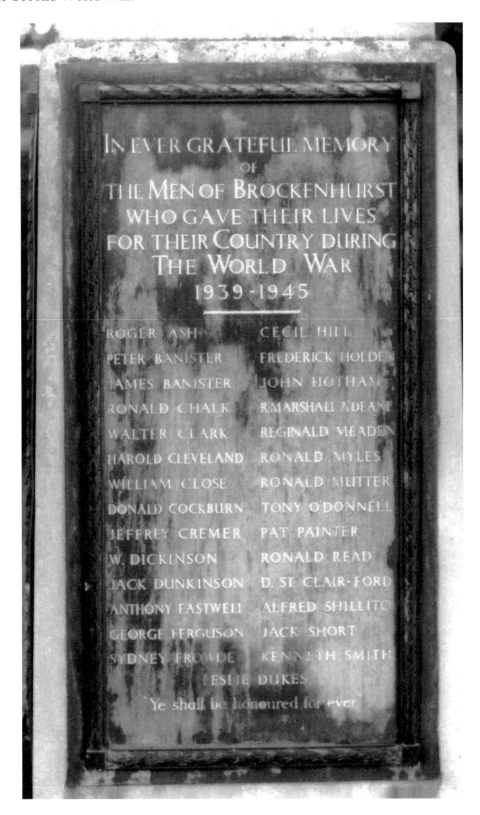

The estimate for this work was £58.15.00d.

During the war, however, a bullet of unknown origin had struck the 1914-1919 tablet on the Memorial. In 1948, therefore, the Lettering Centre was tasked with its repair. This was estimated to cost an additional £2.17.00d. To add an additional name and to repair damage to the tablets occasioned whilst in the hands of the Southern Railway cost a further sum of £23.11.00d. The total, of £85.03.00d exceeded income raised for the project.

Both tablets were fixed to the War Memorial in time for Remembrance Day, 1948. The bill was finally settled one year later!

In 1921 the Morant Trustees had began the process of conveying the War Memorial land to become the absolute property of the parish Council. The Council established a Memorial Committee to deal with this matter. After an exchange of fifteen letters and the loss of the first Deed of Gift in the post whilst in transit from the Stamping Office we still find a letter from Ellis Peirs & Co to the Parish Council dated 3rd April 1952 recording that John Morant

> *"Is desirous of making a gift to the Parish council*
> *of the land pertaining to the War Memorial."*

The transfer of ownership was finally completed later that year!

Remembrance Sunday. The names of those who died and are remembered on the Memorial are read out during the Remembrance Sunday service.

One additional name, that of **Nigel John Noel Sutton**, is included in this practice. Nigel died, aged 30, on 14th August 1973 from injuries received whilst serving as a Captain in the Duke of Edinburgh's Royal Regiment in Northern Ireland. He is buried in **Tidworth Military Cemetery**. There is a memorial seat to him at the lower entrance to **St. Nicholas Churchyard**.

SOLDIERS FROM THE WARS RETURNING

Servicemen and women were slowly demobilised and returned to the village.

In the 1930's and 40's **Stan "Grog" Orchard** ran a cycle business from his shop in Waters Green. He was also a keen photographer who photographed many of the villagers when they were home on leave. His photographs have already appeared in some of the memorials of those who died in the Second World War.

The following photographs of some of those who, happily, returned to Brockenhurst after the war are mostly further examples of his skill in capturing the character of his subject.

JACK ANSON   DOUGLAS BESSANT   BILL BROWNING

TOMMY BURT   JACK COOPER   LES COOPER

BILL DORRICOTT　　　　**BILL DUNKINSON**　　　　**BUSSY ELVE**

EDGAR FRANCIS　　　　**ERN HEAD**　　　　**ERN HIBBS**

ARTHUR HOLT　　　　**FRANK HOUSE**　　　　**FRED HOUSE**

GEORGE HOUSE   **JOE JENVEY**   **GEORGE JOHNSON**

LES JOHNSON   **GWEN JOLLY**   **BERT LEWIS**

TOM MARDEN   **REG MARSH**   **FRED MORGAN**

JACK OLNEY

PETER PHELPS

ARTHUR PURKIS

TONY PURKIS

LES REEVES

MARIAN SHERARD

JOE SHORT

BOB SPRAKE

RON SQUE

REG STREET   **BERT TIGHT**   **JIM TIZZARD**

BERT WALLIS   **JACK WATERMAN**

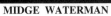

MIDGE WATERMAN   **PHILIP WATERMAN**   **GEORGE WITCHER**

CAN YOU RECOGNISE ANY OF THESE FIVE SERVICEMEN AND WOMEN?

EPITAPH

Survival in war appears to be an almost capricious matter of chance.

Percy Pope was a victim of an ammunition accident, as was *Anthony O'Donnell* a war later. Flying, road or military accidents took the lives of *Alfred Shilleto, Jack Short, Roger Ash, John Hibbs* and *John Janes*. Illness carried off *Ernest Field, William Harrison, Leonard House* and *Harold Cleveland*. *Harold Large* was killed by a stray bullet whilst walking in a rear area. *Christian Patterson* was revealed to the enemy by a vivid flash of lightning. The after-effects of war service led to the deaths of *Leonard Smith, Jack Lancaster* and *Selim Chandler*.

Direct enemy action, however, accounted for 77% of the casualties.

Seventy-nine village men died in the First World War. Of these, forty-two were killed in action and twenty men died of wounds. Five died from accidents, however, and a further twelve from illnesses - some from the Influenza epidemic at the end of the war.

In World War II medical advances and improvements in casualty evacuation procedure appears to have saved all the wounded. Of the forty villagers known to have died, twenty-four Servicemen and two members of the Merchant Navy were killed in action. *Jean Gentle* and the two *Cumberleys* was killed by enemy bombing and three members of the *Street family* died accidentally, as did five Servicemen. *Harold Cleveland* and *Eric Donaldson* died from illness and *Walter Clark* died whilst a prisoner of the Japanese.

The War Memorial does not, therefore, record the names of all the one hundred and seventeen villagers who died as a direct result of the two wars. Twenty-five more Servicemen were killed in the First World War than are shown. The Second World War bronze plate appears to record the names of all Servicemen who died but does not honour those who died in air raids, such as *Jean Gentle*, or those who died at sea in the Merchant Navy. In the early part of the war one in four of all Merchant Navy seamen died when their ships were sunk from attack by torpedoes bombs or mines. *William Judd* is one such, *Edward Smith* another. There may be more.

In short, Brockenhurst freely and fully committed its manpower and resources to both wars. Its losses have influenced its development since 1914 and the cost of both world wars to the village is much greater than is either recorded or collectively remembered.

I hope this book goes some way towards perpetuating the memory of those who died.

"Requiem aeternam dona eis,
domine,
et lux perpetua luceat eis"

APPENDIX 1: VILLAGERS RECORDED AS KILLED IN THE FIRST WORLD WAR

All these villagers are documented as dying whilst serving in the First World War. If their names are not on the Memorial their qualification by birth or residence is indicated.

NAME	RANK	UNIT	DIED	HOW	BURIED	RECORDED
Waterman H	Sgt	1 Hamps	07/11/14	KIA	Plug Street	MEM
Pope P J	OS	BULWARK	26/11/14	Ac'nt	Port NM	MEM
Field E	Pte	RMLI	06/02/15	Illness	Deal	MEM
Large H	Capt	3 Mx	16/02/15	KIA	Ypres	MEM
Groome R	2/Lt	RFA	04/03/15	DOW	Ypres	MEM
Tillyer R	Lt	1 Wark	25/04/15	KIA	Ypres	MEM
Large P	Maj	3 Mx	27/04/15	KIA	Ypres	MEM
Christopher C	Pte	2 Hamps	08/05/15	KIA	Gallipoli	MEM
Hill J	Pte	2 Hamps	08/05/15	KIA	Gallipoli	Born
Moore T	Pte	3 RF	24/05/15	KIA	Ypres	MEM
Tucker C	Pte	1 Wilts	17/06/15	DOW	Ypres	MEM
Janes W	Pte	2/7 Hamps	07/07/15	Ac'nt	India	MEM
Jerrim F	Pte	1 Hamps	07/07/15	KIA	Ypres	MEM
Harris J	Pte	2 Hamps	06/08/15	KIA	Gallipoli	Resided
Hinves A	Pte	10 Hamps	10/08/15	KIA	Gallipoli	MEM
Reynard W	L/Cpl	10 Hamps	10/08/15	KIA	Gallipoli	Resided
Wells W	Pte	10 Hamps	10/08/15	KIA	Gallipoli	MEM
Large H	Capt	10 RB	08/10/15	DOW	Ypres	MEM
Miller J W	Pte	10 Hamps	01/11/15	Died	Home	Born
Dove T L	L/Cpl	1/6 Welsh	16/12/15	DOW	Bethune	Resided
Stokes S D	Pte	2 Dorsets	25/12/15	DOW	Mespot	Resided
Legg J W	Cpl	1 Hamps	02/01/16	KIA	Somme	Resided
Macintosh J	Pte	7 Leic	30/01/16	KIA	Somme	Resided
Kitcher D	Pte	1 E Yorks	01/07/16	KIA	Somme	Born
Hayter G	Pte	14 Lond	01/07/16	KIA	Somme	MEM
Harrison W	Pte	2 Hamps	05/07/16	DOW	Somme	MEM
Holman S	A/Cpl	2 Hamps	13/07/16	KIA	Somme	Resided
Clark G	Pte	2 Hamps	09/08/16	KIA	Ypres	MEM
Rickman J A	Pte	2 Dorsets	18/08/16	Died	Mespot	Resided
Hinves H	Rfm	7 KRRC	18/08/16	KIA	Somme	MEM
Bew R	Pte	15 Hamps	07/10/16	KIA	Somme	Resided
King A	Pte	8 Devons	21/10/16	KIA	Plug Street	MEM
Burton H	Gnr	RA	20/11/16	KIA	Somme	MEM
Patterson C B	Lt	IARO	30/12/16	KIA	Iraq	MEM
Cleveland W	Pte	5 Dorsets	26/01/17	Ac'nt	Rouen	MEM
Raisey F	Pte	2 Berks	04/03/17	KIA	Somme	Resided
Wells J	Gnr	RGA	08/04/17	DOW	Arras	Born
Burton Fred	Pte	2 Wilts	09/04/17	DOW	Arras	MEM

Burton F W	Pte	94 Trg Res	10/04/17	Illness	Swindon	MEM
Salmon L	Cpl	5 Hamps	16/04/17	KIA	Pas'daele	MEM
White G	Pte	20 Canadian	13/05/17	KIA	Vimy	MEM
Lucas T F	Lt	Warwicks	16/06/17	KIA	Ypres	MEM
Moores E W	Pte	14 Hamps	31/07/17	KIA	Pas'daele	Born
Murch A	Pte	6 DCLI	23/08/17	DOW	Pas'daele	MEM
Dunford W	Gnr	RGA	18/09/17	KIA	Pas'daele	Born
Povey W	Pte	12 DLI	20/09/17	KIA	Pas'daele	MEM
Waterman W	Pte	14 Hamps	27/09/17	DOW	Ypres	MEM
Baker C J H	Pte	9 Devons	06/10/17	KIA	Pas'daele	Born
Payne S	Pte	2/5 Hamps	20/11/17	DOW	Egypt	MEM
Payne B	Spr	55 Div Sigs	30/11/17	KIA	Cambrai	MEM
Gates J	Driver	RFA	03/12/17	KIA	Cambrai	MEM
Pope H	Pte	15 Lond	30/12/17	KIA	Egypt/at sea	MEM
Broomfield D	Pte	Lab Corps	31/12/17	Died	Etaples	Born
Hibbs J	L/Stkr	HMS OPAL	12/01/18	Ac'nt	Port NM	MEM
Pullen E G	S.S.M.	RASC	18/01/18	Died	Home	Born
Fisher E	2/Lt	RFA 1	31/03/18	Illness	B'hurst	MEM
White S L B	Pte	8 Berks	09/04/18	KIA	Somme	Resided
White W H	S/Sgt	Canadian	20/04/18	DOW	Canada	MEM
Beard A H	Sgt	2 Ox & Bucks	20/04/18	DOW	Arras	Resided
Tregunna J	Pte	1 Hamps	22/04/18	KIA	Gonnehem	MEM
Johnson F	Pte	15 Hamps	06/05/18	KIA	Ypres	MEM
Hunt H	Cpl	1 Wilts	27/05/18	KIA	Soissons	MEM
Bowden-Smith V	Lt-Cdr	HMML 403	22/08/18	Ac'nt	Port NM	MEM
Elford J F	Pte	2 S Staff	23/08/18	KIA	Arras	Born
Middleton W	L/Cpl	14 Welsh	27/08/18	KIA	Somme	Born
Sibley F	Cpl	2/4 Hamps	28/08/18	DOW	Ligny	MEM
Phillpott W T	Pte	13 Lond	10/09/18	DOW	Boulogne	Born
Christopher G	L/Cpl	2 Hamps	14/09/18	DOW	Chocques	MEM
House M	Pte	2/4 Hamps	29/09/18	DOW	Grevillers	MEM
Cole A	Pte	RDC	19/10/18	Illness	B'hurst	MEM
Kitcher A	Pte	8 Glouc	20/10/18	KIA	Haussy	MEM
Hewlett J E	Pte	2/4 Berks	28/10/18	DOW	Cambrai	Resided
Stride W	Pte	RMLI	09/11/18	KIA	Gibraltar	MEM
House L	Pte	51 Hamps	24/11/18	Illness	B'hurst	MEM
Lancaster J H	L/Cpl	Hamps	26/01/19	DOW	B'hurst	MEM
Harrison W	Pte	Hamps Dep	29/01/19	Illness	B'hurst	MEM
Humphreys D	Pte	Pte RDC	07/03/19	Illness	B'hurst	MEM
Chandler S	PO	RN	02/09/19	Illness	B'hurst	MEM
Smith L E	?	?Hamps	??/??/21	DOW	B'hurst	MEM

APPENDIX 2: VILLAGERS RECORDED AS KILLED IN THE SECOND WORLD WAR

NAME	RANK	UNIT	DIED	HOW	BURIED	RECORDED
Chalk R	O/S	ROYAL OAK	14/10/39	KIA	Port NM	MEM
Dickinson W	Major	RTR	29/05/40	KIA	Dunkirk M	MEM
Holden F	P/O	61 Sqn RAF	18/04/41	KIA	Cherbourg	MEM
Dunkinson J	AB	GLOUCESTER	22/05/41	KIA	Ply NM	MEM
A'Deane W	Cdr	GREYHOUND	22/04/41	KIA	Port NM	MEM
Banister P	Lt RN	UMPIRE	20/07/41	Ac'nt	Port NM	MEM
Short J	Cpl	RAF	03/08/41	Ac'nt	S. Africa	MEM
Painter P	L/Cpl	44RTR	22/11/41	KIA	Egypt	MEM
Fergusson G	Lt-Cdr	PR OF WALES	12/12/41	KIA	Ply NM	MEM
Moore A	Lt	AUDACITY	22/12/41	KIA	Ply NM	MEM
Cockburn D	Sgt	50 Sqn RAFVR	14/01/42	KIA	Run'mede	MEM
Smith E J	Cadet	SS Traveller	26/01/42	KIA	Tower Hill M	Resided
Hotham J	Major	6 RTR	27/07/42	KIA	Alamein M	MEM
Street Phyllis/Molly/Beryl			18/10/42	Ac'nt	B'hurst	Resided
Judd W G		Seaman Merchant Navy	14/11/42	KIA	Tower Hill	Resided
St. Clair-Ford	Lt-Cdr	TRAVELLER	12/12/42	KIA	Port NM	MEM
Read W	Sgt	83 SQN RAF	17/01/43	KIA	Kiel	MEM
Cremer J	F/O	610 Sqn RAF	14/03/43	KIA	Run'mede	MEM
Close W	Pte	2 Hamps	16/03/43	KIA	Tunisia	MEM
Smith K	W/Cdr	9 Sqn RAF	11/04/43	KIA	Rhineberg	MEM
Meaden R	WO 2	5 Hamps	22/04/43	KIA	Tunisia	MEM
O'Donnell A	AC2	RAF SNAITH	19/06/43	Ac'nt	Selby	MEM
Hodder F	Gp Cpt	RAF SYERSTON	6/9/43	KIA	Rheinberg	MEM
Ash R	Capt	31 Fd Regt RA	23/09/43	Ac'nt	Israel	MEM
Donaldson E	Cdr	KONGONI	26/10/43	Illness	S. Africa	MEM
Clark W	Dvr	RASC	13/11/43	POW	Thailand	MEM
Hill C	Pte	1 Queens	02/12/43	KIA	Burma	MEM
Gentle J			15/05/44	Bomb	B'hurst	Resided
Cumley William & Geoffrey			15/05/44	Bomb	B'hurst	Resided
Banister J	F/O	7 (P) AFU	21/04/44	KIA	B'hurst	MEM
Eastwell A	Pte	1 Seaforths	24/04/44	KIA	Rangoon	MEM
Shilleto A	Flt/Lt	14 OTU	13/07/44	Ac'nt	B'hurst	MEM
Cleveland H	Gnr	144 Fd Regt	01/09/44	Illness	Beirut	MEM
Dukes L	Pte	1/4 Hamps	09/10/44	KIA	Italy	MEM
Myles L	Corp	Royal Dragoons	18/11/44	KIA	Holland	MEM
Frowde S	Corp	5 Hamps	04/12/44	KIA	Italy	MEM
Mutter R	Lieut	2 Scots Guards	27/04/45	KIA	Germany	MEM

Buried. The BURIED column also includes the Portsmouth and Plymouth Naval Memorials and Memorials at Alamein, Dunkirk, Tower Hill and Runneymede.

FORMAL BIBLIOGRAPHY

Regimental Histories

Atkinson, C.T.	The Royal Hampshire Regiment (1952)
Farndale, General Sir Martin	History of the Royal Regiment of Artillery
Forty, George	Royal Tank Regiment (1988)
Sym, Colonel John	Seaforth Highlanders (1962)
Wyrall, Everard	The Die-Hards in the Great War(1926)

Service

Chorley, W.R.	R.A.F. Bomber Command Losses of WW II
Jones, H. A	The War in the Air Vols 2 and 3.
Watts Anthony J	The Royal Navy (1994)

First World War

Banks, Arthur	A Military Atlas of the First World War
HMSO (1936)	Order of Battle of Divisions 1914-18
The Times	History of the War
Fisher, H. A. L.	An Unfinished Autobiography (1940)

The Second World War

Falls, Cyril	The Second World War (1948)
Fuller, J. F. C	The Second World War 1939-1945 (1948)
Matanle, Ivor	World War II

General

Hughes-Wilson, John	Military Intelligence Blunders
Michelin Guide	Ypres (1919)
Taylor, Richard	Before We Go (1995)

Public Record Office

ADM 137/3726 HMS OPAL, ADM 137/3771 H Pope , ADM 159/193 E Field, ADM 196/122 E Donaldson, WO /00/339 H Large, WO 95/2269 R Groome,   WO 95/2279 R Fusiliers, WO 95/2279 H Large, WO 95/2279 P Large, WO 95/2279 T Moore, WO 95/5111 C Patterson, WO 169/9481 R Ash, WO 339/478 T Lucas.

INDEX

Names indexed in **bold** are of those who died in war. Names recorded in ***bold italics*** are to be seen on the War Memorial. Personal photographs are shown in **bold**.

INDEX

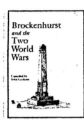

Brockenhurst and the Two World Wars

ADDITIONAL ACKNOWLEDGEMENTS

Maps: From **Battlefields Review**, the bi-monthly magazine
for Battlefields Enthusiasts; Pages 21, 44.
Tel.: 01226 734333 to subscribe.
From **The Royal Navy, An Illustrated History** by
Anthony J.Watts, published by Cassell&Co; Page 178

Drawing: M. S. **"Warwick Castle";** by permission of the family
of John H. Isherwood; Page 209.
Original held by Southampton City Records Office.

Photographs: Courtesy of the **Imperial War Museum, London**;
Pages 17: Q21052; 98: SP2017; 134: Q46036;
161: Q18144; 183: FL3925; 185: FL2766; 192: A6786
195: A5449; 205: E13533; 212: A9823.
Courtesy of the **National Maritime Museum,
London;**
Pages 135: N21210; 188: N2371.